Simulated Worlds

Simulated Worlds
A Computer Model of National Decision-Making

Stuart A. Bremer

PRINCETON UNIVERSITY PRESS

Copyright © 1977 by Princeton University Press
Published by Princeton University Press, Princeton, New Jersey
In the United Kingdom: Princeton University Press, Guildford, Surrey

All Rights Reserved

Library of Congress Cataloging in Publication Data will be found on the last
printed page of this book

This book has been composed in Times Roman

Printed in the United States of America
by Princeton University Press, Princeton, New Jersey

To my father and mother:
All that I really am, and will be, I owe to them.

Contents

List of Figures and Tables

Figures

Tables

Preface

THIS book reports one man's effort to formulate and test a macro-theory of international relations that encompasses and interrelates a variety of inter- and intra-national political and economic phenomena. This theory is embodied in a computer simulation model named SIPER (Simulated International ProcessER), and an effort is made to assess the sensitivity and validity of the model.

This work is both grand in design and limited in scope. The grandness of the endeavor is inherent in the objective of formulating a precise, operational, and general theory of international relations; the limitations stem from the obvious impossibility of any one individual's ability to satisfactorily achieve this goal, given the present state of our knowledge.

The obvious questions then are: why should anyone make such an attempt, and, more specifically, why should you, the reader, devote any time to learning about a laudable, but impossible quest? Chapter One is, in part, intended to answer the first of these questions, but the second question deserves immediate attention since it concerns what the reader can expect to find in this book.

We suspect that any benefit derived from a book is determined not solely by the contents of the volume, but also by what the reader wishes to get from it. Thus, a desirably diverse audience makes it especially difficult to specify in advance what merit individual readers may find in the following pages. Nevertheless, I would like to speak to certain segments of this anticipated audience and suggest some reasons why I think the material that follows is relevant.

First and foremost, I hope that present and future scholars who favor the scientific approach to the study of world politics, as I do, will be in this audience. I am referring to that invisible college of world politics scholars who identify themselves as "quantitative" or "behavioral" in their approach to conducting research. Within this group, however, significant differences exist as to whether the dominant mode of inquiry should be *inductive* or *deductive*. Those who prefer the inductive approach will, I trust, find several things of value in the following pages. First, they will see how diverse empirical findings can be integrated into a single model, and gain some appreciation of the desirability of doing so in the earlier, rather than in the later stages of research. Second, they will see where the lacunae are in our empirical knowledge base, as revealed by one individual's efforts to construct a complete and self-contained theory. Third, they will recognize the potential of the deductive approach to theory construction, and how these strengths differ from those of the inductive approach.

It may be of interest to those favoring the deductive approach to see how formal modeling can be done, even without a Ph.D. in Mathematics. Second, through a demonstration of how more complex and comprehensive models can be built and evaluated, scholars will be encouraged to construct substantively richer and more relevant models. Third, they may see the validity of the position, articulated by Gregg and Simon, that process models, as this branch of simulation has come to be called, represent more powerful theoretical formulations than mathematical models.[1]

Those world politics scholars who prefer the traditional or "classical" approach may be interested to find that grand theory has not been forgotten in contemporary international relations research. No doubt such readers will have many objections to the content of the theory, and I welcome criticisms of this nature. My anticipation is that they will not allow themselves to be alienated by the form of the theory but will see that, to a certain extent, this work represents "old wine in new bottles." The principle difference between what the traditionalist does and what is done here is largely a matter of rigor. The theory offered here is specified more precisely, and therefore more falsifiable, and the deductions that are made are perfectly logical in nature, since they are produced by the computer. In part then, this book offers a challenge to my traditionally oriented colleagues: organize your theoretical expectations and represent them in a computer model, making all assumptions explicit, and let the computer deduce the consequences. It is rather demanding, for the computer does only what it is told to do and will neither tolerate ambiguous instructions nor "fudge" logical inconsistencies; however, the experience will be a rewarding one. Finally, I hope to demonstrate that judgment and intuition, the twin pillars of traditional knowledge, can exist side by side with more empirically verified statements and that the two can be made to work together.

I feel confident that political scientists in fields other than world politics will see the importance of their work in relation to the advancement of world politics. My colleagues in comparative politics, for example, will no doubt have reservations about the somewhat primitive political system the model contains, and perhaps they will be moved to suggest improvements. Or, what is even more desirable, this work might serve as a stimulus in constructing simulations in their field, as I was stimulated by others' efforts.

Scholars from other disciplines should see the need for more inter-disciplinary work and the value of cross-fertilization. The problems of the globe require a concerted effort, and it is my intention to exhibit in these pages how relevant the work from diverse fields is to world politics and vice versa. Finally, these scholars may find in the pages that follow a useful adaptation of a method that is more widely used in their own fields, while containing some useful innovations, thus allowing me to return a small portion of the vast amount I have borrowed from them.

Perhaps more than a few practitioners of world politics will wander into the audience, and I expect that they will be uncomfortable with the level of abstraction and apparent lack of direct policy relevance. For two reasons, I would urge such readers to persevere. First, they may find the macro-perspective refreshing, and a periodic exposure to it is probably healthy. Second, and more important, I think this book represents a portent of things to come. Clearly, this is only a beginning. Better models, with more direct policy relevance, will be developed, especially if these practitioners can be persuaded that the general approach is worthy of investment.

At this point I would like to acknowledge the support and assistance that various people have given me throughout the enterprise. First and foremost among these individuals is Harold Guetzkow, who has facilitated so much research in world politics.

PREFACE

Without his support of the dissertation research that forms the basis of this book, it could not have been done. I am also greatly indebted to Rufus Browning, who, as my dissertation adviser and friend, encouraged and guided the present endeavor. Words cannot adequately express my gratitude to these two individuals.

Paul Smoker and Cleo Cherryholmes were also influential in the early stages of this research, as J. David Singer has been in the later stages of its development. I would like to express my thanks to the American Political Science Association for the Helen Dwight Reid Award in 1972, a presentation that encouraged me to carry the research through to the stage reported here. Acknowledgement is gratefully made to Cynthia Cannizzo, Teresa Frantz, and Pat Coffey for their labors in typing the manuscript, to Dorothy LaBarr for her assistance in editing the work, and to Hugh Wheeler who graciously read and commented on the final draft of this volume.

PREFACE NOTE

1. Lee W. Gregg and Herbert A. Simon, "Process Models and Stochastic Theories of Simple Concept Formation," In John M. Dutton and William H. Starbuck, eds., *Computer Simulation of Human Behavior* (New York: Wiley, 1971), pp. 127–146.

Simulated Worlds

ONE

Introduction

IT seems to me that an introduction to a book reporting scholarly research should answer the following questions: what is it all about, why was it undertaken, what context does it fit into, and what specifically can the reader expect to find in the remainder of the volume? I shall endeavor to supply the answers to these questions in this chapter.

THE ESSENCE OF THE RESEARCH

In essence, the work that follows represents an attempt to construct and evaluate a macro-level theory of international politics. This, by itself, is not particularly new or distinguishing in the field of world politics, for scholars have been engaged in this activity for decades, if not centuries. This work is distinguished from prior efforts at theory construction in that the theory is embodied in an operating computer simulation model. This has several implications. Translating a theory into a computer program demands that the theory be explicitly and unambiguously specified, while permitting it to be complex. Representing a theory in a computer simulation model allows one to observe the theory in action and discover the implications of alternative theoretical formulations, in spite of the complexity of the model. And finally, the model is capable of predicting or deducing what should be observed in the referent world if it is a valid representation of that world. The number and specificity of these predictions make the model and the theory it contains eminently testable and, more important, falsifiable.

At the same time, this work is not without parallel in the field of world politics. Kaplan's pioneering effort to specify rules of behavior in a prescriptive sense for various types of international systems[1] and the subsequent effort to construct a computer simu-

3

lation model of the balance of power system[2] is closely related to what is reported here. Although few are aware of it, and even fewer know about it in detail, Abt and his associates designed and built a computer simulation of the contemporary world called TEMPER[3] for the Department of Defense. As far as I know, no sustained attempt to subject the model to empirical testing was undertaken and, for all intents and purposes, it seems to have disappeared. Alker and his associates developed a computer simulation of United Nations peace-making operations,[4] and more recently Bonham and Shapiro have embarked on the construction of a simulation of the cognitive processes of foreign policy decision-makers[5] drawing upon the earlier work of Pool and Kessler.[6]

Simulation has been used quite extensively in fields other than world politics. Within political science itself we find Crecine's model of the municipal budgetary process,[7] Shapiro and Cherryholmes' simulation of congressional role call voting.[8] Brunner's model of political development,[9] and Browning's simulation of the political recruitment process,[10] to name just a few. Computer simulation has been used profitably in other social sciences, including economics,[11] sociology,[12] psychology,[13] and organizational behavior,[14] and has been extensively employed in the physical sciences. A survey of the simulation literature up to 1969 revealed almost 1,000 publications which contained a description of a working simulation model.[15] Thus, although computer simulation is a relatively new technique, it has been used in a variety of ways.

What is particularly unusual about the computer simulation effort that is described in these pages is that it draws heavily upon prior work with a man-machine simulation in Inter-Nation Simulation (INS). For those who are not familiar with this model, a brief description might be helpful.[16] In one sense, the Inter-Nation Simulation is a complex game with teams of participants attempting to formulate domestic and foreign policies within the rules of the game. The rules are unlike those usually associated with the concept of a game, for they specify primarily the consequences of decisions rather than kinds of moves which are permitted. Thus, a team of national decision-makers, confronting the possibilities of internal revolution, economic depression, external invasion, and electoral defeat, must formulate national and international policies that seek to avoid these pitfalls. In other words, INS attempts to replicate the kinds of dilemmas and decisional trade-offs that real world decision-makers confront.

These rules are contained in a set of programmed relationships that specify under what conditions certain decisions have particular outcomes, hence, the designation man-machine simulation. In reality, they constitute a partial macro-theory of how some important aspects of inter- and intra-national phenomena are interrelated. As we shall see later on in this chapter, a considerable amount of activity has been devoted to evaluating, revising, and enriching the INS model as a man-machine simulation.

My effort to build upon this model led me in a different direction. I concluded that if the participants in the INS could be successfully replaced with sets of decision-making and information processing rules, and incorporated in a computer program with the programmed assumptions present in the INS, the result would be a complete and self-contained model of some important aspects of world politics. Had I realized the implications of such a procedure, I may not have undertaken the task.

On the other hand, there were obvious advantages which stemmed from beginning my work with half a model in hand. A number of the hard decisions were already made, since the INS model defined many of the critical ones. For example, the INS model specifies how the allocation of national resources to consumption, investment, and defense affect the political stability, economic growth, and national security of the nation. Thus, it was clear that I needed to include decision processes dealing with the allocation of resources. This, in turn, necessitated the inclusion of decision processes that dealt with the question of national goals. As it turned out, the INS portion of the model represents only about one-tenth of the completed model's contents rather than the anticipated one-half.

To recapitulate, then, the essence of this book is a description of the model that emerged from my efforts to convert the INS into a complete theory of international relations and subject that theory to empirical testing.

THE REASONS FOR THE RESEARCH

When scientists are asked why they study stars that are millions of light-years away, or a civilization that vanished from the face of the earth many millennia ago, or a disease that takes the lives of large numbers of people, the replies are often not essentially different from George L. Mallory's famous explanation for climbing Mt. Everest: "Because it is there." At some point, all scholars select the subjects they study because they sense an intellectual challenge, as well as an opportunity for achievement, if the freedom to make such a choice is theirs.

There are some who might argue that such a justification is unacceptable and is even irresponsible, because it ignores the related issues of value and relevance. On the one hand, there is the Mannheimian position that all scientific knowledge is value-bound: that is, reflective of and subservient to the prevailing value structure. Therefore, a scientist cannot be objective, and any protestations of dispassionate, intellectual curiosity should be dismissed as a smoke screen, or more generously, as a kind of false consciousness. On the other hand, one finds many scholars, particularly in the social sciences, who feel that intellectual curiosity without moral concern is a kind of scholastic degeneracy that is not to be encouraged.

The decision to study something because "it is there" is also challenged, because it allegedly leads one away from the pressing problems of the human condition into the realm of angels dancing on the heads of pins. In the field of world politics, this frequently manifests itself in the call for more "policy relevant" research. The more general statement of the position alleges that research not readily applicable to the solution of our immediate problems is largely a waste of time.

As I survey the history of science, however, I find little correlation between the motivations of the researcher and the quality of his contribution. Consider for a moment the origins of our knowledge concerning the movement of the stars and planets. Much of what we know about the heavens draws heavily upon the patient compilation of data by astrologers interested in using this information to advise their particular patrons as to the wisdom of undertaking a war against some recalcitrant neighbor. We have found their observations to be valuable, but not for the same reasons that these observations were made. Still, those like Newton, who sought to score the "music of the spheres," founded a body of knowledge upon which every bridge and building rests.

My point is not that we should immediately turn our attention to angels and pins, but rather that we recognize the legitimacy of curiosity, even serendipity, in the scientific tradition. For example, substantial research has been undertaken on the subject of how individuals play chess. Personally, I think this research is fascinating, but why should anyone be interested in studying that? After all, chess is merely an abstract representation of warfare and diplomacy in the pre-modern era. The answer is simply that we hope to learn more about human problem-solving in complex situations in order to improve and refine that capability at some later date.

All this is intended as a preface to discussing one key reason I undertook this research; that is, I saw a challenge and an opportunity in synthesizing three basic elements in order to achieve a more coherent and comprehensive theory of international relations than has heretofore been presented. These elements were: (1) a macroscopic view of world politics; (2) a knowledge of and belief in the potential of the INS model; and (3) an admiration for the way in which Herbert Simon and his associates approach the problem of modeling the behavior of complex, adaptive systems.

The first and most basic of these three elements is the conviction that the problems of the world are not due primarily to the idiosyncratic behavior of particular decision-makers, for the decision-makers changed but the problems remained, but rather due to political and economic factors in the decision-making environment and the propensity of decision-makers to react to these factors in uniform, but often maladaptive ways. I feel that the major determinants of international politics are not only very

7

macro in nature but also relatively slow to change, and are capable of exerting their influence over a long period of time. In addition, I thought that our problems rise from a complex set of economic and political relationships and that these problems would remain until we gain a better understanding of these relationships. Thus, I began the research with the states-as-actors perspective and embraced what Russett termed the ·"macroscopic perspective" with the object of studying "the role of social, economic, and technological factors in providing the menu for political choice."[17] In a general sense, then, this research began with the "state centric paradigm" as its point of departure.

Many scholars, perhaps a majority, in world politics have a similar orientation but have not been led to construct simulation models. In my case, an early exposure to the INS was critical in the intellectual development of this project. As an undergraduate student, I participated in a run of the INS and was intrigued by the model, not so much as a laboratory setting for conducting experiments, but rather as a partial macro-theory. After entering graduate school, I discovered that I was virtually alone in having had this experience, and, since there was a number of students and faculty interested in participating, I organized and executed a run of the simulation. Throughout my graduate education, I continued to use the INS in the classroom, as I do today. Thus, the second element of the synthesis was almost accidently acquired.

The final key ingredient in the synthesis was supplied when I became familiar with the simulation work of Simon and his associates, and I am indebted to Browning for this. I found in this body of work, and particularly that of Cyert and March, an exciting approach to the simulation of complex systems, sometimes referred to as process modeling. Simon has very elegantly outlined the basic philosophy of the approach in lectures given at the Massachusetts Institute of Technology in the spring of 1968.[18] A full exposition of this approach is clearly beyond the scope of this chapter, but a brief discussion of some of its assumptions are in order. First, entities are viewed as goal-directed and adaptive, although not necessarily rational, in nature. As in the TOTE (Test-Operate-Test-Exit) model put forth by Miller, Galanter, and

Pribram,[19] behavior is seen as purposive and feedback-controlled. Second, entities behave according to relatively simple decision rules, which specify how the entity is to act in order to approach a given set of objectives within the set of constraints and opportunities that the environment offers. The third major principle, which in a sense is a deduction stemming from the first two, is that the apparent complexity of an entity's behavior stems mostly from the complexity of the environment, and not from the complexity of the entity itself. Simon describes an ant crossing a beach heading for its home: "Viewed as a geometric figure, the ant's path is irregular, complex, hard to describe. But its complexity is really a complexity in the surface of the beach, not a complexity in the ant. On that same beach, another small creature, with a home at the same place as the ant, might well follow a very similar path."[20]

Simon contends that entities that are "artificial" in the sense of being as they are only because they are "being molded, by goals and purposes, to the environment in which [they] live,"[21] can best be studied by computer simulation. In reply to the question of how a simulation can ever tell us anything that we do not already know, Simon suggests two ways in which simulation can provide new knowledge. The first of these stems from the ability of the computer model to deduce the consequences of a particular set of assumptions. As he points out, "even when we have correct premises, it may be very difficult to discover what they imply. All correct reasoning is a grand system of tautologies, but only God can make direct use of that fact. The rest of us must painstakingly and fallibly tease out the consequences of our assumptions."[22]

The second way in which simulation can contribute to our knowledge is particularly appropriate for what he calls "poorly understood systems" like the one we are dealing with here. As he notes, "we are seldom interested in explaining or predicting phenomena in all their particularity; we are usually interested in only a few properties abstracted from the complex reality."[23]

The more we are willing to abstract from the detail of a set of phenomena, the easier it becomes to simulate the phenomena.

Moreover, we do not have to know, or guess at, all the internal structure of the system, but only that part of it that is crucial to the abstraction.

It is fortunate that this is so, for if it were not, the top-down strategy that built the natural sciences over the past three centuries would have been infeasible. We knew a great deal about the gross physical and chemical behavior of matter before we had a knowledge of molecules, a great deal about molecular chemistry before we had an atomic theory, or a great deal about atoms before we had any theory of elementary particles—if, indeed, we have such a theory today.

This skyhook-skyscraper construction of science from the roof down to the yet unconstructed foundation was possible because the behavior of the systems at each level depended on a very approximate, simplified, abstracted characterization of the system at the next level beneath.[24]

Thus, he concludes, the possibility of simulating a system ". . . does not depend on having an adequate microtheory of the natural laws that govern the systems components. Such a microtheory might indeed be simply irrelevant."[25]

I think these words have profound implications for the field of world politics. They suggest that we do not have to await the development of satisfactory micro-theories before a potentially successful attempt to construct macro-theory can be made. In other words, it is not necessary to understand the behavior of individual decision-makers before we can understand the behavior of the nations they represent; very approximate, simplified, abstracted characterizations may be sufficient.

An examination of two specific applications of the general approach may further clarify this matter. Cyert and March, in their attempt to understand the way in which modern business firms operate, postulate a set of decision-making processes that such organizations are assumed to follow.[26] Organizations are conceived as pursuing goals, learning, searching for alternatives, and other forms of behavior that we would normally ascribe only to individuals making up the organization. It is not alleged that these rules are consciously followed by any single individual in the firm, but rather that the sum total of the individual behaviors is to produce behavior at the organizational level like that described by the decision rules. A comparable approach in world politics might specify the Department of State as a single actor behaving in accordance to a set of relatively simple decision rules.

Crecine's simulation model of municipal budgeting illustrates how the application of these principles may lead to the inclusion of several actors in the same model that represent different levels of aggregation.[27] His model includes such diverse actors as Department Heads, the Mayor's Office, and the City Council. Only the first of these can be identified as a person following the proposed decision-rules, but all three of the "actors" are postulated as following decision rules at the same level of generality. In world politics, this might be comparable to treating the Department of State, the President, and the United Nations as three comparable actors, each following a different set of decision rules.

Both of these applications demonstrated to me the value of assuming that higher level theories do not depend upon knowledge of lower level theories, and that the computer could be a powerful tool for deriving the consequences of relatively simple, but complexly interrelated, assumptions about how an actor behaves. It required only a small additional step to see that an application of these principles would enable me to convert the partial macro-theory of international relations embedded in the INS into a complete macro-theory. I believed that by doing so I would learn more about the analysis of complex systems, and by example, perhaps encourage others to undertake similar and even more fruitful efforts. Perhaps the most important contribution is the attempt to define a middle ground between two of the main contending foci in the study of world politics: the decision-making and state-as-actor approaches. By raising our focus above the level of individual decision-makers, while retaining the critical element of decision-making, it may be possible to synthesize the best of both approaches in way that other scholars will find useful.

11

INTRODUCTION

The computer simulation model described and evaluated in this book offers many opportunities for exploring the implications of different sets of decision-rules, and anyone interested in working with the model is invited to do so. To this point, I have been able to undertake only a limited exploration of this potential, but it is my desire that one result of this book will be the encouragement of others to undertake similar projects. These, then, are the reasons for this research.

The Context of the Research

No research project springs *de novo* out of the head of the researcher; it has an intellectual heritage and ancestry that includes the work of others who contributed to the development of one particular body of literature. Thus, in order to understand the full import of a piece of research, it must be seen in its proper context.

Since this research draws so heavily upon the INS and the work that Guetzkow and his associates began nearly two decades ago, a brief outline of their work is clearly in order.[28] The simulation project located at Northwestern University and directed by Guetzkow has served as a catalyst for much research in world politics, including that which follows.

Development of the INS

Development of the INS began in 1956 and 1957 while Guetzkow was at the Center for Advanced Study in the Behavioral Sciences. At that time, he thought that a synthesis of a free-form war game like those being used at RAND, and a controlled social-psychological experiment that he had used in the study of organizations might prove to be a useful research vehicle for investigating various hypotheses concerning foreign policy decision-making.

Following his year at the Center, Guetzkow joined the International Relations Program at Northwestern University and began in 1957 to develop a man-machine simulation model through a series of pilot runs. The principle objective of these early runs was to test and improve the workability of the model. The process of

12

incremental modification continued during 1958 and 1959,[29] when elements such as decision latitude, programmed war outcomes, and revolution routines were added. In each case, the decision to revise some aspect of the model was based on intuitive judgments about the adequacies and inadequacies of the simulation.

By 1960, these incremental modifications had produced a model which has remained, at least structurally, more or less constant for many years. The model is described in many places, but the first definitive description appeared in *Simulation in International Relations*.[30] Partial descriptions have also been published,[31] and, more recently, Alker has described the model, using a Lasswell-McDougal framework.[32] At the conclusion of the developmental work, Guetzkow and his associates had produced a partial macro-theory of international relations, a method of addressing research questions in a quasi-laboratory setting, and a potentially useful educational tool.

Application of the INS

In 1960, then, the designers apparently felt that they had a reasonably complete and workable model, so they turned to the matter of application and utilization in the areas of education and research. As early as 1959, the INS was used in classroom instruction at Northwestern. Alger describes the early experiences, using the model in an undergraduate class in international organizations, and many of the student reactions he reported are familiar to those of us who still use it today.[33] In 1961 Robinson proposed to undertake in the classroom a comparative analysis of the use of simulation and case studies. The results were not heartening to those who thought simulation might produce a breakthrough in the teaching of international relations. They found no clear evidence to support the assertion that students were more interested in the course, or learned more from it, through the use of simulation, as opposed to case studies.[34] Cherryholmes partially substantiated these findings later, and, since that time (to my knowledge), little more has been done to evaluate the INS as a teaching device.[35] Richard Snyder was especially interested in the training and educational potential of the INS, and in 1965, the National Science

13

Foundation was approached for support of a project that would concentrate on this area. Unfortunately, the project was not begun.

It appears that use of the simulation began to spread to other universities during this period, but in informal ways. Often this occurred when someone who had worked with the project in one capacity or another moved to another university and carried with him the "seeds" of an INS game. The relatively early use of the INS at The University of Michigan seems to have come about in this way. Skinner worked as an assistant for the Brody-Driver runs in the summer of 1960 and later attended law school at The University of Michigan. While at Michigan, Skinner, in conjunction with a graduate student in political science, Robert Wells, developed the "Michigan INS",[36] and it was used for several years in the Introductory International Relations course, where I received my first exposure to the model.

The educational usage of the INS was greatly facilitated by the production of an improved version of the model in 1966. Cherryholmes and Guetzkow designed a college and high school version that is distributed by Science Research Associates, and countless other educators have developed their own versions, drawing upon their experiences with the INS.

The idea of using the INS as an experimental research vehicle for a variety of purposes was first laid out by Guetzkow in 1959. The research questions he suggested then were important and interesting ones, but unfortunately only a handful of the studies was executed. The first research application of INS occurred in INS–8, or the "Brody-Driver" runs, in the summer of 1960. Although principally designed to investigate the effects of nuclear proliferation,[37] several other published and unpublished reports also resulted. Driver investigated, among other things, the effect of some key personality variables on the propensity of the simulated decision-makers to use force.[38] Caspary examined some of the factors relating to the occurrence of war in these runs.[39] Brody, Benham, and Milstein later re-examined the data from these runs in terms of a model relating hostile communication,

14

threat perception, and armament production.[40] Pruitt examined the role of trust and responsiveness in international behavior within the simulated worlds;[41] Wright examined inter-group communication and attraction;[42] and Shapiro focused on the relationship between the cognitive rigidity of participants and their tendency to perceive things in moral terms.[43]

In the summer of 1961, Charles and Margaret Hermann, with support from Project Michelson and assistance from the Stanford project, attempted to simulate the events just prior to the outbreak of World War I.[44] It was, of course, a feasibility study rather than a complete research project, a fact that some critics have failed to take into account, but some interesting innovations in the use of the simulation were introduced. Specific referent nations served as the basis for specifying the initial characteristics of the simulated system, more detailed histories were supplied to the decision-makers, the time scale was changed from years to days, and—perhaps most important—an effort was made to match the surrogate decision-makers with their real world counterparts in terms of certain personality characteristics.

The next research run occurred in the summer of 1962, and it was designed to investigate some social-psychological aspects of bilateral negotiations.[45] For this purpose, certain programmed negotiation processes were added to the model. Bartos also investigated the applicability of the Nash bargaining solution to international trades within the INS and found that it had substantial predictive power.[46]

The second major research application of the INS was carried out by James Robinson and Charles and Margaret Hermann in the fall of 1963, again with the support of Project Michelson. Charles Hermann was interested in identifying and defining crises and the ways in which crisis and non-crisis decision-making differ.[47] Margaret Hermann tested a model of psychological stress, as well as some relationships between self esteem, defensiveness, and coping behavior.[48] Charles Hermann later re-analyzed some of the data from this set of runs and re-examined crisis decision-making behavior differentiating between the participants' and the

15

experimenters' measurement of crisis.[49] In addition, these runs were used as a basis for investigating the question of whether decision-makers who are given information that an attack on their nation is likely chose to counter-attack immediately or delay their response.[50] Robinson used the INS to examine the role of maximizing-versus-satisficing in the search for information and alternatives in crisis and non-crisis situations.[51]

This set of runs also contained some interesting modifications of the basic simulation. For example, additional role specifications for the decision-making positions were established, special-task subgroups within the simulated governments were created, mediated intra-national communication was introduced, and a more clearly defined hierarchy of authority of decision-makers was added. All of these were aimed at achieving a more realistic representation of the organizational context of foreign policy decision-making. In addition, the decision-makers were assigned different sets of national goals, and their performance was monitored in relation to these goals. A world bank was also introduced and the actions of blockade, propaganda, and subversion were added to the repertoire of international behaviors that nations might initiate.

Project Michelson served as a base of support for some other interesting research applications of the INS, not directly connected with the Northwestern project. Crow and Solomon, of the Western Behavioral Science Institute, undertook two feasibility studies in the summer of 1962, dealing with the utility of the INS as a research vehicle for studying strategic doctrines.[52] One of these experimental runs dealt with the strategic effects of the capacity to delay response to a nuclear attack, and the other, more successful effort was aimed at examining Osgood's GRIT (Graduated Reciprocation In Tension-reduction) strategy.[53] They were sufficiently pleased with the results to undertake several other studies for Project Michelson under the auspices of the Western Behavioral Science Institute.

This initial effort was followed by a more extensive attempt to evaluate the consequences of the capacity to delay response (CDR), known as the WINSAFE II runs.[54] Among other things, they found that the possession of CDR made the decision-makers *more* belligerent, aggressive, and war-prone. A replication of the experiment, using Mexican students, essentially supported the findings of the first study,[55] although cultural differences did appear to affect certain behaviors. In part, these findings led Crow, in conjunction with Robert Noel, to undertake the "East Algonian Exercise" using a highly modified version of the INS. They sought to systematically vary the participants' psychological characteristics, their social context, and the decision-making situation confronting them.[56] It was found that psychological factors seemed to have the strongest and most consistent association with decision-making behavior, and they suggested that more attention be paid to the psychological characteristics of real and simulated decision-makers in the future. Raser, with support from Guetzkow's project, conducted a literature review to examine the personal characteristics of political decision-makers in the "real" world.[57] One of the reasons for this study was to enable simulators to match participants with their real world counterparts on some general personality dimensions. Druckman's study of ethnocentric perceptions and behavior in the INS also had a psychological orientation.[58] Later research applications of the INS, not directly supported by the project, include Forcese's study of some factors that affect alliance cohesion[59] and Burgess and Robinson's examination of some implications of the theory of collective goods for alliance behavior.[60]

In surveying the diverse research applications of the INS model, one is struck by its use in interesting and innovative ways to address important questions drawn from a variety of disciplines. Certainly it is to the credit of the designers of the INS that it lends itself to so many different kinds of questions.

Validation of the INS

Between 1963 and 1968, the bulk of the project's work seems to have involved attempts to assess the validity of the INS, and clearly it is the case that no other social science simulation model has received such intense scrutiny from so many different angles. The methodology of validating simulations was not (and is not) well developed, yet I think it has benefited from some of the methodological studies that the project encouraged or supported. Beginning with a conference in 1965 on validating simulation models, a number of project papers wrestled with the thorny problems of validation.[61]

The validation studies themselves are quite numerous, but fortunately Guetzkow has provided us with a summary of the findings from most of them.[62] His over-all assessment of fifty-five relationships, derived from twenty-four different studies, indicated that there was "some" or "much" correspondence between the referent and simulated worlds in about two-thirds of the cases. Modelski, after independently reviewing the same studies that Guetzkow examined, arrived at very similar conclusions.[63] The studies are too numerous for me to review here, and the interested reader is directed to Guetzkow's discussion.

One of the more ambitious attempts to assess the validity of the INS was the "Event Simulation Project" undertaken by Meier and Stickgold in 1963, and followed up by Targ and Nardin in 1964.[64] The original intent of these runs was to match the simulation world's starting conditions to those of the real world in 1963–1964, and to run the simulation forward a year or so in time, with one period of simulation time equal to six weeks of real time. After the events of 1964 and 1965 had unfolded in the real world, there was to be an assessment of the simulation's ability to predict these events in advance. This predictive power was to be compared with that of policy-makers, scholars, and journalists, using predictions collected by Jensen for the same period of time. The venture, unfortunately, was never carried to completion. Jensen published his findings separately, and his work would appear to be the principal substantive contribution of this ambitious undertaking.[65] However, Nardin and Cutler used the data from these runs to analyze the correspondence of simulated nations' dyadic interaction patterns to those of referent world dyads,[66] while McGowan attempted to carry out the original intention of the designers of the predictive validity assessment, and his effort represents one of the richest validation studies to date.[67]

Beyond the INS

Although the years 1967-1968 seem to mark another shift in the project's focus, the change was not an abrupt about-face, but rather a logical extension of the validation studies. During this period, a new man-machine simulation was developed by Smoker through the International Processes Simulation (IPS), and work was begun on a number of all-computer simulation models.

Some of the elements that were eventually incorporated into the IPS were first utilized by Smoker and others in an earlier effort to use the INS in studying the Vietnam conflict.[68] This joint Canadian-English effort was a creative application of the INS, and it is interesting to note that the participants reported severe feelings of frustration due to their inability to control the unfolding situation (the ''slippery slope syndrome''), indicating some support for the fidelity of the situational factors incorporated in the model.

Some of Smoker's other early work also fed directly into the eventual structure of the IPS. The adoption of a Parsonian framework for conceptualizing world politics enabled him to incorporate economic and cultural trans-national phenomena within a coherent theoretical schema.[69] His work on arms races enabled him to improve the Validator Satisfaction with respect to National Security (VSns) relationship, which had proved so problematical in the INS.[70]

Working from these materials, and others provided by the validation studies, Smoker created a truly ingenious simulation model. A description of this very complex model is clearly beyond our scope, yet it is difficult to appreciate the richness of it without knowledge of its structure. This new model incorporates an answer to almost all of the specific criticisms that were made about the INS. The economic system includes a private economic sector composed of corporations, partially programmed trade flows, a monetary unit, diminishing marginal costs of production, as well as economic sanctions that governments can apply against each other. In the political sector, the powers of the decision-makers have been restructured so that they more closely resemble those possessed by governmental decision-makers. Their resources, for example, were derived from taxation of corporations and citizens, a welcome change from the INS formulation. New decision-making roles were created; each nation has a citizen who earns income, pays taxes, and may engage in demonstrations (peaceful and violent) against his own or another government, as well as local and general strikes against corporations. The corporation executive director similarly has a variety of activities he may engage in. The result is a much more intra-nationally and inter-nationally pluralistic world. As a successor to the INS, the IPS is, indeed, a substantial contribution.

In order to achieve a higher degree of realism, the complexity of the model was greatly increased and its operating procedures also became more complex. Part of this burden was shifted to the computer, since all the "programmed" portions of the simulation are truly programmed. The logistical demands of the simulation are, nevertheless, quite high. In spite of this, the IPS is an excellent example of how theoretical insight, empirical evidence, and practical experience can be blended together in a man-machine simulation. In my opinion, the IPS is the best man-machine simulation to be found in the social sciences today.

Smoker immediately began to conduct validation studies, and he proposed eight different ones covering foreign and domestic conflict, economic characteristics, aggression and conflict, alliance formation, crises, arms races, and integration. To date, about one-half of these have been completed. Since the simulation runs included high school participants in some and adult participants in others, a nation-state system in some and an inter-nation system in others, Smoker has been better able to separate the effects due to the structure of the model from those related to the nature of the participants. His analysis of conflict behaviors in the IPS and referent world revealed interesting differences within the simulation runs, and between these and the referent world.[71] A replication of Chadwick's work on the INS indicated that the IPS represented a substantial improvement on the INS, and a study parallel to that undertaken by Singer and Small, concerning alliance patterns and war,[72] revealed substantial convergence between the IPS and the Singer-Small findings.[73] Remy explored the relationship between trade and defense for simulated and referent dyads.[74] Soroos examined cross-national activities in the IPS and referent system of the period 1966–1968 and some aspects of crisis behavior in the IPS, in comparison to the findings of

McClelland with regard to Berlin.[75] Hoole and Pirro separately examined some hypotheses derived from frustration-aggression theory in the IPS and referent worlds.[76]

These studies give a mixed validity picture for the IPS, but, on balance, the results look good, although there are areas that apparently need some revision. One of the advantages of the IPS over the INS is that it makes more predictions (and more specific predictions) and, therefore, it is more testable and more amenable to revision than the INS.

While Smoker was proceeding to enrich the environment of the participant decision-makers, others were leaning more towards the elimination of human participants through all-computer simulation. Among others, Leavitt, Krend, Pelowski, and I were engaged in the construction and evaluation of computer simulation models of international politics from about 1969 until the project ended recently. Leavitt developed a computer model of alliance formation and dissolution, utilizing propositions drawn from the traditional literature.[77] Krend reconstructed and updated Benson's "Simple Diplomatic Game," and worked on the development of computer modules embodying various formulations drawn from international relations theory;[78] Pelowski experimented with an event-based simulation of the Taiwan straits crisis.[79] The work reported in this volume was begun during that stage of the project's work.

This review of the project's literature demonstrates that its output has been both massive and diversified; at the same time, however, a clear evolutionary pattern is readily apparent. As the work moved from the development of the basic model to the development of second and third generation models, the theoretical foundations of these models became more complex, sophisticated, and complete. The work described in this volume is an effort to build upon, and continue, the work that began nearly two decades ago.

OUTLINE OF THE BOOK

In the next chapter, a description of the simulation model named SIPER (Simulated International ProcessER) is presented.

We differentiate between environmental processes, taken from the INS model, and decision processes, which are new. A combination of verbal, mathematical, and diagrammatic representations is employed in order to make the description as complete and comprehensible as is possible. In spite of this, I anticipate that some readers will find this chapter difficult, and my only advice is that it be read slowly and carefully.

The model itself, as you shall see, is a collection of interrelated processes that could generate a wide variety of behavioral profiles, depending upon the values assigned to its parameters and the variables that describe the initial state of an international system and its component members. Chapter Three examines this question and describes the basic design of this first set of twenty-four simulation runs. By varying certain parameters across runs, the simulated nations are made to use different decision algorithms, and by varying the initial conditions across runs, we give to the different systems and nations different historical pasts.

Chapter Four is concerned with determining the degree to which the behavior of the model is a result of different *decision processes,* as opposed to *different historical beginnings.* This analysis will enable us to make a preliminary assessment of the sensitivity of the model *qua* model to changes in input.

Obviously, we are interested not only in the sensitivity of the model, but in its validity as well. Chapter Five reports the first of two validation studies contained in this book. The first study encompasses a wide range of national behavior, and comparisons are made between simulated nations (both SIPER and INS generated), and a sample of contemporary nations.

The second validation study, contained in Chapter Six, concentrates on fewer variables, but raises the analytical focus to the level of simulated and referent international systems. In addition, we are concerned with assessing both static and dynamic correspondences of the simulated systems to both contemporary and historical referent systems.

Finally, in Chapter Seven we offer our conclusions as to what may be learned from the research, and what directions future research should take.

CHAPTER ONE NOTES

1. Morton Kaplan, *System and Process in International Politics* (New York: Wiley, 1957).

2. Donald L. Reinken, "Computer Explorations of the 'Balance of Power'," in Morton Kaplan, ed., *New Approaches to International Relations* (New York: St. Martin's Press, 1968), pp. 459–482.

3. *TEMPER: Technological, Economic, Military, and Political Evaluation Routine* (Bedford, Mass.: Raytheon Company, Vol. 1–7, 1965–1966).

4. Hayward R. Alker, Jr. and Cheryl Christensen, "From Causal Modelling to Artificial Intelligence," in Jean A. Laponce and Paul Smoker, eds., *Experimentations and Simulation in Political Science* (Toronto: University of Toronto Press, 1972), pp. 177–224.

5. Michael J. Shapiro and G. Matthew Bonham, "Cognitive Process and Foreign Policy Decision-Making," *International Studies Quarterly,* 17, No. 2 (June, 1973), pp. 147–174.

6. Ithiel de Sola Pool and Allen Kessler, "The Kaiser, the Tsar, and the Computer: Information Processing in a Crisis," *The American Behavioral Scientist,* 8, No. 9 (May, 1965), pp. 31–38.

7. John P. Crecine, *Governmental Problem-Solving* (Chicago: Rand McNally, 1969).

8. Cleo H. Cherryholmes and Michael J. Shapiro, *Representatives and Roll Calls* (New York: Bobbs-Merrill, 1969).

9. Ronald D. Brunner, "Some Comments on Simulating Theories of Political Development," in W. Coplin, ed., *Simulation in the Study of Politics* (Chicago: Markham Publishing Company, 1968), pp. 329–342.

10. Rufus P. Browning, "Hypotheses about Political Recruitment: A Partially Data-Based Computer Simulation," in William D. Coplin, ed., *Simulation in the Study of Politics* (Chicago: Markham Publishing Company, 1968), pp. 303–326.

11. See Thomas H. Naylor, *Computer Simulation Experiments with Models of Economic Systems* (New York: Wiley, 1971), Chapter 4, for a brief summary of the applications of simulation to economics.

12. A discussion of sociological applications can be found in James S. Coleman, "Mathematical Models and Computer Simulation," in Robert E.L. Faris, ed., *Handbook of Modern Sociology* (Chicago: Rand McNally, 1964), pp. 1027–1062.

13. See Rufus P. Browning, "Simulation: Attempts and Possibilities," in Joanne N. Knutson, ed., *Handbook of Political Psychology* (San Francisco: Jossey-Bass Inc., 1974), pp. 383–412.

14. Organizational behavior simulations are discussed in Kalman J. Cohen and Richard M. Cyert, "Simulation of Organizational Behavior," in James G. March, ed., *Handbook of Organizations* (Chicago: Rand McNally, 1965), pp. 305–334.

15. John M. Dutton and William H. Starbuck, eds., *Computer Simulation of Human Behavior* (New York: Wiley, 1971).

16. A more complete description of the model and its usage is in Harold Guetzkow, et. al., *Simulation in International Relations* (Englewood Cliffs, N.J.: Prentice-Hall, 1963).

17. Bruce Russett, "A Macroscopic View of International Politics," in James N. Rosenau, Vincent Davis, and Maurice A. East, eds., *The Analysis of International Politics* (New York: Free Press, 1972), pp. 109–124.

18. Herbert A. Simon, *The Sciences of the Artificial* (Cambridge, Mass.: The M.I.T. Press, 1969).

19. George A. Miller, Eugene Galanter, and Karl H. Pribram, *Plans and the Structure of Behavior* (New York: Holt, Rinehart and Winston, 1960).

20. Herbert A. Simon, *The Sciences of the Artificial,* p. 24.

21. *Ibid.,* p. ix.

22. *Ibid.,* p. 15.

23. *Ibid.,* p. 16.

24. *Ibid.,* pp. 16–17.

25. *Ibid.,* pp. 19–20.

26. Richard M. Cyert and James G. March, *A Behaviorial Theory of the Firm* (Englewood Cliffs, N.J.: Prentice-Hall, 1963).

27. John P. Crecine, *Governmental Problem-Solving* (Chicago: Rand McNally, 1969).

28. Those who are interested in a more extensive evaluation of the INS project should consult the forthcoming volume, *Quantitative International Politics: An Appraisal,* edited by Dina A. Zinnes and Francis A. Hoole. The papers by myself, Stuart Thorson, and Cheryl Christensen all discuss the project from various perspectives.

29. Robert Noel, "Evolution of the Inter-Nation Simulation," in H. Guetzkow et. al., *Simulation in International Relations* (Englewood Cliffs, N.J.: Prentice-Hall, 1963), pp. 69–102.

30. Harold Guetzkow et al., *Simulation in International Relations* (Englewood Cliffs, N.J.: Prentice-Hall, 1963).

31. Harold Guetzkow, "Simulation in International Relations," *Proceedings of the IBM Scientific Computing Symposium on Simulation Models and Gaming* (1964), pp. 249–278, and "Some Uses of Mathematics in Simulation of International Relations," in John M. Claunch, ed., *Mathematical Applications in Political Science* (Dallas: Southern Methodist University Press, 1965), pp. 21–40.

32. Hayward R. Alker, "Decision-Makers' Environments in the Inter-Nation Simulation," in W. Coplin, ed., *Simulation in the Study of Politics* (Chicago: Markham Publishing Company, 1968), pp. 31–58.

33. Chadwick Alger, "Use of the Inter-Nation Simulation in Undergraduate Teaching," in H. Guetzkow, et. al., *Simulation in International Relations* (Englewood Cliffs, N.J.: Prentice-Hall, 1963), pp. 150–189.

34. James Robinson, Leroy Anderson, Margaret Hermann, and Richard Snyder, "Teaching with Inter-Nation Simulation and Case Studies," *American Political Science Review,* 60, No. 1 (March, 1966): 53–65.

35. Cleo Cherryholmes, "Developments in Simulation of International Relations in High School Teaching," *Phi Delta Kappa,* (January, 1965): pp. 227–231, and "Some Current Research on Effectiveness of Educational Simulations: Implications for Alternative Strategies," *American Behavioral Scientist,* 10, No. 2 (October, 1966): 4–7.

36. Donald D. Skinner and Robert D. Wells, *Michigan Inter-Nation Simulation* (Ann Arbor: The Department of Political Science and the Center for Research on Learning and Teaching, University of Michigan, 1965).

37. Richard A. Brody, "Some Systemic Effects of the Spread of Nuclear Weapons Technology: A Study Through Simulation of a Multi-Nuclear Future," *Journal of Conflict Resolution,* 7, No. 4 (December, 1963): 665–753.

38. Michael J. Driver, "A Cognitive Structure Analysis of Aggression, Stress, and Personality in an Inter-Nation Simulation," (Lafayette, Ind.: Purdue University, August, 1965).

39. William Caspary, "The Causes of War in INS-8" (Evanston, Ill.: Northwestern University, ditto, 1962), and "Simulation Studies in Inter-Nation Conflict: Part II, Application." Presented at the meeting of the Midwest Sociological Association, April 19, 1963.

40. Richard Brody, Alexandra Benham, and Jeffrey Milstein, "Hostile International Communication, Arms Production, and Perceptions of Threat: A Simulation Study," *Peace Research Society (International) Papers,* 7, (1967): 15–40.

41. Dean Pruitt, "Two Factors in International Agreement," (Evanston, Ill.: Northwestern University, ditto, 1961).

42. George Wright, "Inter-Group Communication and Attraction in Inter-Nation Simulation" (Ph.D. dissertation, Washington University, St. Louis, Missouri, 1963).

43. Michael Shapiro, "Cognitive Rigidity and Perceptual Orientations in an Inter-Nation Simulation" (Evanston, Ill.: Northwestern University, 1966).

44. Charles F. Hermann and Margaret G. Hermann, "An Attempt to Simulate the Outbreak of World War I," *American Political Science Review,* 61, No. 2 (June, 1967): 400–416.

45. Allen W. Sherman, "The Social Psychology of Bilateral Negotiations," (Unpublished Masters thesis, Department of Sociology, Northwestern University, 1963).

46. Otomar J. Bartos, "Prediction of Trades in Inter-Nation Simulation" (Evanston, Ill.: Dept. of Sociology, Northwestern University, 1963).

47. Charles F. Hermann, *Crises in Foreign Policy: A Simulation Analysis* (Indianapolis: Bobbs-Merrill, 1969).

48. Margaret G. Hermann, "Testing a Model of Psychological Stress," *Journal of Personality,* 34, No. 3 (September, 1966): 381–396.

49. Charles F. Hermann, "Threat, Time and Surprise: A Simulation of International Crisis," in idem, ed., *International Crises: Insights from Behavioral Research* (New York: Free Press, 1972), pp. 187–211.

50. Charles F. Hermann, Margaret Hermann and Robert Cantor, "Counter-

25

attack on Warning or Delay.'' Presented at the Midwest Political Science Association Meetings, Chicago, Ill., April 27–29, 1972.

51. James Robinson, Charles Hermann, and Margaret Hermann, "Search Under Crisis in Political Gaming and Simulation," in Dean Pruitt and Richard Snyder, eds., *Theory and Research on the Causes of War* (Englewood Cliffs, N.J.: Prentice-Hall, 1969), pp. 80–94; and James Robinson and Alan Wyner, "Information Storage and Search in Inter-Nation Simulation" (Columbus, Ohio: Ohio State University, mimeo, 1965).

52. Wayman Crow, "A Study of Strategic Doctrines Using the Inter-Nation Simulation," *Journal of Conflict Resolution*, 7, No. 3 (September, 1963): 580–589.

53. Charles Osgood, *An Alternative to War or Surrender* (Urbana: University of Illinois Press, 1962).

54. John Raser and Wayman Crow, *Capacity to Delay Response: Explication of a Deterrence Concept, and Plan for Research Using the Inter-Nation Simulation* (La Jolla, Ca.: Western Behavioral Science Institute, 1963); *WINSAFE II: An Inter-Nation Simulation Study of Deterrence Postures Embodying Capacity to Delay Response* (La Jolla, Ca.: Western Behavioral Science Institute, 1964); and "A Simulation Study of Deterrence Theories," in Dean Pruitt and Richard C. Snyder, eds., *Theory and Research on the Causes of War* (Englewood Cliffs, N.J.: Prentice-Hall, 1969), pp. 136–149.

55. Wayman Crow and John Raser, *A Cross Culture Simulation Study* (La Jolla, Calif.: Western Behavioral Science Institute, 1964).

56. Wayman Crow and Robert Noel, *The Valid Use of Simulation Results* (La Jolla, Calif.: Western Behavioral Science Institute, 1965).

57. John Raser, "Personal Characteristics of Political Decision-Makers: A Literature Review," *Peace Research Society (International) Papers*, 5 (1966): 161–181.

58. Daniel Druckman, "Ethnocentrism in the Inter-Nation Simulation," *Journal of Conflict Resolution*, 12, No. 1 (March, 1968): 45–68.

59. Denis Forcese, "Power and Military Alliance Cohesion" (Unpublished Ph.D. dissertation, Washington University, 1968).

60. Philip Burgess and James Robinson, "Alliances and the Theory of Collective Action: A Simulation of Coalition Processes" in James N. Rosenau, ed., *International Politics and Foreign Policy* (New York: The Free Press, 1969), pp. 640–653.

61. See, for example, Charles F. Hermann, "Validation Problems in Games and Simulations with Special Reference to Models of International Politics," *Behavioral Science*, 12 (May, 1967): 216–231; Richard Chadwick, "An Empirical Test of Five Assumptions in an Inter-Nation Simulation, About National Political Systems," *General Systems Yearbook*, 12 (1967): 177–192; Richard Chadwick, "Theory Development through Simulation: A Comparison and Analysis of Associations Among Variables in an International System and an Inter-Nation Simulation," *International Studies Quarterly* 16, No. 1 (March, 1972): 83–127;

and John Raser, Donald Campbell, and Richard Chadwick, "Gaming and Simulations for Developing Theory Relevant to International Relations," *General Systems Yearbook,* 15 (1970): 183–204.

62. Harold Guetzkow, "Some Correspondences between Simulations and 'Realities' in International Relations," *New Approaches to International Relations,* ed. Morton A. Kaplan (New York: St. Martin's Press, 1968), pp. 202–269.

63. George Modelski, "Simulations, 'Realities' and International Relations Theory," *Simulation and Games,* 1, No. 2 (June, 1970): 111–134.

64. Dorothy Meier, "Progress Report: Event Simulation Project," (Evanston, Ill.: Simulated International Processes Project, Northwestern University, 1965); Dorothy Meier and Arthur Stickgold, "Progress Report: Analysis Procedures" (St. Louis, Missouri: Event Simulation Project, Washington University, 1965); and Harry Targ and Terry Nardin, "The Inter-Nation Simulation as a Predictor of Contemporary Events" (Evanston, Ill.: Northwestern University, 1966).

65. Lloyd Jensen, "Foreign Policy Elites and the Prediction of International Events," *Peace Research Society (International) Papers,* 5 (1966): 199–209; and "Predicting International Events," *Peace Research Reviews,* 4, No. 6 (August, 1972): 1–65.

66. Terry Nardin and Neal Cutler, "Reliability and Validity of Some Patterns of International Interaction in an Inter-Nation Simulation," *Journal of Peace Research,* 6, No. 1 (1969): 1–12.

67. Patrick McGowan, "Some External Validities of the Inter-Nation Simulation" (Evanston, Ill.: Northwestern University, 1972).

68. John MacRae and Paul Smoker, "A Vietnam Simulation: A Report on the Canadian/English Project," *Journal of Peace Research,* 4, No. 1 (1967): 1–25; and Jerome Laulicht, "A Vietnam Peace Game: A Computer Assisted Simulation of Complex Relations in International Relations," *Computers and Automation,* 16, No. 3 (March, 1967): 14–18.

69. Paul Smoker, "A Preliminary Empirical Study of an Inter-Nation Integrative Subsystem," *International Associations,* 17, No. 11 (1965): 638–646; and "Nation-State Escalation and International Integration," *Journal of Peace Research,* 4, No. 1 (1967): 60–75.

70. Paul Smoker, "Trade, Defense, and the Richardson Theory of Arms Races: A Seven Nation Study," *Journal of Peace Research,* 2, No. 2 (1964): 65–76; and "A Study of an Arms Race," (M. Sc. thesis, University of Lancaster, England, 1966).

71. Paul L. Smoker, "An International Process Simulation: Theory and Description" (Evanston, Ill.: Simulated International Processes Project, Northwestern University, 1968).

72. J. David Singer and Melvin Small, "Alliance Aggregation and the Onset of War, 1815–1945," in J. David Singer, ed., *Quantitative International Politics* (New York: Free Press, 1968), pp. 247–286.

73. Paul Smoker, "International Processes Simulation: An Evaluation." Pre-

27

sented at the Events Data Conference, East Lansing, Michigan, Michigan State University, 1970.

74. Richard C. Remy, "Trade and Defense in the IPS and Selected Referent Systems" (Evanston, Ill.: Northwestern University, 1967).

75. Marvin Soroos, "Patterns of Cross-National Activities in the International Processes Simulation and a Real World Reference System" (Raleigh, N.C.: North Carolina State University, 1971): "Crisis Behaviors in the International Processes Simulation and the Berlin Reference System," (Raleigh, N.C.: North Carolina State University, 1971); "International Involvement and Foreign Behaviors in the International Processes Simulation and a Real World Reference System" (Ph.D. dissertation, Dept. of Political Science, Northwestern University, 1972); and "An Interpretation of Patterns of Discrepancies between the International Process Simulation and an International Reference System," in Joseph Ben-Dak, ed., *The Simulation of Intersocietal Relations*. Forthcoming.

76. Frank Hoole, "Societal Conditions and Political Aggression" (Bloomington, Ind.: Indiana University, mimeo, 1972); and Ellen Pirro, "Frustration-Aggression: A Causal Model Analysis" (Evanston, Ill.: Northwestern University, 1972).

77. Michael Leavitt, "A Computer Simulation of International Alliance Behavior" (Ph.D. dissertation, Dept. of Political Science, Northwestern University, 1971).

78. Jeffrey Krend, "A Reconstruction of Oliver Benson's 'Simple Diplomatic Game'" (Evanston, Ill.: Simulated International Processes Project, Northwestern University, 1970); "War and Peace in the International System: Deriving an All-Computer Heuristic." Proceedings, Summer Simulation Conference, San Diego, Ca., 1972; and "Computer Simulations of International Relations as Heuristics for Social Status, Action and Change" (Evanston, Ill.: Simulated International Processes Project, Northwestern University, 1972).

79. Allan L. Pelowski, "An Event-Based Simulation of the Taiwan Straits Crisis," in J. Laponce and P. Smoker, eds., *Experimentation and Simulation in Political Science*, (1972), pp. 259–279.

28

TWO

The Simulation Model

THE purpose of this chapter is to describe the computer model as it stands today and to provide some of the supporting rationale for the way in which it is presently structured. As I have already indicated in the previous chapter, the SIPER model draws upon the INS model for some of its components, and the description that follows is organized in order to make clear where INS ends and SIPER begins.

The simulation model is composed of two parts. The larger and more complex part of the model specifies how a national decison-making unit attempts to achieve its goals in a changing environment. The smaller and less complex part of the model, borrowed essentially from INS,[1] defines the decision-making environment and specifies the ways in which it changes in response to the behavior of the national decision-making units. It is this second part of the model that we will examine first.

THE DECISION-MAKING ENVIRONMENT

The national decision-making unit is embedded in an environment composed of three basic systems: an international system, the national economic system, and the national political system. Each of these presents the decision-making unit with opportunities for achievement, as well as obstacles to be overcome.

The International System

The behavior of other nation states in the international system is a major influence on the national decision-making unit. Figure 2-1 presents in diagrammatic form the essential features of a typical simulated international system. The system is small, since it contains only five actors, and tight bipolar, since the alliance

29

bonds define two mutually exclusive blocs. Furthermore, each bloc is composed of a leader nation who is primarily responsible for coordinating the defense policy of the bloc, and a variable number of member nations who may or may not wish to follow the advice of their bloc leader. The current model does not permit non-alignment, so every member of the system must be affiliated with one of the two blocks.

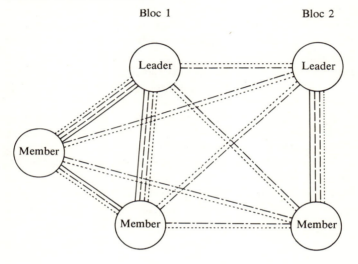

Bloc 1   Bloc 2

Key:

——————— = Alliance Bond
—·—·—·— = Trade Flow
— — — — = Aid Flow
············· = Conflict Flow

FIGURE 2-1
THE INTERNATIONAL SYSTEM

The size limitation and bipolarity requirement were necessitated by considerations of economy and parsimony. Although the model was originally designed to accommodate ten nations, it became clear that the exponential nature of the cost increase for the larger system capability outweighed the advantages of such a capability at this state of the research. With a few technical modifications, the computer model can accommodate any number of national actors.

The tight bipolarity restriction is a more important and limiting assumption and less easily relaxed within the current model. After much deliberation, it became clear to me that for some purposes I would need to conceptualize an international system as a 2-bloc system.[2] In the future, it is my intention to provide for the inclusion of nonaligned nations, but the modifications required are theoretical, not technical.

As Figure 2–1 indicates, there are three kinds of interactions that link the national actors. Trade is an important way for nations to acquire economic and military goods, while aid serves as an instrument for bloc leaders to reward and bolster the economies of bloc members. Hostile interactions are represented in the model as well. A good number of the decision-making rules to be discussed later in this chapter govern the amount and direction of these flows, and further discussion will be postponed until that time. It should be noted here that, unless exogenously changed, the alliance structure remains constant for the duration of a simulated international system.

The National Economic System

The national economic system is composed of three sectors of economic activity: consumption, investment, and government. Consumption refers to that sector of economic activity concerned with the production of ''final goods'' with which ''the population replenishes or increases its energies and ministers to its wants and needs. . . . ''[3] The value produced by this sector will be referred to as Consumption Satisfaction (CS).

Investment refers to that sector of economic activity concerned with the production of value that has the characteristic of being able to produce more value.[4]

For our purposes, the government sector will be equated with that aspect of economic activity concerned with the maintenance of the internal and external security of the system.[5] Other gov-

31

ernmental economic activities are considered to be either consumption (such as government transfer payments) or investment (such as subsidies to industries). The value produced by activity in this sector has the characteristic of being capable of destroying other value. This will be called Force Capability (FC).

Value production occurs when resources are allocated to an economic sector. These resources, the factors of production, are represented in the model by a unidimensional measure of resource capability, Total Basic Capability (TBC). Allocation to the investment sector increases the resource capability of the national system in the future; hence, Total Basic Capability may be thought of as the accumulated past Basic Capability (BC) production.

The value produced by an allocation of TBC to an economic sector depends upon the size of that allocation and the efficiency of the economic sector. Each sector has associated with it a generation rate that states the output of the sector given a unit input of TBC. For example, the CS sector may have a generation rate of 1.4 for a particular nation, in which case an allocation of 100 TBC units will produce 140 units of CS value. Each nation has a set of three generation (GR) rates (CSGR, BCGR, FCGR) that may be considered analogous to what the economists call opportunity costs, and these rates will differ from nation to nation in response to their level of development and degree of specialization.

There is a second kind of value accumulation that occurs in the economic system. FC value accumulates in such a way that at least part of the value produced in the present time period will be available for use in a future time period. Accumulated force capability is called Total Force Capability (TFC), and the level of this variable determines the amount of force capability that can be used in defense of the nation at any time.

These two value reservoirs, TBC and TFC, are assumed to depreciate, and, to maintain constant levels, allocations to the investment and defense sectors are necessary. The rate of depreciation for TBC (DBC) is either 2 percent, 5 percent, or 10 percent, depending upon a stochastic determination in which each rate is given an equal probability of being used. The rate of depreciation for TFC (DFC) is 20 percent, 30 percent, or 40 percent, depending upon a stochastic determination as discussed above.

We can now establish some basic relationships in equation form.[6] The amount of CS value produced in a particular time period is

$$CS = CSP \bullet TBC \bullet CSGR$$

where CSP is the proportion of national resources allocated to consumption. Similarly the BC value produced in one time period is

$$BC = BCP \bullet TBC \bullet BCGR$$

and the FC value produced is

$$FC = FCP \bullet TBC \bullet FCGR$$

CS value is completely consumed in a period of time, but BC and FC value accumulate in the following ways:

$$TBC_{t+1} = TBC_t + BC_t - (DBC_t \bullet TBC_t)$$

$$TFC_{t+1} = TFC_t + FC_t - (DFC_t \bullet TFC_t)$$

DBC and DFC are the selected depreciation rates discussed earlier. That is, the levels of basic capability and force capability at the next time point are simply the present level plus the current production, minus depreciation.

The allocation of resources to consumption, investment, and defense and the setting of values for CSP, BCP and FCP, constitute major decisions which have far-ranging political consequences for the simulated national systems, and it is to the nature of these consequences that we now turn our attention.

The National Political System

In the previous section, we discussed a set of decisions concerned with the allocation of resources to the production of value. This set of decisions involves the authoritative allocation of value, which, according to Easton, is the domain of the political system.[7]

The making of decisions necessarily entails the existence of a set of decision-makers, and in this context the term decision-makers may be thought of as parallel to the concept of elite. Whether we consider them the "influential" as Lasswell does,[8] or the "active population" as Rashevsky does,[9] "by an 'elite' we mean a very small (usually less than .5 percent) minority of people who have very much more of at least one of the basic values than have the rest of the population. . . . "[10] In an Eastonian sense, our "decision-makers" are the authoritative allocators of the system.

In the previous section, we specified that economic activity in the consumption sector produced value that was consumed by the "population." These consumers, which, in conformity with the INS model, we shall call validators, may be thought of as the masses or non-elite. We need not be concerned at this level of abstraction with the question of who *is* and who *is not* a member of the elite and, therefore, a part of the decision-making unit. We need only postulate that the population of a nation can be divided up for analytical purposes into those who have more, and those who have less, control over the behavior of the nation.

We begin our discussion of the programmed relationships between the decision-makers and validators with a consideration of the demands the validators make upon the decision-makers. The demands fall into two areas.

1. The validators expect a certain flow of CS value into their hands.
2. The validators expect a certain level of national security.

The specification of these demand functions follows the formulations used in the INS.[11]

With regard to the first demand, let us assume the existence of a minimum level of CS value flow below which the nation cannot fall without ceasing to exist. This may be thought of as the subsistence level or simply the maximum deprivation that the validators will endure. We will call this variable CSmin, and it is a function of the CS value production potential of the nation (CSmax). CSmax is, in turn, a function of the value productive resources of

34

the nation, TBC, and the productivity of the consumption sector, CSGR.[12]

$$CSmax = TBC \bullet CSGR$$

Thus, CSmax is the amount of consumption goods that would be produced if all of a nation's resources were allocated to that purpose.

The minimum CS value flow (CSmin) is defined as[13]

$$CSmin = CSmax - a_1 CSmax^2$$

Since a_1 is assigned a small value less than one, the effect of this equation is to stipulate that when the maximum possible consumption production is rather small, the minimum fraction of national resources which must be allocated to consumption will be large; but the size of this non-discretionary proportion decreases as the CS production maximum increases. Thus, larger and more developed nations must devote proportionately less to meeting the minimum demands of their population than smaller and less develped nations. CSmax and CSmin represent the maximum and minimum demands of the validators with respect to CS value flow.

The validators give support to the decision-makers in response to the level of CS value flow at any point in time as related to this minimum and maximum. This support is manifested in the variable of validator satisfaction with respect to consumption satisfaction (VScs). As specified in the INS, VScs is dependent on three factors.

1. For consumption near minimum consumption standards, validator satisfaction depends on the relation of consumption satisfaction to minimum consumption levels.
2. Once minimum consumption standards have been met, larger and larger increases in consumption are necessary to produce corresponding changes in validator satisfaction.
3. This saturation effect is more pronounced for wealthier nations.[14]

The formulation of this in the INS is as follows:[15]

$$VScs = a_2 + a_3 \left[\frac{CS}{CSmin} - 1 \right] - a_4 \left[\frac{CSmax}{CSmin} \right] \left[\frac{CS}{CSmin} - 1 \right]^2$$

This rather formidable looking equation is merely a mathematical formulation of the above factors. The first value, a_2, is a constant term used to rescale VScs, while the second term specifies the amount of validator satisfaction resulting from a specified amount of CS production. Thus, when the level of consumption is at the minimum level, no support from the validators will be forthcoming. As the ratio of CS production to CSmin increases, validator satisfaction increases proportionately. The final term incorporates the marginally decreasing nature of this support for wealthier nations. In an aggregate sense, then, the support the validators give to the decision-makers is partially a function of the level of the CS value flow, the value productive resources of the nation, and the efficiency of the mechansims that produce the CS value.

The second area of validator demands is national security. Here we postulate that the validators expect a distribution of world FC favorable to their national security, as well as a favorable distribution of potential Force Capability. The support the validators give to the decision-makers in response to the satisfaction of this demand is called Validator Satisfaction with respect to national security (VSns). However, in determining the distribution of world force capability, the validators do not perceive internal coercive forces as factors in their decision. Since TFC includes forces for the control of external and internal systemic threat, we want to remove the Force Capability devoted to internal control (FCic) from the support equation. That equation is[16]

$$VSns = a_5 \left[\frac{\sum\limits_{non\text{-}allies}^{self\,+\,allies} (TFC - FCic + a_6 TBC)}{\sum (TFC - FCic + a_6 TBC)} \right] + a_7$$

The minimum value of VSns is 1.0, and the maximum is 10.0. A VSns of less than 1.0 indicates that the nation should be considered "disengaged from the armaments race,"[17] and a favorable balance of forces ceases to be a demand for the validators. In this case, support is solely dependent on consumption flow.

The aggregate support for the decision-makers, called VSm, is a weighted average of the two support factors discussed above.[18]

$$VSm = a_8 VScs + a_9 VSns$$

It is clear that political systems differ in the degree to which decision-makers are dependent upon validator support for their continuation as decision-makers. The power to disregard the wishes of the validators is called Decision Latitude (DL).[19] Political systems with low decision latitude may be considered open,[20] flexible,[21] non-directive,[22] or accessible.[23] In any event, this may be considered a structural variable that mediates the relationship between the decision-makers and validators.

DL is not necessarily constant. It is assumed that the validators will periodically seek to change the political system by making it more responsive to their wishes or demanding more leadership from the decision-makers. In the model, a unit increment in DL, a unit decrement in DL, and no change in DL are equally likely outcomes of a stochastic decision process in any given period of time. The variable DDL introduces random shocks into the relationship between the decision-makers and validators, to which the nation must adapt.[24]

Returning now to the question of the relationship between the degree to which the validators are satisfied and the stability of the political system, we assume, as INS does, that[25]

$$POH = a_{10} + a_{11} VSm - a_{12} VSmDL + a_{13} DL$$

POH, as it is used here, is a measure of the stability of the system as suggested by Elder and Pendley.[26]

We see then, that as validator support goes up, stability also increases, and as decision latitude rises, stability increases. The middle term, however, specifies that when the political system is more democratic (low DL), each unit increase in VSm brings a greater increase in stability than when the system is more authoritarian (high DL). The rationale is that an authoritarian nation whose stability rests primarily on oppression, gains relatively little additional stability from increased validator satisfaction, while the opposite is true for more democratic nations.

It will be recalled that in the VSns formulation, there was a term FCic, or Force Capability devoted to internal control. The role of coercive forces in relation to the control of internal threats to the political system is well established,[27] and it is assumed that the decision-makers will allot some proportion of their total force capability to the performance of this function. The importance of this force will become clear when we consider another way in which the validators may manifest their support, or lack of support, for the decision-makers.

Revolutions may occur in the simulated nations, and their occurrence is dependent on four factors. If the overall Validator Satisfaction (VSm) is above a revolution threshold, a_{14}, revolution is not considered possible. If this threshold value is not reached, then the probability of revolution is dependent upon the nature of the political system and the level of coercive forces, in the following manner:[28]

$$PR = a_{15}DL - a_{16}\left[\frac{FCic}{TFC}\right] + a_{17}$$

According to this equation, the more authoritarian the regime, the greater the probability of a revolution *unless* this tendency is offset by the maintenance of a relatively large internal security force.

The final decision as to whether or not a revolution occurs depends upon a stochastic decision process. Should a revolution occur, however, there are substantial costs to the national system. All FC devoted to internal control (FCic) is considered lost in defense of the system. Furthermore, there are substantial losses in the productive capacity of the system; 20 percent of the nation's TBC is assumed lost in the event of a revolution. On the other hand, there are benefits to be gained from a revolution in the form of momentary increases in the overall validator satisfaction. In the period following the revolution, an increase in VSm of two units is credited and a one unit bonus is given in the period after that.[29]

It should be clear by now that we have described a set of conceptual variables, which we may use to define the predecisional and post-decisional states of a simulated nation, and a set of relationships that determine the transformation of the system given the outcome of the decisional stage. It is to this stage that we now turn our attention.

THE DECISION-MAKING PROCESSES

Having specified the national and international environment of the decision-making units, we can attend to the decision-making and information processing rules that govern the behavior of the national actor. These rules can be viewed as a substitute for the human participants found in the INS model, and they consist of nine basic processes, which are diagrammatically presented in Figure 2–2. Tracing through this diagram, we can see the sequence of operations that a simulated decision-making unit undertakes in the course of one unit of time. After assessing the environment, the decision-making unit first sets its general goals for the current period (Goal Formation), and then proceeds to identify the specific things that should be done if these goals are to be attained (Goal Operationalization). The next four processes (Trading, Resource Allocation, Aid Requesting, and Aid Granting) are used in an attempt to meet these specific needs by utilizing international and national resources. After all these alternatives have been explored, a final set of decisions concerning resource allocation is made (Allocation Finalization) and expressions of hostility and friendship are transmitted to other members of the international system (Conflict Generation). The set of decisions made in such a way modifies the decision environment according to the formulations discussed in the previous section. The remaining process (Expectation Formation) is used for making predictions about the future behavior of other states. These predictions are used in the Goal Formation and Conflict Generation processes. In the remaining part of this chapter, we will examine each of these nine processes in detail.

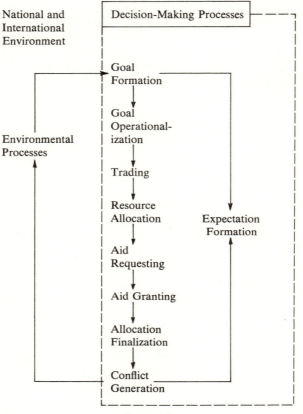

FIGURE 2-2
DECISION-MAKING SEQUENCE

Goal Formation

Nations are open, complex, adaptive systems and, as such, their behavior is purposive. Their behavior is intended to reduce the perceived discrepancy between the present state of the nation and some desired future state of the nation. We are concerned here with the national definition of that desirable future state.

Defining completely the state of a complex system, be it present or future, would require an extraordinarily large number of dimensions. Theory and prudence tell us, however, that it is essential for us to carefully select a subset of these dimensions for scrutiny.

The first goal area to be so isolated is political stability. Decision-making elites have, as a major goal of their behavior, the retention of their decision-making positions. The elites will endeavor to use the resources of the political and economic systems at their command to make their positions of command secure. This can, of course, have far ranging consequences. As North pointed out, "during the summer of 1914. . . the Austro-Hungarian leadership, feeling threatened by the spectre of Pan-Slavism, put forward the preservation of the dual Monarchy at all costs as their major policy goal."[30]

The second goal area that will guide the behavior of the decision-making elite of a nation is economic growth. The expansion of national productive capability has been, particularly in this century, a major objective. Organski has stated, "wealth is [a] goal that is sought to some extent by every nation."[31]

The third end toward which national behavior is directed is national security. By this, we mean that nations act to further the continuation of their existence in the face of real or imagined external threats, "Each political unit aspires to survive. Leaders and led are integrated in and eager to maintain the collectivity they constitute together by virtue of history, race or fortune."[32] Political stability, economic growth, and national security by no means constitute an exclusive set of national objectives; they are, however, universal among nations and clearly prominent in the literature of international relations.

Our task of specifying the goals that guide nations is far from complete, however, for as Singer has stated, ". . . goals and motivations are both dependent and independent variables, and if we intend to explain a nation's foreign policy, we cannot settle for the mere postulation of these goals; we are compelled to go back a step and inquire into their genesis and the process by which they become the crucial variables that they seem to be in the behavior of nations."[33] In specifying the process by which goals are set and reset, we have relied heavily on the work of Cyert and

41

March.[34] Their formulation of goal determination in a business firm suggests a pattern for such behavior in all complex organizations, including nation-states.

Organizations set levels of aspiration in areas of meaningful achievement, and in the short run seek to attain these levels. In the long run, however, these aspiration levels themselves are subject to change. The result of this process is a dynamic homeostatic equilibrium of aspiration and achievement. In what follows, we will show how this formulation is applied in the political stability and economic growth goal areas.

The Goal of Political Stability

We have posited that decision-makers act to make their positions secure. The degree of security they seek at any given time, we will call the nation's Aspiration Level of Political Stability (ALPOH). The current value of the aspiration level for political stability is dependent upon three factors: (1) the past aspiration level for political stability; (2) the degree to which the past aspiration was achieved; (3) the achievement of a significant other nation with regard to political stability relative to one's own achievement. The way in which these three factors enter into the setting of the Aspiration Level for Political Stability (ALPOH) is outlined in Figure 2–3. Initially, the aspiration level for this period is set equal to a pre-determined proportion, b_1, of last period's level. If b_1 is greater than 1.0, then the present aspiration level will be higher than the past aspiration level unless subsequently altered; if b_1 is less than 1.0, the opposite holds true. The value of b_1 represents the teleological inertia of the system with respect to the goal of political stability. Since goals change slowly and incrementally, this coefficient indicates the influence of past goals upon present goals.

The second step in this decision process represents an adaptive or learning component. It is a simple feedback loop with b_2 and b_3 being the rates of adaptation. Both coefficients are positive, hence over-achievement leads to a higher aspiration level and under-achievement leads to a lower one. The relationship between over- and under-achievement is not symmetrical, however.

We will assume that nations (given encouragement) will more

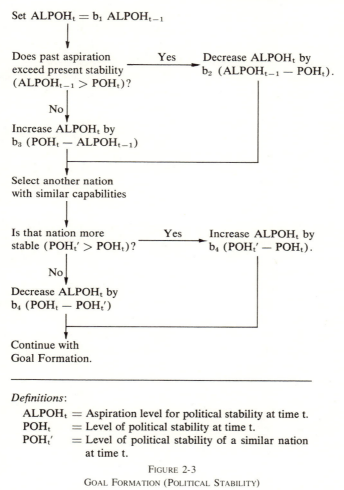

Set $ALPOH_t = b_1\ ALPOH_{t-1}$

Does past aspiration exceed present stability $(ALPOH_{t-1} > POH_t)$?

Yes → Decrease $ALPOH_t$ by $b_2\ (ALPOH_{t-1} - POH_t)$.

No ↓

Increase $ALPOH_t$ by $b_3\ (POH_t - ALPOH_{t-1})$

Select another nation with similar capabilities

Is that nation more stable $(POH_t' > POH_t)$?

Yes → Increase $ALPOH_t$ by $b_4\ (POH_t' - POH_t)$.

No ↓

Decrease $ALPOH_t$ by $b_4\ (POH_t - POH_t')$

Continue with Goal Formation.

Definitions:

$ALPOH_t$ = Aspiration level for political stability at time t.
POH_t = Level of political stability at time t.
POH_t' = Level of political stability of a similar nation at time t.

FIGURE 2-3
GOAL FORMATION (POLITICAL STABILITY)

readily raise their aspiration levels and more reluctantly lower them when failure is encountered. Hence, b_2, the amount that the aspiration level for political stability will be decreased (given failure to achieve the aspiration level set in the previous period), is less than b_3.

The third consideration in setting this aspiration level centers on the relative achievement of other nations in this goal area. That is, it is assumed that the achievement of significant other nations with regard to political stability in relation to one's own achievement will condition the aspiration level. The coefficient b_4, may be considered the propensity to emulate. Since its value is assumed to be greater than zero, the aspiration level of a nation will be increased by the attainment of a higher level of political stability by another nation that is deemed to be significant.

The significant other nation is chosen on the basis of similarity of resource capability and level of development. The nation most similar to the self nation on these factors will be selected for comparison.

The Goal of Economic Growth

The Aspiration Level for Economic Growth (ALGRO) is assumed to operate in the same manner as the aspiration level for political stability. The steps involved in setting this aspiration level are outlined in Figure 2–4. The coefficients b_5 through b_8 correspond to the coefficients b_1 through b_4. The first, b_5, specifies the propensity to raise or lower the aspiration level for economic growth, regardless of what has happened internally or externally in the immediate past. The next two parameters, b_6 and b_7, govern the degree to which success or failure in fulfilling previous aspirations modify present aspirations. Once again, we assume that b_6 is less than b_7; hence, success fosters a greater amount of increase in the aspiration level than failure engenders in the opposite direction. The last parameter, b_8, determines the degree to which the achievement of other nations in the area of economic growth causes a nation to increase or decrease its own aspirations in this area.

The Goal of National Security

As we indicated earlier, nations are assumed to be grouped into alliances, and the model, as it presently stands, does not allow for the position of non-alignment. Furthermore, the international system is bipolar in nature, with a major power functioning as the leader or dominant member in each bloc. The perspectives of bloc

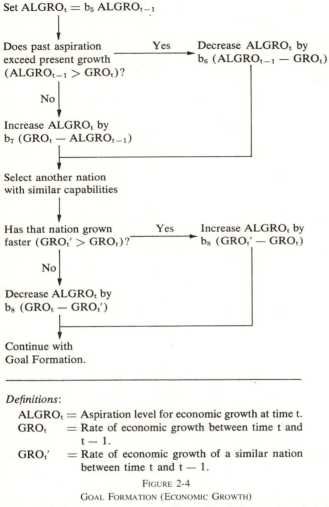

Set $ALGRO_t = b_5 \, ALGRO_{t-1}$

Does past aspiration exceed present growth $(ALGRO_{t-1} > GRO_t)$? —— Yes —— Decrease $ALGRO_t$ by $b_6 \, (ALGRO_{t-1} - GRO_t)$

No

Increase $ALGRO_t$ by $b_7 \, (GRO_t - ALGRO_{t-1})$

Select another nation with similar capabilities

Has that nation grown faster $(GRO_t' > GRO_t)$? —— Yes —— Increase $ALGRO_t$ by $b_8 \, (GRO_t' - GRO_t)$

No

Decrease $ALGRO_t$ by $b_8 \, (GRO_t - GRO_t')$

Continue with Goal Formation.

Definitions:

$ALGRO_t$ = Aspiration level for economic growth at time t.
GRO_t = Rate of economic growth between time t and $t - 1$.
GRO_t' = Rate of economic growth of a similar nation between time t and $t - 1$.

FIGURE 2-4

GOAL FORMATION (ECONOMIC GROWTH)

leaders and bloc members are sufficiently different that their behavior in regard to national security questions deserves separate treatment.

However, there are some common elements in their decision

processes. National security is identified with the ability to successfully counter the use of coercion by other nations. Hence, when we speak of the aspiration level for national security (for both bloc leaders and bloc members), we will be referring to the level of defense that is considered adequate for countering external threat.

Since national goal setting behavior is anticipatory in nature, we have modified Singer's threat equation (Threat = Intent x Capability).[35] That is, the national desire is for an ability to counter not simply *present* threat, but also *future* threat. Accordingly, our formulation equates expected threat to the product of expected intent and expected capability. In a later section, we will discuss specifically how these expectations are arrived at in the model, when we examine the Expectation Formation process.

When a nation scans its environment for possible threats to its security, the search pattern must be selective. The limitations of time and resources prevent the nation from treating all nations as potentially equally threatening. In the present model, a simulated nation assumes that those nations in the international system with whom it has not entered into mutual security agreements are potentially threatening. The alliance structure serves as a guide in simplifying the search for enemies.

The Bloc Leader

When the leader of an alliance bloc ponders the question of national security, the nation perceives the question in terms of bloc security. As the leader of a bloc, the nation takes upon itself the duty of evaluating the security position of its alliance vis-a-vis an opposing alliance. Leadership confers larger responsibilities than membership, and the security interests of the leader become intertwined with those of the group; accordingly, the goal of national security merges with the goal of bloc security.

The gap that the alliance leader watches closely, then, is the difference between the amount of threat expected from the opposing bloc and the amount of threat-countering ability that his own bloc will have in the future.[36] If the bloc's counter-threat capability is adequate, then the alliance leader will be content with cur-

46

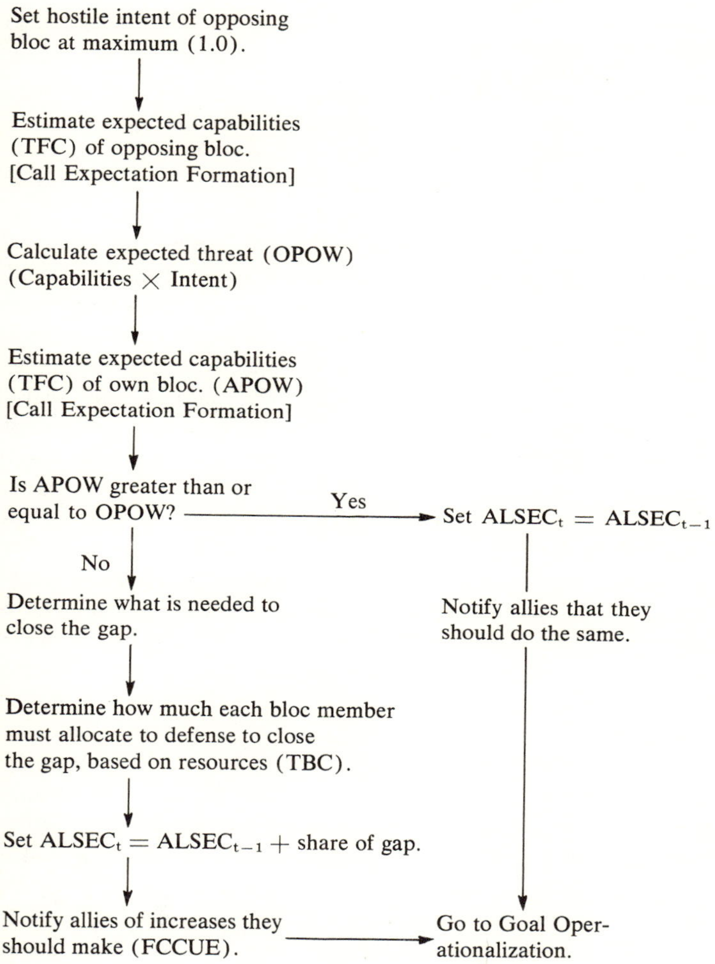

Set hostile intent of opposing
bloc at maximum (1.0).

Estimate expected capabilities
(TFC) of opposing bloc.
[Call Expectation Formation]

Calculate expected threat (OPOW)
(Capabilities $\times$ Intent)

Estimate expected capabilities
(TFC) of own bloc. (APOW)
[Call Expectation Formation]

Is APOW greater than or   Yes
equal to OPOW? ───────────────────────→ Set $ALSEC_t = ALSEC_{t-1}$

    No

Determine what is needed to   Notify allies that they
close the gap.   should do the same.

Determine how much each bloc member
must allocate to defense to close
the gap, based on resources (TBC).

Set $ALSEC_t = ALSEC_{t-1} +$ share of gap.

Notify allies of increases they   ──────→   Go to Goal Oper-
should make (FCCUE).   ationalization.

Definitions:

$ALSEC_t$ = Aspiration level for national security at time t.
OPOW   = Expected threat from opposing bloc.
APOW   = Expected threat-countering capability of own
             bloc.
FCCUE = Suggested level of force capability allocation
             for bloc members.

FIGURE 2-5
GOAL FORMATION (NATIONAL SECURITY, BLOC LEADER)

rent defense commitments and those of his allies. If, on the other hand, the counter-threat capability is not judged adequate, then a revision of alliance security policy will be sought.

Figure 2–5 outlines the decision processes that the bloc leader executes in setting his own aspiration level for national security and deciding upon what defense allocation his allies should make. As mentioned above, nations are sensitive to expected threat, and expected threat is equal to the product of expected intent and expected capability. One of the differences between bloc leaders and bloc members is their estimate of expected intentions. Intent in the threat calculation is considered to be the probability that a given nation's force capability will be used against one's own nation. Hence, the upper bound of intent is 1.0 and the lower bound is 0.0.

The first step in the decision process incorporates the assumption that, in the case of alliance leaders, expected intent is always at the maximum value of 1.0, and the reasons for this are several. It is assumed that the special responsibilities of leadership make a nation more cautious in its security calculations, and therefore the nation will, in all likelihood, wish to be able to counter the worst of all possible situations. It can do so, in part, because of its larger resource base and the associated consequence of being able to work with such a pessimistic view without being overwhelmed. And, of course, there is some realism contained in the special paranoia of bloc leaders as their prominence and centrality in the international system make them primary targets for other nations.

The next two steps in Figure 2–5 involve computing the amount of threat that the opposing alliance is likely to present in the next time period (OPOW). Since intent has been set at 1.0, the calculation reduces to this:

$$OPOW = \sum^{\substack{\text{non-} \\ \text{allies}}} TFC_{t+1}$$

The expected value of TFC_{t+1} is given by the application of one of the information processing rules to data concerning a nation's past behavior with regard to total force capability levels, and is described in a later section.

The next step is to simply estimate the amount of counter-threat capability (APOW) of the leader's own alliance; this is calculated according to the following formula:

$$\text{APOW} = \sum^{\text{self +}}_{\text{allies}} \text{TFC}_{t+1}$$

With these estimates of the future threat capabilities of both blocs in hand, the bloc leader is ready to decide whether a change in its aspiration level for national security is necessary. If APOW is greater than OPOW, then the leader's Aspiration Level for National Security (ALSEC) will remain unchanged. If this relationship does not hold, then a series of steps is undertaken to formulate a defense policy for the alliance that will close the gap.

The leader first considers the amount by which the alliance, as a whole, must increase its military strength to counter the expected threat. The leader then computes the share of the increase that each ally should contribute, based on its respective resource capability. The leader then modifies the aspiration level for national security in accordance with what is considered to be its fair share of the additional defense burden. In addition, the leader transmits cues (FCCUE) to his allies, suggesting to them an appropriate level of defense allocation. This completes the determination of the aspiration level for national security for a bloc leader.

The Bloc Member

Turning to Figure 2–6, we see that the bloc member (like the bloc leader) reacts to the expectation of threat. For the most part, however, the member cannot afford to assume the worst, and is not so much concerned about the security of the bloc as its own security. These and other factors compel the alliance member to be more discriminating in an assessment of threat. To do so, the alliance member examines the verbal conflict behavior, Hostile Communication (HOST), of each non-allied nation in order to make estimates concerning the future intentions of these nations. The following formula summarizes the first three steps in Figure 2-6:

49

$$OPOW = \sum^{\substack{\text{non-}\\\text{allies}}} b_9 \bullet HOST_{jt+1} \bullet TFC_{jt+1}$$

where TFC has the same meaning as above, and HOST (jt + 1) is the amount of verbal hostility the nation expects to receive from nation j in the next time period. The coefficient, b_9, is a parameter that indicates the propensity to discount verbal statements, when estimating intentions.

The fourth step in the decision process entails the use of the Expectation Formation process to predict the level of armaments the bloc member can expect to have available next period (IPOW). After this determination, the member nation compares expected threat (OPOW) to his own expected threat-countering capability (IPOW). If the comparison is favorable for the bloc member, then the aspiration level for national security is tentatively assigned the same value as it had in the previous period. If, on the other hand, IPOW is less than OPOW, the aspiration level is raised by an amount sufficient to close the expected gap.

The bloc member now has a tentative aspiration level for national security, but it also has received a cue (FCCUE) from its bloc leader suggesting a certain level of armaments that would be appropriate according to the leader's assessment of the world situation. The last steps in Figure 2–6 deal with reconciling these views and setting a final ALSEC. If the leader's estimate (FCCUE) is less than, or equal to, the member's own estimate (ALSEC), then the member acquiesces and accepts the leader's policy. If, on the other hand, the bloc leader's estimate is more pessimistic than the member's, and the leader's estimate is greater than the member's, a negotiation process is begun, and the outcome is determined in the following way.

The outcome of the negotiation process is dependent upon the amount of power the leader exercises over the member at the time of the negotiation. Etzioni identified three basic types of power in his discussion of political integration.[37] These are utilitarian or economic power, identive or ideological power, and coercive or military power. Working with this power typology, Denis Forcese

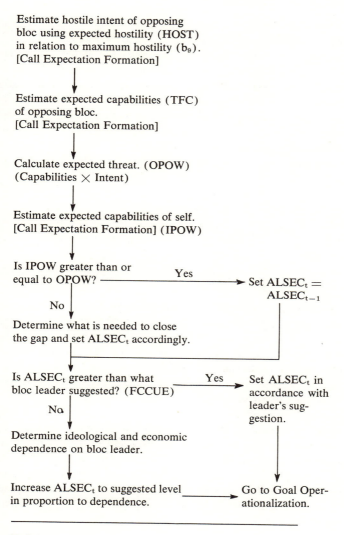

Estimate hostile intent of opposing
bloc using expected hostility (HOST)
in relation to maximum hostility (b_9).
[Call Expectation Formation]

Estimate expected capabilities (TFC)
of opposing bloc.
[Call Expectation Formation]

Calculate expected threat. (OPOW)
(Capabilities $\times$ Intent)

Estimate expected capabilities of self.
[Call Expectation Formation] (IPOW)

Is IPOW greater than or
equal to OPOW? ——— Yes ———→ Set $ALSEC_t =$
                                  $ALSEC_{t-1}$

No

Determine what is needed to close
the gap and set $ALSEC_t$ accordingly.

Is $ALSEC_t$ greater than what   Yes   Set $ALSEC_t$ in
bloc leader suggested? (FCCUE) ———→   accordance with
                                        leader's sug-
No   gestion.

Determine ideological and economic
dependence on bloc leader.

Increase $ALSEC_t$ to suggested level ———→ Go to Goal Oper-
in proportion to dependence.   ationalization.

Definitions:

$ALSEC_t$ = Aspiration level for national security at time t.
HOST   = Hostile communication.

FIGURE 2-6
GOAL FORMATION (NATIONAL SECURITY, BLOC MEMBER)

found that only the first two of these were effective in coordinating the behavior of alliance leaders and members.[38] Forcese's findings were based largely on data generated by the INS model. We have made the outcome of the bargaining process dependent upon the amount of utilitarian and identive power that the leader exercises over the member.

Utilitarian power is likely to be most effective when the bloc member is highly Economically Dependent upon the leader (EDEP) by virtue of past trade and aid flows. This latter condition varies from 0 to 1.0 and is computed in the following way:

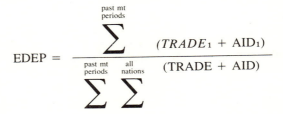

$$EDEP = \frac{\sum\limits_{\substack{past\ mt \\ periods}} (TRADE_1 + AID_1)}{\sum\limits_{\substack{past\ mt \\ periods}} \sum\limits_{\substack{all \\ nations}} (TRADE + AID)}$$

The numerator in this equation indicates how much trade and aid the bloc member has received from its bloc leader (nation l) in the past, and the denominator is the total amount of trade and aid it has received from all nations during the same period of time. Thus, economic dependency reflects the degree to which the bloc member's economic transactions with the outside world have been dominated by its bloc leader.

Identive power reflects a kind of moral suasion that an alliance leader can exert by the manipulation of symbolic rewards. We postulate first that the greater the ideological difference between leader and member, the less identive power the leader will be able to exercise over the member. Since we are again looking at the situation from the bloc member's point of view, we are interested in measuring Ideological Dependency (IDEP). The preliminary formulation states:

$$IDEP = 1 - \frac{|DL_i - DL_1|}{DL_i + DL_1}$$

where IDEP varies from 0 to 1.0, and l is member i's bloc leader. The numerator of the term on the right hand side of the equation measures the absolute difference in decision latitudes of the member and leader. The denominator normalizes this difference so that the value will be between 0 and 1.0. The result is that IDEP will be at its maximum when the member's DL is the same as its leader's, and it is at its minimum when they are on opposite ends of the decision latitude continuum. Thus, the further apart the member and leader are ideologically, the less dependence.

Identive power will be maximally effective and identive dependency will be higher when the world is ideologically heterogeneous and less effective when ideological differences are slight. Consequently, IDEP is modified by a term that takes into account the between-nation variance in decision latitude. This variance is greatest when one-half of the nations are on each end of the DL continuum, and smallest when they all have the same DL. Hence, the standard deviation of the distribution of DL values among the nations in the international system is normalized by the maximum value it may attain with a given system size.

The complete equation for IDEP is

$$\text{IDEP} = \left[1 - \frac{\text{DL}_i + \text{DL}_l}{\text{DL}_i - \text{DL}_l} \right] \bullet \frac{\sigma_{dl}}{\text{Max } \sigma_{dl}}$$

In general, then, when the leader and member are quite *similar* ideologically, as reflected in their DL values in a world that is characterized by high ideological diversity, the bloc leader will be able to greatly influence the member's behavior by the manipulation of symbols. If they are considerably *different* ideologically the world is relatively homogeneous, then this type of influence is not likely to be as effective.

The compromise forged between the bloc leader and member, if only tacitly, is based upon the average of EDEP and IDEP in the following manner:

$$\text{ALSEC} = \text{ALSEC} + (\text{FCCUE} - \text{ALSEC}) \bullet \left(\frac{\text{EDEP} + \text{IDEP}}{2} \right)$$

Consequently, if a bloc leader has absolute power over a member

53

(EDEP and IDEP equal to 1.0), that member would raise its own estimate of security needs, ALSEC, to the level, FCCUE, suggested by its leader. Proportionately less power means proportionately less increase, and if the bloc leader has no power over the member (EDEP and IDEP equal to 0), then the bloc member would totally disregard the leader's wishes.

At this point we have completed the setting of aspiration levels for the simulated nations. We now turn to the consideration of how these aspiration levels are to be attained.

Goal Operationalization

At this stage, each nation has a set of aspiration levels it wishes to attain. The next thing the simulated nation does is to operationalize these goals in terms of laying out a tentative resource allocation budget and the steps in this procedure are outlined in Figure 2–7. The first steps involve making preliminary estimates as to what proportion of its resources will have to go to consumer goods (CSP) to achieve its Aspiration Level for Political Stability (ALPOH). In equation form, the procedure looks like this:

$$CSP_t = CSP_{t-1} + b_{10} (ALPOH_t - POH_t) \bullet CSP_{t-1} + b_{11} PR_t$$

The first term embodies the idea that such decisions are incremental in nature, and the second states that the amount of revision is related to the degree that goal achievement has failed in the past. The third term causes the system to react when political stability is threatened by crisis. Parameter b_{10} is the goal operationalization rate and b_{11} represents the propensity of the regime to react to crisis of support by acceding to the validator's wishes with an emergency CS allocation.

The proportion of resources needed to achieve the Growth Aspiration Level (ALGRO) is the next concern of the simulated nation. The proportion (BCP) is determined in the following way:

$$BCP_t = BCP_{t-1} + b_{12} (ALGRO_t - GRO_t) \bullet BCP_{t-1}$$

GRO_t is the proportionate change in total basic capability from time $t - 1$ to the present time t. As in the case of the consumption

54

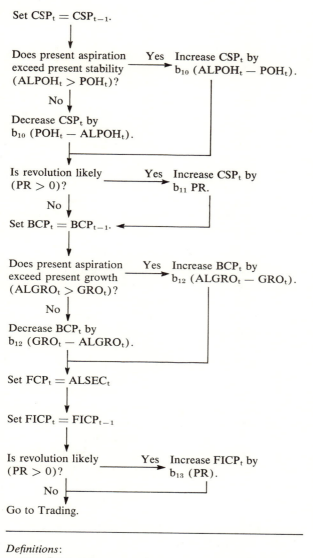

Set $CSP_t = CSP_{t-1}$.

Does present aspiration exceed present stability $(ALPOH_t > POH_t)$? — Yes → Increase CSP_t by $b_{10} (ALPOH_t - POH_t)$.

No ↓

Decrease CSP_t by $b_{10} (POH_t - ALPOH_t)$.

Is revolution likely $(PR > 0)$? — Yes → Increase CSP_t by $b_{11} PR$.

No ↓

Set $BCP_t = BCP_{t-1}$.

Does present aspiration exceed present growth $(ALGRO_t > GRO_t)$? — Yes → Increase BCP_t by $b_{12} (ALGRO_t - GRO_t)$.

No ↓

Decrease BCP_t by $b_{12} (GRO_t - ALGRO_t)$.

Set $FCP_t = ALSEC_t$

Set $FICP_t = FICP_{t-1}$

Is revolution likely $(PR > 0)$? — Yes → Increase $FICP_t$ by $b_{13} (PR)$.

No ↓

Go to Trading.

Definitions:

CSP_t, BCP_t, FCP_t = Proportion of resources allocated to consumption, investment, and defense sectors, respectively.

$FICP_t$ = Proportion of force capability devoted to internal security.

FIGURE 2-7
GOAL OPERATIONALIZATION

allocation decision, the past allocation for capital goods is adjusted, based on how successful the nation has been in attaining its growth goal. A higher than desired rate of growth will produce a drop in capital investment, while the opposite condition will cause the proportion of resources devoted to capital goods to increase.

The proportion of resources devoted to national security concerns (FCP) is set equal to the ALSEC level previously established.

$$FCP_t = ALSEC_t$$

The remaining allocation decision involves the establishment of the proportion of current Total Force Capability (TFC) that will be used for internal control (FICP).

$$FICP_t = FICP_{t-1} + b_{13}PR_t$$

The maximum value of FICP is .30, as it is in the INS model. The form of this equation is such that if the Probability of a Revolution (PR) is zero, then the proportion of forces allocated to internal control does not change. As revolution becomes more likely, then, the internal security forces are increased proportionately. Hence, a threat of revolution prompts the decision-making unit to attempt raising both consumption levels and internal security force levels.

This set of decisions completes the goal operationization process of a simulated nation. It now has a set of concrete objectives, which, although not necessarily consistent with one another, can serve as a basis for evaluating and selecting specific alternatives.

One major profitable alternative open to the nation is the exchanging of goods with other nations, and it is this process that we will consider next.

Trading

International trade entails certain non-economic costs, which we will call sovereignty costs. The kinds of costs referred to here have been alluded to by John Maynard Keynes. "Let goods be home-spun wherever it is reasonably and conveniently possible. . . We do not wish. . . to be at the mercy of world forces. . . . We wish to be our own masters, and to be as free as

56

we can make ourselves from the interferences of the outside world.''[39]

Jan Pen concluded, ''. . . nationalism leads to protection, the deliberate choking-off of imports with the intention of reserving the home market for home producers.''[40] The methods by which nations accomplish this are through import duties, quotas, excise taxes, manipulation of public health and administrative rules, government purchase restrictions, import permits, and, of course, the state trading monopoly.

The process that governs this activity is outlined in Figure 2–8. The simulated nations set import limits for each of the three kinds of goods. These Import Limits (IMLIM) are a function of the size of the national economy and the particular priority that a specific type of goods has in the tentative allocation mix. The import limit on all imports (TOTIM) is

$$TOTIM = b_{14}TBC$$

where b_{14} is the international trade autarky factor, or propensity to import. This total figure is apportioned among the three types of goods according to the relative magnitude of the sector values produced by the goal operationalization process. Thus, the import limit for a specific good, such as BC's would be

$$IMLIM_{bc} = \frac{BCP}{CSP - CSMF + BCP + FCP} \bullet TOTIM$$

where CSMF is the proportion of national resources that must be allocated to the consumption sector to satisfy the CSmin requirement. Hence, if CSP, BCP, and FCP were .86, .10, and .04 respectively, and the fraction of resources that must go to consumption, CSMF, is .8, then the CS, BC, and FC shares of the total imports would be 30 percent, 50 percent, and 20 percent respectively.

In addition to deciding in the preliminary trading stage how many foreign goods will be allowed to enter the nation, the nation must also decide the prices at which it is willing to sell its goods to other nations. The national set of Export Prices (EXPRC) is a function of a series of factors.

The basic unbiased price, or what might be considered the

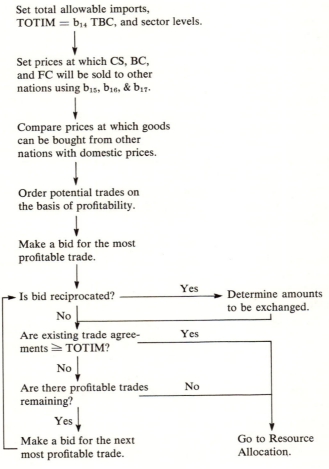

FIGURE 2-8
TRADING

equal profit price, is given by the following rather formidable formula:

$$EXPRC_{ijkl} = \frac{GR_{jl} \bullet GR_{il} \bullet (GR_{ik} + GR_{jk})}{GR_{ik} \bullet GR_{jk} \bullet (GR_{il} + GR_{jl})}$$

This formula states the amount of good 1 that nation i would want from nation j in exchange for one unit of good k. GRi1, GRi2, and GRi3 are nation i's generation rates for CS, BC, and FC goods respectively. The terms of trade given by this formula are such that nation i and j would derive an equal amount of profit by concluding a trade on these terms.

The 50–50 profit split appears to be a powerful norm in human interaction. Simmel, Durkheim, Homans, and Schelling are just a few of the authors who have noted its prominence.[41] In referring to the INS trade negotiations, Sherman commented, "these findings demonstrate the pervasiveness and importance of the 50–50 profit splitting norm for the prediction of the negotiation outcome."[42]

On the other hand, we have reason to suspect that there are factors which produce a departure from the equal profit price. The first one we shall consider is the preference among allies for trading with one another.

If we may define alliances as formal agreements among nations to be responsive to one another, then we may postulate that this general state of responsiveness will lead allies to reduce their export prices to one another. Furthermore, it is reasonable to suggest that allies frequently interact and negotiate on a wide range of matters, and consequently the costs of trading are reduced.[43] By the same reasoning, the cost of trading with nations that are not frequently interacted with, and to which one is not responsive, are higher. Consequently, EXPRC is modified in the following way:[44]

$$EXPRC_{ijkl} = EXPRC_{ijkl} - b_{15} (2 \bullet ALLY_{ij} - 1) \bullet EXPRC_{ijkl}$$

where $ALLY_{ij}$ equals 1 if i and j are allies and 0 otherwise. The parameter, b_{15}, is the alliance preference pricing factor, or, alternately, the price increase (expressed as a proportion) that a non-ally receives.

The relative economic strengths of the two nations involved is yet another factor that may affect export prices. There are, of course, two ways this can be manifested. One line of argument states that the terms of trade are such that, in effect, richer nations

59

charge poorer nations more than they charge other richer nations and in this way are able to exploit poorer countries. On the other hand, Sherman observed in INS trading patterns a "paternalistic attitude toward the smaller under-developed countries" on the part of larger countries.[45] The consequence of this would be that richer nations charge poorer nations less than they charge other richer nations. Both of these factors are embodied in the following modification of EXPRC:

$$EXPRC_{ijkl} = EXPRC_{ijkl} + b_{16} \left[\frac{TBC_j}{TBC_j + TBC_i} - \frac{1}{2} \right] \bullet EXPRC_{ijkl}$$

If b_{16}, the economic strength pricing factor, is greater than zero, then export prices are adjusted according to the ability to pay, thus being of benefit to poorer nations. If, on the other hand, b_{16} is less than zero, trade prices are biased in favor of the wealthier nations. The fractional term following this parameter assesses the relative size of the national resource bases, as they differ from equality. For example, if a potential trading partner has twice the total basic capability of the price setting nation, then the price for each good would be increased (or decreased, depending upon the sign of b_{16}) proportionately by one-sixth of the value of b_{16}.

The final factor that enters into pricing decisions is risk, and in international trade, two kinds of risk are involved. The first of these is the possibility that one nation will fulfill its part of the bargain, while another nation will not. And, since trade is not a simultaneous exchange, the risk involved requires compensation. The second, more indirect form of risk is that associated with whether or not the goods sold to a nation will enable it to act contrary to the selling nation's interests at some future time. Trading-with-the-enemy legislation is one means by which nations attempt to minimize this latter type of risk. Accordingly, the following formula stipulates an increase in the profit derived from trading with a hostile or distrusted nation to compensate for the increased risk.[46]

60

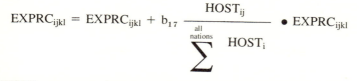

$$EXPRC_{ijkl} = EXPRC_{ijkl} + b_{17} \; \frac{HOST_{ij}}{\sum\limits^{\text{all nations}} HOST_i} \; \bullet \; EXPRC_{ijkl}$$

$HOST_{ij}$ represents the hostile feelings that nation i feels for nation j at the present time. If the price setting nation, i, feels no hostility towards the potential trading partner, j, then no price increase is made. If, on the other hand, all of i's hostility (represented by the denominator in the equation above) is directed at nation j, then the full degree of increase stipulated by b_{17} is made.

This completes the setting of export prices for the simulated nations, and we can return to Figure 2–8 in order to best understand the rest of the trading process. The trading process itself begins with each nation computing the foreign and domestic prices for each commodity and preparing a list of profitable trades, rank-ordered by profitability. A trade round consists of each nation making a bid to trade a given commodity to a specific nation for another specific commodity. After each nation has bid its most profitable trade, a check is made to see if any trade offers have been reciprocated. If this is not the case, then a new trade round is begun and the nations bid for their next most profitable trade. This again is followed by a reciprocity check, but this check includes bids made in both the first and second rounds. Trade rounds continue until all nations, except one, have either reached their import limit and/or have no profitable trades yet to bid. When this state is reached, trade ceases.

The reciprocation of bids entails agreement on the terms of trade, and it is only the actual quantities that remain to be determined. These quantities are based on the smaller of the two import limits of the two nations involved, and the trading continues.

Resource Allocation

At this stage in the decision processes, a simulated nation begins to evaluate its over-all position with reference to all goal areas. Prior to this point, activity in each goal area was carried on

61

independently from activity in the other goal areas. The problem of goal conflict is considered at this point, and a resolution of any such conflict is sought; Figure 2–9 outlines the steps in this process.

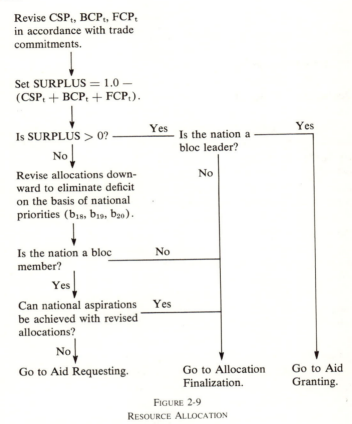

Revise CSP_t, BCP_t, FCP_t in accordance with trade commitments.

Set SURPLUS $= 1.0 - (CSP_t + BCP_t + FCP_t)$.

Is SURPLUS > 0? ——Yes—— Is the nation a bloc leader? ——Yes——

No

Revise allocations downward to eliminate deficit on the basis of national priorities (b_{18}, b_{19}, b_{20}).

No

Is the nation a bloc member? ——No——

Yes

Can national aspirations be achieved with revised allocations? Yes

No

Go to Aid Requesting.

Go to Allocation Finalization.

Go to Aid Granting.

FIGURE 2-9
RESOURCE ALLOCATION

Before this evaluation can take place, however, the nation must adjust its allocation decisions in accordance with any trade commitments that may have been made. This process involves the shifting of resources into sectors where export commitments have been made and away from sectors where import commitments have been received. Consequently, the values for CSP, BCP, and FCP (the tentative proportional allocation decisions) may require some adjustment.

The nation, at this point, considers the possibility that it may have over-extended itself. If the sum of CSP, BCP, and FCP is greater than one, the nation is faced with a deficit and a budget crisis. In the event of this situation, the following processes are activated to resolve the crisis.

First, a new emergency budget is drafted, based on two factors: (1) the size of the commitment that has been made in each sector, as indicated by the tentative proportional allocation decisions; and (2) the national priority for each sector. This latter set of values, which may be considered budget-crisis-resolution weights, indicates in a critical situation the degree of importance ascribed to each sector. Accordingly, the revised CS allocation would be

$$CSP = \frac{b_{18}CSP}{b_{18}CSP + b_{19}BCP + b_{20}FCP}$$

where b_{18} is the parameter denoting relative priority assigned to the area of political stability. The new values for BCP and FCP are calculated in an analogous way with the parameters b_{19} and b_{20} indicating the relative priorities of economic growth and national security. The nation now has a budget that is acceptable, but not necessarily desirable, in terms of its consequences.

Aid Requesting

The nation may find, for example, that the resulting level of consumption (after adding CS to be imported and substracting CS to be exported) is far short of its perceived need, if its aspiration level for political stability is to be achieved. It may, under these circumstances, make a request for a grant of CS value from another nation in the international system. The steps in this process are outlined in Figure 2–10.

However, there are some basic rules constraining nations in making aid requests. At some future time we may want to relax some of these constraints, but for the moment they are considered necessary simplifications.

63

Determine sectors where
deficits are expected.

↓

Estimate amount needed
to achieve goals in each
area.

↓

Formulate aid request and
transmit it to bloc leader.

↓

Go to Allocation Finali-
zation after bloc leader
acts on request.

FIGURE 2-10
AID REQUESTING

The first of these constraints specifies that alliance leaders may
not make aid requests since such requests would compromise their
position of authority and undermine their prominence in their
alliance. Alliance members, on the other hand, when aid is required, direct requests only to the leader of their alliance. This is a
constraint that we reluctantly impose and resolve to relax in the
future.

Within these constraints, a nation requests aid of specific commodities to the degree that its prior considerations revealed a
discrepancy between the value level needed to achieve a goal and
the value level that is expected as a consequence of fulfilling
budget decisions.

Aid Granting

A bloc leader, then, may be confronted with a large number of
aid requests, and the rendering of decisions concerning these requests proceeds in the manner outlined in Figure 2–11. There are
four factors that exert control over the granting-of-aid decisions.
First consideration is given to the leader's economic ability to
fulfill the aid requests it has received. If the leader has found that
it can meet its aspiration levels and have uncommitted resources

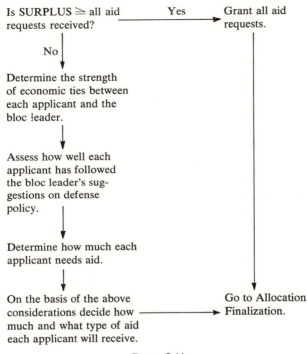

Is SURPLUS ≧ all aid requests received? — Yes → Grant all aid requests.

No ↓

Determine the strength of economic ties between each applicant and the bloc leader.

↓

Assess how well each applicant has followed the bloc leader's suggestions on defense policy.

↓

Determine how much each applicant needs aid.

↓

On the basis of the above considerations decide how much and what type of aid each applicant will receive. → Go to Allocation Finalization.

FIGURE 2-11
AID GRANTING

remaining, it will consider aid requests; if not, any aid requests it has received will be ignored. On the other hand, if the leader's surplus permits all aid requests to be granted without sacrificing the attainment of its own goals; it will grant all requests.

In the event of a situation where the leader has a surplus, but this surplus is not adequate to satisfy all the aid requests, the leader must decide how much and to whom aid will be given. There are three criteria that a bloc leader uses to make such decisions.

The first consideration for the bloc leader is the degree to which the requesting nation's economy and its own are interdependent. The greater the economic linkages between the two nations, the

65

greater the share of available aid resources the requesting nation will receive. The economic linkage with nation j, $ETIE_j$ is

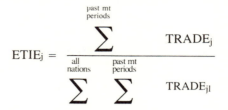

$$ETIE_j = \frac{\sum\limits_{\substack{\text{past mt} \\ \text{periods}}} TRADE_j}{\sum\limits_{\substack{\text{all} \\ \text{nations}}} \sum\limits_{\substack{\text{past mt} \\ \text{periods}}} TRADE_{jl}}$$

The numerator of this equation indicates the amount of exports that the aid-requesting nation, j, has directed to the bloc leader who is considering the request, over the past mt periods of time. The denominator yields the aid-requesting nation's total exports to all nations over the same period of time. Thus, $ETIE_j$, which varies from 0 to 1, indicates the degree to which nation j, the aid-requesting nation, has concentrated its trade with its bloc leader.

The second consideration of the bloc leader is the degree (reflected in the value of $DTIE_j$) the aid-requesting ally has followed previous suggestions concerning defense policy. This value is produced by an algorithm, which has as its essential component, a Pearson product-moment correlation coefficient. The TFC levels of the alliance leader and aid requester are correlated over time and the resulting coefficient is rescaled in such a way that an r of -1.0 yields a $DTIE_j$ value of 0 and an r of $+1.0$ corresponds to a $DTIEj$ value of $+1.0$.

Finally, consideration is given to the need of the aid-requesting nation as embodied in its request relative to other nation's requests. Relative need is assessed according to the following formula by relating each nation's request of aid to the total requests that have been received.

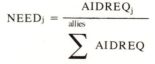

$$NEED_j = \frac{AIDREQ_j}{\sum\limits_{\text{allies}} AIDREQ}$$

where AIDREQ is defined as the value of an aid request measured in the number of units of TBC that the leader would need to allocate so as to meet the request. The total value of aid that the requesting nation, j, receives from its bloc leaders, l, designated $TAID_{lj}$; is as follows.

$$TAID_{lj} = \frac{(NEED_j + ETIE_j + DTIE_j)}{3} \bullet SURPLUS_l$$

We then can see that need, economic ties, and defense ties are weighted equally in the determination of the share of the bloc leader's available resources (SURPLUS) that each aid-requesting nation receives. The total for each receiving nation is then divided among the various commodities, in relation to the degree that each commodity was originally requested by the nation.

Allocation Finalization

The final steps in the resource allocation process are outlined in Figure 2–12. If aid has been given, then the value production schedule must be adjusted to produce the CS, BC, and FC units that have been promised. If aid has been received, then the production mix may need to be altered to take into account the type

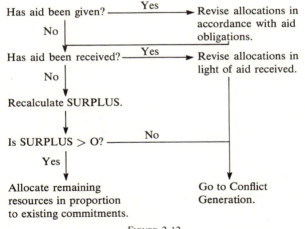

FIGURE 2-12
ALLOCATION FINALIZATION

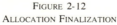

and amount of aid received. It is possible that the nation may still have uncommitted recources (SURPLUS greater than 0), and in the event this is true, the remaining resources are allocated to the value sectors, proportionate to the relative size of the existing sector commitments.

Conflict Generation

Nations may express hostility toward one another during each time period, and the process that generates these conflict flows in outlined in Figure 2–13. The first step in the determination of hostility levels involves a reaction factor. The action-reaction phenomena has been frequently discussed, and the work of Zinnes is particularly relevant here.[47] Zinnes examined both historical and simulated data and found a positive relationship between "x's expression of hostility to y and y's perception of unfriendliness," and that "there is a positive relationship between the perception of unfriendliness and the expression of hostility."[48] However, we will add to this basic formulation the proposal that nations react to expected hostility by anticipating how hostile another nation will be in the future, with the aim of deterring that behavior. Accordingly, the Expectation Formation process, to be discussed shortly, is used to yield a value for $HOST_{(ji\ t+1)}$, and the equation is

$$HOST_{ijt+1} = b_{21}HOST_{jit+1}$$

where $HOST_{ji\ t+1}$ is the amount of hostility nation i expects from nation j in the next period and $HOST_{ij\ t+1}$ is the amount of hostility that nation i is considering sending to nation j in that same next period.

There are factors that work to repress the expression of hostility, and three kinds of factors that modify the expression of hostile feelings have been included. The first of these factors comes into play when there are great power differences between actor and target. Rummel reports a significant positive association between the discrepancy in military power between a pair of nations and the level of threats, accusations, and protests that pass between the nations.[49] Brody, Benham, and Milstein found that if a weaker simulated nation perceived hostility emanating from a

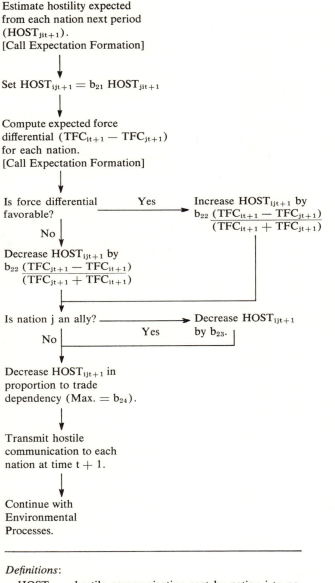

Estimate hostility expected from each nation next period ($HOST_{jit+1}$).
[Call Expectation Formation]

Set $HOST_{ijt+1} = b_{21} HOST_{jit+1}$

Compute expected force differential ($TFC_{it+1} - TFC_{jt+1}$) for each nation.
[Call Expectation Formation]

Is force differential favorable? — **Yes** → Increase $HOST_{ijt+1}$ by $b_{22} \dfrac{(TFC_{it+1} - TFC_{jt+1})}{(TFC_{it+1} + TFC_{jt+1})}$

No

Decrease $HOST_{ijt+1}$ by $b_{22} \dfrac{(TFC_{jt+1} - TFC_{it+1})}{(TFC_{jt+1} + TFC_{it+1})}$

Is nation j an ally? — **Yes** → Decrease $HOST_{ijt+1}$ by b_{23}.

No

Decrease $HOST_{ijt+1}$ in proportion to trade dependency (Max. $= b_{24}$).

Transmit hostile communication to each nation at time $t + 1$.

Continue with Environmental Processes.

Definitions:

$HOST_{ijt}$ = hostile communication sent by nation i to nation j at time t.

FIGURE 2-13
CONFLICT GENERATION

stronger one, it was less likely to respond with verbal hostility than if it emanated from a weaker one.[50] This finding has been partially supported in analyses using real world data, as well. Erich Weede reports, "powerful states are more likely to engage in verbal conflict activities than relatively powerless states."[51]

Hence, the next steps outlined in Figure 2–13 involve computing the expected force differential, again calling upon the Expectation Formation process. If the force differential is positive, then HOST is increased by the following amount:

$$b_{22} \frac{TFC_{it+1} - TFC_{jt+1}}{TFC_{it+1} + TFC_{jt+1}}$$

The division term normalizes the force differential value so that is varies from —1.0 to 1.0, and this modified value determines the fraction of b_{22} that will be added to the value of HOST. Thus, if the expected levels of force capability are two to one in favor of the acting nation, i, then one-third of the value of b_{22} would be added to the hostility level.

If, on the other hand, the expected force differential is negative, then the level of hostility will be lowered by a certain fraction of b_{22}. This fraction is also determined by the above equation. Thus, if the expected levels of force capability are two to one in favor of the target nation, then the acting nation will lower his hostility level by one-third the value of b_{22}. The second factor operating in the conflict generation process takes into account the effects of alliances on the expression of hostility between nations. Zinnes found that there is a tendency for a nation to perceive less hostility from an ally than a non-ally, and to express less hostility to an ally than a non-ally.[52] Consequently, it is postulated that a nation will be willing to overlook a certain amount of hostility from an ally in the interests of preserving the alliance. Hence, the next set of steps in Figure 2–13 involves determining whether or not the target nation is an ally, and if so, the level of hostility is decreased by the amount b_{23}.

The third and final set of steps in Figure 2–13 takes into account the effect of close economic ties on the expression of hostility. The reasons for including this term are similar to those given

70

above for the alliance factor. The stronger the economic dependence, the more effort will be made to repress the expression of hostility, up to a maximum value, for the sake of maintaining economic ties. The relevant formulation is:

$$b_{24} \frac{TRADE_{ji}}{\displaystyle\sum_{\substack{\text{all} \\ \text{nations}}} TRADE_i}$$

The numerator in this equation indicates the amount of exports the target nation, j, sent to the acting nation, i, in the last trading round, while the denominator indicates the total amount of exports the acting nation received in that trading round. In the context of the total equation, the reduction in the level of hostility will be proportional to the target nation's share of the acting nation's total imports. The greater the import dependency of the latter on the former, the more the hostility level will be decreased, up to the maximum, b_{24}.

Putting all these component parts together yields the following equation:

$$HOST_{ijt+1} = b_{21}HOST_{jit+1}$$

$$+ \; b_{22} \frac{TFC_{it+1} \; - \; TFC_{jt+1}}{TFC_{it+1} \; + \; TFC_{jt+1}}$$

$$- \; b_{23}ALLY_{ij}$$

$$- \; b_{24} \frac{TRADE_{ji}}{\displaystyle\sum_{\substack{\text{all} \\ \text{nations}}} TRADE_i}$$

Expectation Formation

In the previous sections, reference has been made to the development of expectations by one nation vis-a-vis the future behavior of another nation. In this section, I will discuss how these estimates of future behavior are formulated.

71

The central thesis here is that nations use information processing rules to forecast the behavior of other nations. Since much national behavior is, in part, anticipatory in nature, it is a matter of no small importance how this future behavior is estimated. An underlying assumption of all the information processing rules to be discussed here is that the best estimate of future behavior is to be found in the analysis of past and present behavior.

The particular type of forecasting rule used seems to be dependent on two considerations: (1) the perceived accuracy of the information at hand; and (2) the underlying pattern that is thought to characterize the behavior of the nation being considered. Each of these two dimensions has been divided into two categories. The information at hand may be considered accurate or approximate, and the behavior pattern may be either stable or changeable. Thus, there are four combinations:

1. Approximate information, changeable behavior.
2. Approximate information, stable behavior.
3. Accurate information, changeable behavior.
4. Accurate information, stable behavior.

As we shall see, there is an information processing rule corresponding to each pair of assumptions.

Before considering each of these in turn, it may be useful to gain an over-all view of the entire Expectation Formation process. The steps in the process are laid out in Figure 2–14, and, as is apparent, a single parameter, b_{25}, governs the whole process. Looking at the first step on the left, we see that the assumptions about information and behavior need not be made by the decision-making unit. (We will return later to this alternative and explain in more detail what happens when b_{25} is set equal to zero, and for the moment take the yes branch of the assumptions question.)

The next two steps are branching operations that determine which of the four pairs of assumptions is held by the decision-making unit. Moving from right to left in Figure 2–14, we will examine accurate information, stable behavior.

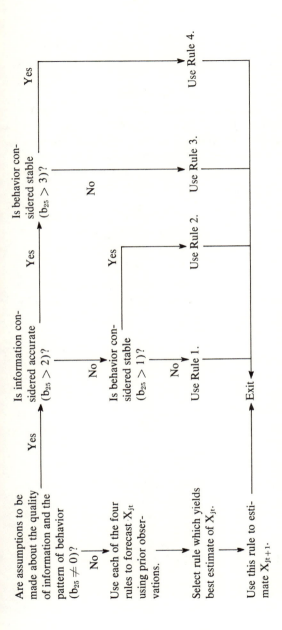

FIGURE 2-14
EXPECTATION FORMATION

Definitions:

X_{jt} = The level of behavior X by nation j at time t.

Rule 4 = Set $X_{jt+1} = X_{jt}$ [No change]

Rule 3 = Set $X_{jt+1} = X_{jt} + (X_{jt} - X_{jt-1})$ [Disjoint change]

Rule 2 = Set $X_{jt+1} = E(X_j)$ [Central tendency]

Rule 1 = Set $X_{jt+1} = \alpha + \beta (t+1)$ [Trend]

Accurate Information, Stable Behavior. Setting b_{25} equal to four invokes rule 4 as the forecasting rule to be used, and rule 4 specifies that:

$$X_{jt+1} = X_{jt}$$

That is, the level of behavior by nation j in the next time period is assumed to be equal to that emitted in the present time period. This rule stipulates that, under the conditions of accurate information and stable behavior, the best estimate of what is likely to happen in the future is what is happening presently. For obvious reasons, this has been labeled the No Change rule.

Accurate Information, Changeable Behavior. When the appropriate value has been assigned to the controlling parameter, the decision-making unit is forced to use rule 3, which is:

$$X_{jt+1} = X_{jt} + (X_{jt} - X_{jt-1})$$

Thus, the level of behavior by nation j in the next time period is taken as the present level plus the last change. Since changes in behavior are seen as disjoint and incrementalistic in nature, this rule is labed the Disjoint Change rule.

Approximate Information, Stable Behavior. Under these circumstances, rule 2 is invoked for forecasting purposes and it states that:

$$X_{jt+1} = \frac{\sum^{\substack{\text{past mt} \\ \text{periods}}} X_j}{mt}$$

The level of behavior to be emitted in the next time period is estimated as the average level of behavior over the last mt time points. Since the error in the information is assumed to be normally distributed, the mean value is thought to be the best estimate, given that no fundamental change in the behavior pattern is expected. This rule is labeled the Central Tendency rule.

Approximate Information, Changeable Behavior. The last in this set of four rules, rule 1, specifies that:

74

$$X_{jt+1} = \alpha + \beta \,(t+1)$$

where α and β are the constant and slope of the regression line relating the behavior X to time over the last mt time points. Error is assumed to be normally distributed, but the expectation is that there is a linear trend in the pattern of behavior. This rule is identified as the Trend rule.

Thus, by setting b_{25} equal to one of the four values discussed, we can force the decision-making unit to consistently use one of the four information processing rules. As we suggested earlier, there is still another option that remains to be discussed. This is the Best Fit rule.

Setting b_{25} equal to zero specifies that only empirical considerations will be used to develop forecasts, and no a priori assumptions will be made about the accuracy of information and stability of behavior. Simply stated, rule zero stipulates the use of that rule (from among the four previously discussed) that hindsight suggests would have yielded the most accurate prediction had it been used in the previous period. As we can see in Figure 2–14, this is done by using all four rules to estimate the present level of behavior, X_{jt}, and then using the rule that produces the best estimate to predict the future value, X_{jt+1}. Hence, the designation Best Fit rule. With this rule, a nation may not constantly use the same rule if, by experience, it learns that another rule is more accurate, and some elementary learning and adaptation is possible with respect to the Expectation Formation process.

This set of five rules by no means exhausts the variety of rules that could be formulated, but the rules do represent some interesting and different prediction processes. Since there are five nations, each of which may be assigned a different rule, and five rules, there are twenty-five possible combinations. In the simulation runs reported in the next chapters, it will be apparent that only a few of these combinations have been explored.

Before turning to a discussion of these simulation runs, let me trace the few remaining steps in the model's execution sequence. At this point, each of the simulated nations has made decisions about resource allocation, trade, aid, and conflict in light of its knowledge and expectations about the environment, and these decisions become inputs into the processes (described in the first part of this chapter) that specify how the environment is altered. Following these alterations, the cycle begins again as the simulated nations endeavor to cope with their redefined environment.

CHAPTER TWO NOTES

1. See Harold Guetzkow, et al., *Simulation in International Relations* (Englewood Cliffs, N.J.: Prentice-Hall, 1963), Chapter 5, "Structured Programs and their Relation to Free Activity within the Inter-Nation Simulation," pp. 103–149.

2. This is not an uncommon response to this type of problem. Newton resolved his n-body problem by reducing it to a 2-body problem (the sun and each planet individually), and one solution to the problem of the n-person game involves transforming it into a 2-person game by merging two of the players into one coalition.

3. Robert L. Heilbroner, *Understanding Macro-Economics* (Englewood Cliffs, N.J.: Prentice-Hall, 1966), p. 13.

4. *Ibid.,* p.14.

5. This assumption does not seem unreasonable since governments are typically defined as social institutions having a legal monopoly over the use of force.

6. In many of the equations which follow subscripts will be used to denote variables. The following will be true, unless otherwise noted.

Subscript	*Referant*
i	the decision-making nation
j	a nation other than the decision-making nation
l	a bloc member's bloc leader
t	the present time period
t+1	the next time period
t−1	the preceeding time period

When the variables used in an equation pertain to the decision-making nation, i, and/or are measured at the present time period, t, the subscripts are omitted. Thus, a fuller notation of the equation: $CS = CSP \bullet TBC \bullet CSGR$ would be: $CS_{it} = CSP_{it} \bullet TBC_{it} \bullet CSGR_i$.

7. David Easton, *A Framework for Political Analysis* (Englewood Cliffs, N.J.: Prentice-Hall, 1965).

8. Harold D. Lasswell, "Introduction: The Study of Political Elites," in Harold D. Lasswell and Daniel Lerner, eds., *World Revolutionary Elites* (Cambridge, Mass.: The M.I.T. Press, 1965), pp. 4–6.

9. Nicholas Rashevsky, *Mathematical Theory of Human Relations: An Approach to a Mathematical Biology of Social Phenomena* (Bloomington, Ind.: Principia Press, 1947), pp. 146–149.

10. Karl W. Deutsch, *The Analysis of International Relations* (Englewood Cliffs, N.J.: Prentice-Hall, 1968), p. 63.

11. Guetzkow, *Simulation in International Relations,* pp. 122–127.

12. *Ibid.,* p. 123.

13. *Ibid.,* p. 124.

14. *Ibid.*

15. Ibid., p. 125.

16. *Ibid.*, p. 126. In order to simplify the equations which follow we will denote summation operations in the following way.

Notation	*Meaning*
$\sum^{\text{all nations}}$	Sum of the indicated variable(s) for all nations in the system.
$\sum^{\text{allies}}$	Sum of the indicated variable(s) for those nations allied to the decision-making nation.
$\sum^{\text{non-allies}}$	Sum of the indicated variable(s) for those nations not allied to the decision-making nation.
$\sum^{\text{past mt periods}}$	Sum of the indicated variable(s) over the past mt time points, including the present.
$\sum^{\text{self+ allies}}$	Sum of the indicated variable(s) for the decision-making nation and its allies.

17. *Ibid.*, p. 127.

18. *Ibid.*, p. 114.

19. *Ibid.*, pp. 115–117.

20. James N. Rosenau, ''Pre-theories and Theories of Foreign Policy,'' in R. Barry Farrell, ed., *Approaches to Comparative and International Politics* (Evanston, Ill.: Northwestern University Press, 1966), pp. 27–92.

21. Quincy Wright, *The Study of International Relations* (New York: Appleton-Century-Crofts, 1955), pp. 543–553.

22. Morton A. Kaplan, *System and Process in International Politics* (New York: Wiley, 1957), pp. 55–56.

23. Phillip M. Gregg and Arthur S. Banks, ''Dimensions of Political Systems: Factor Analysis of a Cross-Polity Survey,'' *American Political Science Review,* 59, No. 3 (September, 1965): 602–614.

24. In the original INS model, provision was made for the decision-makers to initiate increases in decision latitude. It was not included in this extension because an inspection of INS data indicated the option was seldom used by participants and it was thought desirable to simplify the model somewhat by its exclusion.

25. Guetzkow, *Simulation in International Relations,* p. 11. This is a rearrangement of the original equation.

26. Robert E. Pendley and Charles D. Elder, "An Analysis of Office-Holding in the Inter-Nation Simulation in Terms of Contemporary Political Theory and Data on the Stability of Regimes and Governments" (Evanston, Ill.: Simulated International Processes Project, Northwestern University, November, 1966).

27. Ted R. Gurr, *Why Men Rebel* (Princeton, N.J.: University Press, 1970).

28. Guetzkow, *Simulation in International Relations,* pp. 130–131. We have collapsed two of the INS equations into one here.

29. *Ibid.,* pp. 131–132.

30. Robert C. North, "Decision-making in Crisis: An Introduction," *Journal of Conflict Resolution,* 6, No. 3 (September 1962): 198.

31. A. F. K. Organski, *World Politics* (New York: Alfred A. Knopf, 1958), p. 57.

32. Raymond Aron, *Peace and War* (New York: Praeger, 1967), p. 72.

33. J. David Singer, "The Level-of-Analysis Problem in International Relations," in Klaus Knorr and Sidney Verba, eds., *The International System: Theoretical Essays* (Princeton, N.J.: Princeton University Press, 1961), p. 86.

34. Richard Cyert and James March, *A Behavioral Theory of the Firm* (New York: Prentice-Hall, 1963), pp. 26–43.

35. J. David Singer, "Threat-perception and the Armament-Tension Dilemma," *Journal of Conflict Resolution,* 2, No. 1 (March, 1958): 90–105.

36. This formulation is similar to the Lagerstrom-North anticipated-gap model. See Richard P. Lagerstrom and Robert C. North, "An Anticipated-Gap, Mathematical Model of International Dynamics" (Stanford, Ca.: Institute of Political Studies, Stanford University, April, 1969).

37. Amitai Etzioni, *Political Unification* (New York: Holt, Rinehart and Winston, 1965).

38. Denis Forcese, "Power and Military Alliance Cohesion" (St. Louis, Mo.: unpublished Ph.D. dissertation, Department of Sociology, Washington University, 1968).

39. John Maynard Keynes as cited in Jan Pen, *A Primer of International Trade* (New York: Vintage Books, 1966), p. 93.

40. *Ibid.,* p. 94.

41. Georg Simmel, *The Sociology of Georg Simmel,* trans. and ed. Kurt H. Wolf (Glencoe, Ill.: Free Press, 1950). Emile Durkheim, *Professional Ethics and Civic Morals* (London: Routledge and Paul, 1957). George C. Homans, *Social Behavior: Its Elementary Forms* (New York: Harcourt, Brace and World, 1961). Thomas C. Schelling, *The Strategy of Conflict* (Cambridge, Mass.: Harvard University, 1963), p. 47.

42. Allen W. Sherman, "The Social Psychology of Bilateral Negotiations" (unpublished Masters thesis, Department of Sociology, Northwestern University, 1963), p. 47.

43. See Dean G. Pruitt, "An Analysis of Responsiveness between Nations," *Journal of Conflict Resolution,* 6, No. 1 (March, 1962): 5–18.

44. The notation scheme used in some of the equations that follow is a mixture

79

of mathematical and computer convention. For example, in strictly mathematical terms, the equation a = a•b makes sense only if b is equal to one, since a•b = a must also be true. In computer languages, however, the equal sign indicates that the value on the left of the equal sign is to be assigned that value which results after the operations on the right of the equal sign have been performed. Thus, a = a•b is sensible, but a•b = a is not. This is the explanation of why, in some of the following equations, the same variable will be found on both sides of the equal sign.

45. Sherman, "Social Psychology of Bilateral Negotiations," p. 32.

46. For a recent discussion of the effects of hostility on trade see Richard E. Gift, "Trading in a Threat System: The U.S.-Soviet Case," *Journal of Conflict Resolution,* 13, No. 4 (December, 1969): 418–437.

47. Dina Zinnes, "A Comparison of Hostile Behavior of Decision-Makers in Simulate and Historical Data," *World Politics,* 18, No. 3 (April, 1966): 474–502.

48. *Ibid.,* p. 477.

49. Rudolph J. Rummel, "A Social Field Theory of Foreign Conflict Behavior," *Peace Research Society (International) Papers,* 4 (1965): 143.

50. Richard A. Brody, Alexandra H. Benham, and Jeffrey S. Milstein, "Hostile International Communications, Arms Production, and Perception of Threat: A Simulation Study" (Stanford, Ca.: Institute of Political Studies, Stanford University, July, 1966).

51. Erich Weede, "Conflict Behavior of Nation-States." Paper delivered at the Midwest meeting of the Peace Research Society (International) on April 17, 1969, p. 1.

52. Zinnes, "Comparison of Hostile Behavior," pp. 484–486.

THREE

The Simulation Runs

THE model described in the previous chapter may be used to simulate the behavior of different nations and different systems of nations, depending upon the values assigned to the parameters of the model, and to the basic variables which define the initial state of a simulated international system. In this chapter we want to discuss one particular set of simulation runs that were conducted with the model. It should be emphasized that these constitute only a limited exploration of the capabilities of the model, and it is clear that many different kinds of runs could have been designed. Thus, any conclusions about the model must be tentative.

The specific objective of this chapter is to describe the particular set of parameter settings and variable initializations used to generate the international systems that are the central concern of the remainder of this book. An infinite number of international systems could be generated using the model described above, but we will be focusing on only twenty-four here. The design is simple: six different initial system configurations were run under four different sets of parameter values, thus generating twenty-four different, but related, five-nation international systems. Let us begin by examining the six-system configurations.

THE SIX SYSTEM CONFIGURATIONS

A system configuration, as we are using the term here, is composed of three elements: (1) the values of those variables that define the environment of the national decision-making units at the very beginning of a system's existence: (2) the values of the decisional variables that reflect the first period of activity on the part of the decision-making unit; and (3) the values of the environmental variables, as they have been redefined by the behavior of the decision-making units.

Given values for these three sets of variables, and the parameter values to be discussed in the next section, the computer model is free to trace out a path of behavior. We shall consider each of these three factors in turn.

Environmental Variables: Initial Values

A few select variables define the environments of the national decision-making units at the beginning of a simulation run. Each of the five nations must be assigned values for the following environmental variables: Total Basic Capability (TBC), Total Force Capability (TFC), Validation Satisfaction Over-all (VSm), Probability of Office-Holding (POH), Decision Latitude (DL), Probability of Revolution (PR), the Generation Rates, and the Initial Alliance Structure. This set of variables determines the pre-decisional state of each national system, and the values given in Table 3–1 for the five nations listed were used in all twenty-four systems.

These starting values were derived from those used in the WINSAFE II INS runs conducted by John Raser and Wayman Crow,[1] and we shall often have occasion to refer to this series of INS runs in the setting of variables and parameters.

The WINSAFE II INS runs were designed to explore the ramifications of the capacity to delay response to a nuclear attack; that is, the "invulnerability and deliverability of a retaliatory force after accepting the most devastating blow or series of blows the initiator of a nuclear attack can deliver."[2] The experimental intervention involved giving to nations, for short periods of time, the capacity to delay response. The changes in national behavior were then noted and conclusions drawn about the effects of this capacity.

This set of INS runs will be compared to the SIPER runs in some of the following chapters, and we must keep in mind that the behavior of the INS model is, in part, due to these special experimental conditions as well as to basic nature of the model. However, this set of data is the best that is presently available, and the intervention effects appear to be less pronounced than in the Brody-Driver INS runs, for example.[3]

82

TABLE 3–1
INITIAL CHARACTERISTICS OF SIMULATED NATIONS

Characteristic	Nation				
	1	2	3	4	5
Total Basic Capability (TBC)	7,500	17,000	9,000	34,000	37,000
Total Force Capability (TFC)	100	1,000	800	2,850	2,713
Validator Satisfaction (VSm)	4	4	5	6.5	6
Probability of Office-Holding (POH)	.8	.6	.7	.7	.9
Decision Latitude (DL)	6	4	3	5	7
Probability of Revolution (PR)	0	0	0	0	0
Generation Rates (GR)					
Consumption	1.2	1.0	1.1	1.4	1.4
Investment	1.0	1.2	1.0	1.3	1.2
Defense	1.5	0.7	0.9	2.0	2.1
Allied Nations	3 and 5	4	1 and 5	2	1 and 3

Returning to the assignment of initial values to this first set of variables, an examination of Table 3–1 reveals five nations of the following nature.

Nation 1. In terms of productive resources, this nation is the smallest of the five, and its low level of force capability makes it the weakest militarily. With the second highest level of decision latitude, it has a somewhat authoritarian political system that enables it to maintain a high level of political stability. It is moderately efficient in the production of consumption goods, but rather inefficient in the production of capital goods. On the other hand, defense goods are relatively inexpensive for this nation to produce. Nation 1 has two allies, nations 3 and 5, with the latter being its bloc leader.

Nation 2. This is a medium sized nation with significant military power, a relatively democratic political system, and also the lowest initial level of political stability. In terms of economic productivity, capital goods are relatively cheap and military goods quite expensive, while consumer goods are priced in between these two. Its only ally and bloc leader is nation 4.

Nation 3. This nation is slightly larger than nation 1, but significantly more powerful, militarily. It is the most democratic nation in the system, but has attained a moderately high level of political stability. It is very efficient in the production of consumption goods, and moderately efficient in the production of capital goods. Defense goods, on the other hand, are very expensive, relatively speaking, and it is likely that arms have been a principle item of import. It is a member of the 1–3–5 bloc.

Nation 4. This is the second largest nation in the system, and the most powerful militarily. Its political system is mixed in character, having both authoritarian and democratic aspects, thus enabling it to attain a moderately high level of political stability. It is a highly developed country, relative to the three nations we have already examined, as reflected in its generally high Generation Rates, and is the leader of the 2–4 bloc.

Nation 5. This is the largest and second most powerful nation in the system, as well as the most authoritarian. It appears to be politically stable, and, like nation 4, is endowed with high generation rates in all sectors, indicating a highly developed economy. Defense goods are particularly cheap for this nation, which may enable it to help its allies, nations 1 and 3.

Over-all, then, the international system we begin with is composed of three smaller powers and two larger powers. Two of the nations have high decision latitudes, indicating rather authoritarian governments, while the remaining three nations are somewhat more open. All are stable politically, and exhibit no significant likelihood of revolution. Force capability levels are moderately high, with the two bloc leaders possessing the bulk of the force capability units that are to be found in the system. The alliance structure stipulates that nations 1, 3, and 5 form one bloc, with nation 5 as the bloc's leader, and nations 2 and 4 forming the other bloc, led by nation 4. The balance of forces between the blocs is therefore 3,850 to 3,613, indicating a slight advantage for the 2–4 bloc.

Initially, then, all of our twenty-four systems begin as balanced, tight, bipolar systems composed of politically stable, but ideologically heterogeneous, nations.

Three other variables that require initialization, but are unique to the SIPER model, are the aspiration levels for political stability, economic growth, and national security. All five nations begin with the same aspiration levels, and again, all twenty-four systems begin with the same set of national aspiration levels.

The aspiration level for political stability (ALPOH) was assigned an initial value of .8 for all nations. An inspection of the cabinet meeting minutes from the WINSAFE II runs suggested that subjects seemed to desire a POH value of about .8 on a scale of 0 to 1.0. Accordingly, this value was used in this particular series of computer runs.

The initial value for the aspiration level for economic growth (ALGRO) was similarly determined. The value used was five per cent growth per period. The use of this as the initial value for ALGRO seems reasonable, both in terms of what the participants in the WINSAFE II runs appear to have wanted, and in what economists today consider a "good" growth rate for a national economy.[4]

The initial values for the aspiration levels for national security were set equal to the level of force capability allocation (FCP) that was decided upon in the first period of time. This leads us, in turn, to values used in initializing the decisional variables.

Decisional Variables: Initial Values

Due to the incremental nature of the decision processes outlined in the second part of the previous chapter, we need to specify some initial values for the basic decision variables. They are: the proportion of resources allocated to consumption (CSP), investment (BCP), and defense (FCP), as well as the proportion of total force capability assigned the role of internal security (FICP). The dyadic trade, aid, and hostility variables also require initial values, and we must specify as well what changes in the alliance structure are to be exogenously introduced over the system's life span.

In order to explore the sensitivity of the model to different initial system configurations, six different sets of values for the main decisional variables were used. These values reflect the decisions made by each of the five national decision-making teams in the first period of six of the WINSAFE II runs discussed above. In other words, even though all simulated systems begin with the same initial values for the environmental variables, the six different sets of values for the decisional variables will "kick-off" the model in a slightly different direction, thereby creating nations with slightly different histories.

The six sets of numerical values are given in Appendix I, and, with the exception of dyadic trade and aid, values are given for all the variables listed above. The trade and aid matrices were initialized with zero values for all systems. The third element of a system configuration is the subsequent values of the environmental variables, and it is to these that we now turn.

Environmental Variables: Subsequent Values

The six different settings for the decisional variables serve as inputs to the environmental processes, and these processes redefine the decision environment by means of the relationships discussed in the first part of the previous chapter. Thus, the stage is set for the first round of decision-making by the computer model.

The six sets of values for the environmental variables that specify the context for the first period of computerized decision-making are given in Appendix I. Each of the six tables contains a set of values for each of the five nations for the variables Total Basic Capability (TBC), Total Force Capability (TFC), Validator Satisfaction (VS), Probability of Office-Holding (POH), Decision Latitude (DL), and Probability of Revolution (PR). In order to make it easier for the reader to appreciate the similarities and differences between and among these systems, verbal descriptions of each are given below. These system profiles focus on the national decisions concerning resources and conflict and the consequences which stemmed from these decisions.

System Profiles

System 1. Both bloc leaders appear to have de-emphasized consumption in favor of increases in other economic sectors. One sought to hold its force capability level about the same and expand its resource capability, while the other pursued the opposite policy. All three of the bloc member nations made decisions which would reduce their force capability levels, and the released resources tended to be shifted into the consumption sector. Capital investment was set at a level where depreciation would be offset, but no significant expansion of the resource base could be expected for these three less developed nations.

Inter-bloc relations were good, on the whole, with no hostile exchanges between the members of the opposing blocs and only one exchange between the leaders of the opposing blocs. Intra-bloc relations were also quite free of hostility since only one

87

hostile exchange occurred between a bloc leader and one of the members of its bloc.

On the whole, then, this system seems relatively free of both tension and a pre-occupation with national security, with political stability and economic growth appearing to be the primary initial concerns of the system members. The consequences of these decisions were as follows.

Both bloc leaders experienced a slight economic decline, with resource bases 4 to 5 percent lower than the previous period, but they remain approximately equal in this area. One of the bloc leaders has gained a significant edge over the other in force capability, and the disadvantaged power is further threatened by internal revolution. An additional problem for this beleaguered power is posed by its ally, who lost substantial productive resources and force capability in suppressing a revolution. Thus, one of the blocs seems threatened both internally and externally.

Both members of the other bloc registered economic gains by expanding their resource bases 3 to 4 percent, while maintaining approximately the same force capability levels. However, there are signs of internal strife within one of these two nations.

The 1–3–5 bloc appears to have pulled ahead of the 2–4 bloc in many respects; the members of this bloc are, in general, more stable and, in terms of relative force capability levels, more secure, and two of its members have grown economically. The 2–4 bloc, on the other hand, is being pressured externally and internally.

System 2. Both bloc leaders decreased consumption in favor of investment and defense, but one of the bloc leaders sought a substantial expansion of its force capability, while the other's efforts were more modest in this area. The bloc members, on the other hand, pursued dissimilar policies. One sought to marginally increase its force capability by making small cuts in investment and consumption, while another used a similar incremental strategy to marginally increase consumption levels. The third bloc member made substantial cuts in both consumption and defense in order to significantly expand its resource base.

Inter-bloc relations were highly conflictual, although no hostile exchanges occurred between the two bloc leaders. Relations were particularly bad between nations one and four. Their hostile exchanges constitute about three-fourths of all inter-bloc conflict. Parenthetically, these are the same two nations who sought to substantially raise their force capability levels. Intra-bloc relations were also poor since substantial hostile exchanges occurred between each bloc leader and the members of its own bloc.

In general, then, the very high level of conflict, coupled with an apparent desire of one of the bloc leaders to gain a substantial strategic edge over the other (perhaps to deal with the troublesome member of the opposing bloc), indicates a system full of tension and perhaps in the initial stages of an arms race. These decisions produced the following consequences.

Both bloc leaders experienced a modest reduction in productive resources and both achieved high levels of political stability. One of the bloc leaders, nation 4, substantially increased its FC level, so that the ratio of force capabilities for the bloc leaders is now two to one in favor of that nation. Its ally, nation 2, also raised its force capability level somewhat, while expanding its resource base and maintaining a high level of political stability.

Nation 5, on the other hand, has additional problems with its allies. Both of its allies are threatened by internal political resistance, and their collective gains in resource and force capabilities are quite modest.

In summary, then, the 2–4 bloc seems to have an initial advantage over the 1–3–5 bloc, both politically and militarily.

System 3. Both bloc leaders cut consumption in order to expand their resource and force capabilities, while the bloc members' concerns seem to have been more mixed. One member increased consumption and defense by allocating nothing to investment, while a second increased consumption by reducing defense and maintained an investment level sufficient to offset depreciation. The third bloc member, on the other hand, pursued a balanced resource allocation policy aimed at maintaining the status quo.

Inter-bloc conflict was moderately high, most of it concentrated in the relations between one of the bloc leaders and the members of the opposing bloc. Only one hostile exchange occurred between the bloc leaders themselves. Intra-bloc relations were generally non-conflictual, although some signs of strain were present in one of the two blocs.

Large increases in force capability by both bloc leaders, coupled with a moderately high level of conflict, would place this system somewhere between systems 1 and 2 with respect to the prospects for political stability and economic growth.

The relatively high levels of resources devoted to force capability by the bloc leaders resulted in a doubling of their force capability levels, although the two blocs remain approximately equal in this regard. The resource bases of all the nations are approximately the same as before, although both members of the 2–4 bloc have lost some of their resource base to depreciation. Most of the nations remain politically stable, although nation 3 is in some danger of experiencing a revolution.

Over-all, then, both blocs have substantially raised their force capability levels, but without one bloc gaining significant advantage over the other in this area.

System 4. Both bloc leaders reduced consumption levels in order to expand resource and force capabilities. One bloc leader gave a higher priority to investment, while the other gave relatively more emphasis to defense. None of the bloc members, on the other hand, allocated anything to defense production. Two bloc members allocated the released resources to consumption and investment equally, while a third cut consumption as well, in order to substantially increase investment.

Inter-bloc conflict was prevalent, with relations between the bloc leaders being especially bad. One-half of the total inter-bloc conflict involved exchanges between the bloc leaders, while intra-bloc relations were good, with only one hostile interaction between each bloc leader and one of its members.

Most notably characteristic of this system is the high degree of conflictual interaction between the bloc leaders, and the apparent desire of the bloc members not to become involved. This, coupled with an attempt by one of the bloc leaders to secure a strategic edge over the other, suggests that prospects for political stability and economic growth are mixed. These actions produced the following results.

Nation 4's efforts to secure an edge over its rival were successful, for the 2–4 bloc has a total force capability level 37 percent greater than the 1–3–5 bloc. The 1–3–5 bloc is further weakened by the threat of revolution in two of its members. Nations 2 and 3 enlarged their resource bases by about 3 percent, while the remaining nations experienced a slight decline in productive resources.

Generally, then, the 2–4 bloc appears to have secured an edge militarily and politically over the 1–3–5 bloc.

System 5. Both bloc leaders lowered consumption in order to raise force capability levels, while maintaining investment at a level sufficient to offset depreciation. Two of the bloc members allocated no resources to defense production, channeling the released resources into investment and consumption, while the third pursued a more balanced allocation policy aimed at preserving the status quo.

Inter-bloc conflict was at a medium level of intensity, with only one hostile exchange between the bloc leaders. Intra-bloc conflict, on the other hand, was higher than inter-bloc conflict, with relations within one bloc being especially bad.

The most notable characteristic of this system is the apparent disunity within one of the two blocs. In that bloc, the leader has allocated a substantial proportion of its resources to defense production, while its two allies allocated nothing to that sector. Since the amount of hostile inter-action within the bloc was also high, it is likely that the bloc leader will have difficulty organizing bloc security in the face of this non-conforming alliance behavior.

As a result of the first period's decisions, the 1–3–5 bloc appears to have secured a military advantage over the 2–4 bloc. In addition, both the leader and a member of the 1–3–5 bloc have increased their productive resources, while the leader of the 2–4 bloc has slipped economically. The 1–3–5 bloc is stable politically, while both nations 2 and 4 are threatened by revolution.

In short, the 1–3–5 bloc seems better off politically, economically, and militarily than the 2–4 bloc.

System 6. As before, both bloc leaders reduced consumption in order to expand force capabilities, although in this case their allocations are at approximately the same level. Two of the bloc members followed a similar policy of cutting consumption, in order to raise their FC levels. The remaining bloc member allocated nothing to defense and concentrated its efforts in the investment sector.

Inter-bloc conflict was the highest of all six systems, with most of it involving bloc leaders and members of opposing blocs rather than the bloc leaders directly. Intra-bloc conflict was also relatively high and relations were especially bad between the bloc member, who allocated nothing to defense production, and its bloc leader.

In many respects this system is quite similar to system 2. Conflict is high, both between and within blocs, and most of the system members pursued allocation policies designed to increase their force capability levels. The principle difference between this system and system 2 is that here the bloc leaders increased defense production by about the same amount, while in system 2 one bloc leader sought to gain a decisive advantage over the other. In both systems, the prospects for stability and growth do not seem bright. The immediate results of these decisions were as follows.

FC levels for both blocs are very high, but approximately equal. The relatively low consumption allocation levels have produced dire political consequences for the nations with low decision latitude values. Nations 2, 3, and 4 all have high probabilities of a revolution in the next period of time, and nations 2 and 4 have, in fact, had revolutions, causing them a substantial loss in productive resources. Both nations 1 and 5 appear to be politically stable at this time, although they too have experienced a decline in productive resources.

92

Over-all, the 2–4 bloc is economicallly and politically weak, although militarily equal to the 1–3–5 bloc. All nations have experienced some decline in basic capability.

This concludes our discussion of the six system configurations that served as the basis of the simulation runs. Before turning to the matter of assigning values to the parameters of the model, an additional word should be said about the alliance structures present in these six systems. As we indicated earlier, the alliance structure may be changed exogenously while the model is in operation, and in order to make the comparison between SIPER and INS, we need to introduce the changes in the alliance structure that occurred in the six WINSAFE II runs serving as our data base. These changes are listed in Appendix I, and it can be seen that alterations in the alliance structure occur in all but one of the six systems. All of the changes involve a bloc member moving from one bloc to the other.

Having described the six different system configurations that were used to define the initial character or history of our simulated systems, we can now turn to the question of parameter values.

PARAMETERS OF THE MODEL

Before discussing the specific values assigned to the parameters of the model in this set of runs, a more general discussion of some of the issues related to the specification of parameter values in complex simulation models seems to be in order. Simulators differ markedly in the methods they use to arrive at parameter values, and these different approaches reflect, in part, different conceptions of simulation as a research technique.

There are, for example, those who tend to view computer simulation as an extension of, and supplement to, econometric techniques. These simulators are prone to treat the parameters of a simulation model like the parameters of a regression equation, and contend, when estimating simulation parameters, that we should be concerned about the same issues that arise when we estimate regression parameters. In other words, we need a relatively large data set and an estimation method that yields precise values, which are unbiased estimates of the underlying true values of the parameters. Naylor et. al., for example, allege that unless the estimates of the parameters of the system have been estimated "properly" and are known to be statistically significant, then one should not construct a simulation model.[5]

I do not accept this position for a variety of reasons. First, implicit in this position is the assertion that the alternative to statistical estimation is the employment of arbitrary and non-empirical procedures resting on a host of untested assumptions, assumptions that do not have to be made if the "proper" statistical procedures are followed. This is, of course, false. Any estimation procedure rests on a set of untested assumptions, but a statistical procedure assumes such things as independent random sampling, homoscedasticity, normal populations, uncorrelated error terms, etc., and many of these are equally arbitrary. This position, then, simply means that the econometrically oriented simulators feel more comfortable making these assumptions than others.

Second, I think there is a contradiction in this approach, in that they commonly agree that simulation should be used only in those situations where standard analytical techniques, including statistical ones, are inappropriate. Yet, it is similarly argued that these techniques are to be used in estimating the parameters of a simulation model. Thus, one obviously must conclude that in those cases where simulation is the best technique to apply, it should not be used because we cannot estimate parameters "properly." On the other hand, in those cases where we can estimate parameters "properly," simulation is probably not the best technique to use since other analytical procedures will yield a more general solution. I, of course, do not agree with this conclusion.

The third reason I do not find this position attractive, is that it reflects a rather narrow conception of why simulation models are created. Fundamentally, simulation is a deductive analytical technique, and, like all such techniques, it can be used to explore the consequences of a particular set of assumptions without reference to any empirical phenomenon. In my opinion, many of the greatest breakthroughs in science resulted—not from a close adherence to that which is empirically observable—but rather from the exploration of abstract theoretical systems, far removed from any observable phenomenon. In many cases, decades (even centuries) passed before the relevance of such abstract considerations was demonstrated. It is my view, then, that to tie simulation too tightly to data, in the inductivist tradition, is to cripple a potentially powerful tool and ignore the history of science.

On the other hand, we find some simulators who see the question of estimating parameters in an entirely different light. Many of these have been trained in what has been called "system dynamics," and its founder and principal spokesman, Jay W. Forrester, views the matter this way. "In the social sciences, failure to understand systems is often blamed on inadequate data. The barrier to progress in social systems is not lack of data. The barrier is deficiency in the existing theories of structure. When structure is properly represented, parameter values are of secondary importance."[6] Forrester goes on to argue that in complex systems, most of the parameters are unimportant, since changes in their values do not appreciably alter the behavior of the model, while a few are very influential. Since it is impossible to predict these parameters, the argument continues, one should construct a simulation model precisely to determine what the influential ones are. Then, one could proceed to collect the relevant information necessary to more accurately estimate this smaller set of parameters. This position can be translated into an argument that completely contradicts the position outlined above, for it asserts that simulations should be constructed *before* a great investment in parameter estimation is made, not *after*.

I have several reservations about this position also, for while it is true that some simulation models are insensitive to changes in many parameters, it is also true that some are not. I see no reason, in principle, to assume that all complex models are inherently insensitive in this regard. In fact, it can be argued that a model which is insensitive to parameter changes is not a good model, since it is probably over-determined and lacking in parsimony. This counter-argument rests, of course, on the assumption that redundant causality is not characteristic of the world, and that a simpler model is to be preferred to the more complex one.

95

A second consideration is that, while I agree with Forrester that we have often been too concerned with data and insufficiently attentive to theory, I recognize the danger of taking our models too seriously, until such time as we are able to subject them to systematic and rigorous testing. The danger seems particularly acute when we venture to make policy prescriptions using less than fully tested models. Forrester would probably contend that a complex model, even a bad one, is better than the simple mental models that decision-makers now use, since social systems are so counter-intuitive. Yet, this argument rests on a rather simple model of the policy process, which asserts that better advice produces better decisions. Intuitively this seems true, but if the world is as counter-intuitive as Forrester says, we may reasonably expect that better advice will produce worse decisions. In any event, I think the assertion that precisely-determined parameter values and supporting data bases are of secondary importance in simulation is an acceptable working assumption while one is in the exploratory phases of model construction and evaluation. However, at the point one begins to advise decision-makers as to what they should do to produce a more peaceful and prosperous world, these matters become very important.

Finally, I think Forrester's distinction between structure and parameter is too sharply drawn, since, at some point, the distinction between parameter and structure becomes very blurred. In statistical analysis, structure refers to the form of the relationships between variables, and this must be assumed in order to estimate the unknown parameters. From a computer modeling standpoint, however, a parameter is merely a governing value that can be easily changed without reprogramming or recompiling. Parameters are viewed as being those aspects of the model that are more readily manipulable, while the structure of the model is that which is not so easily changed.

Let's examine the distinction between structure and parameter in the following example. Ronald Brunner and Garry Brewer, in demonstrating that one structure with different parameter values could produce quite different behavior patterns, used the following simple models.[7]

96

$$X_{1t} = X_{2t} + X_{3t} - 1$$
$$X_{2t} = \alpha_1 X_{1t-1}$$
$$X_{3t} = \alpha_2 (X_{2t} - X_{2t-1})$$

In one of their examples, they set α_2 equal to zero. The effect of this parameter specification is to implicitly change the structure to the following.

$$X_{1t} = X_{2t} - 1$$

$$X_{2t} = \alpha_1 X_{1t-1}$$

Since X_3 has a constant value of zero under these circumstances, it can be dropped from the structural equations. It is clear that a parameter change can bring about a structural change, and that the specification of a particular structure can be seen as implicitly assigning a parameter value of zero to all those variables not included in the equations. My point is not to further contribute to the ambiguity of the terminology, but rather to suggest that the distinction between structure and parameter is one of convenience, and not principle, as Forrester would have us believe.

Returning to the immediate question at hand, if neither of the two approaches outlined above seems satisfactory, how are we to proceed? I tend to share the view of Cherryholmes and Shapiro. "Parameter estimation in simulation models often must be made in an arbitrary fashion and because of this, predictive power and representativeness must be sacrificed. The extent of these sacrifices, however, can only be estimated after performance of the model has been evaluated."[8] There is an almost Bayesian Spirit about this approach to parameter estimation in simulation models. It recognizes that subjective estimates—to those who do not accept this view, arbitrary estimates—are useful and necessary. In addition, there is the recognition that costs are involved in adopting this strategy, and finally, there is the implication that prior assumptions need to be examined constantly in light of posterior results.

In operational terms, this strategy translates into a set of procedures that incorporate a variety of the methods used here. In some cases, data can be examined and the parameter values inferred from the statistical record. In other cases, values are derived by a kind of pseudo-Monte Carlo method, where different sets of values are introduced into a process, and the decision is based on the reasonableness, or face validity, of the over-all results. In still other cases, parameters are assigned values for experimental purposes, either by varying them over the simulation runs or assigning them a zero value in order to provide a base line sample for additional runs. And finally, the parameters that are derived from the INS model are assigned the values they have been conventionally given. With these general considerations in mind, let us turn to the specific parameter values used in the environmental and decision-making processes.

Environmental Processes Parameters

There are seventeen parameters controlling the environmental processes, and the values assigned to them are given in Table 3–2. These values were derived from the standard INS values reported by Guetzkow.[9] These values are not intrinsically valid nor are they wholly arbitrary, but rather they are conventional in nature. That is, they were developed through a trial and error method by Guetzkow and his associates over the course of several years of experience with the INS model.

Decision-Making Processes Parameters

Altogether there are twenty-five parameters that govern the decision-making processes, and the assigned values are given in Table 3–3. Parameters b_1 through b_9 govern the aspiration level mechanisms in the three goal areas. The first parameter, b_1, determines how much, and in what direction, the ALPOH will change, if there is no pressure for goal change arising from other factors in the process. This parameter allows us to introduce a kind of drift in the goal determination process. If it is given a value greater than 1.0, there will be a tendency for the aspiration level to rise over time, and if it is assigned a value less than 1.0, the aspiration level will tend to drop as time goes by. In this set of runs, we are assuming that this kind of drift does not occur, so b_1 is given a value of 1.0.

TABLE 3–2
ENVIRONMENTAL PROCESS PARAMETERS

Parameter	Value(s)	Function
a_1	2.63×10^{-6}	Set CSmin
a_2	1.0	Determine VScs in
a_3	55.0	relation to CS, CSmax,
a_4	41.0	and CSmin
a_5	3.0	Determine VSns in
a_6	0.5	relation to TFC
a_7	1.3	and TBC
a_8	0.5	Determine VSm
a_9	0.5	from VScs and VSns
a_{10}	$-.10$	Determine POH in
a_{11}	.11	relation to VSm
a_{12}	.01	and DL
a_{13}	.10	
a_{14}	4.0	Determine PR
a_{15}	.05	from VSm, DL, and
a_{16}	1.0	and FICP
a_{17}	0.5	

The next two parameters, b_2 and b_3, determine how much effect prior failure or success has upon the aspiration level; b_2 governs the effect of failure and b_3 the effect of success. Determining values for these parameters is not a simple matter. Since ALPOH is a purely conceptual construct, there is little hope at this time of deriving rigorous measures of the dependent and independent variables and determining parameter values by the use of standard estimation techniques. In view of this, we turned to less rigorous procedures. We postulated that the increase in the aspiration level, when prior efforts had been successful, would be greater than the rate of decrease, given failure, and set the ratio between b_3 and b_2 at two to one. After some trial and error curve fittings, it was found that the values .10 and .05 produced changes in the aspiration level that were neither too extreme and erratic,

TABLE 3–3
DECISION PROCESS PARAMETERS

Parameter	Value	Function
b_1	1.0	Determine aspiration level
b_2	.05	for political stability
b_3	.10	
b_4	.05	
b_5	1.0	Determine aspiration level
b_6	.05	for economic growth
b_7	.10	
b_8	.05	
b_9	0.5	Determine aspiration level
		for national security
b_{10}	.25	Operationalize goals in
b_{11}	.05	stability, growth, and
b_{12}	.20	security areas
b_{13}	.30	
b_{14}	.10	Set import limit
b_{15}	Varied	Determine prices of
b_{16}	Varied	goods for export
b_{17}	0	
b_{18}	1.0	National priorities for
b_{19}	1.0	resolving budget
b_{20}	1.0	crises
b_{21}	1.0	Conflict generation
b_{22}	.25	
b_{23}	1.0	
b_{24}	0	
b_{25}	Varied	Expectation formation

nor so small as to be negligible in consequence. This is essentially the same kind of technique Guetzkow and his associates utilized in developing the original INS model. Using a similar procedure, we assigned the parameter, b_4, which controls the degree to which success or failure by a similar other nations alters the aspiration level, the value of .05. The alternative of setting these last three parameters equal to zero, and permitting no goal change in this first set of runs, was considered and rejected, although in the future we would like to vary these parameters in a systematic fashion, thus determining how they effect the behavior of the model.

The next four parameters, b_5 through b_8, control the goal formation process in the area of economic growth. These parameters parallel b_1 through b_4 in meaning, and they were assigned the same values so that these two aspiration levels would change at about the same rate.

The last of the parameters in the goal formation group is b_9, and the function of this parameter is to enable bloc members to estimate the hostile intentions of other national actors on the basis of hostile communications. An examination of the cabinet meeting minutes made during the WINSAFE II runs suggested that the INS decision-makers tended to become alarmed about the hostile intentions of another nation when they received two or more hostile messages from it in one period of time. For this reason, b_9 was assigned the value of .5.

The next four parameters, b_{10} through b_{13}, control the goal operationalization process. The first of these, b_{10}, determines the rate at which the gap between the aspiration level for political stability and the present level of political stability will be closed by increasing or decreasing consumption levels. This was tentatively assigned the value of .25 for the following reason: in the worst of all possible conditions, that is, the aspiration level equal to 1.0 and the actual level equal to 0.0, the maximum rate of increase in consumption would seem to be about 25 percent of the current level. The second parameter in the group, b_{11}, determines the amount of increase in consumption made when a revolution is likely. In this set of runs, we assigned this parameter the value of .05, which means that when revolution is a virtual certainty, the decision-making unit would try to raise the proportion of resources going to consumption by that amount. Proportionately

101

lower probabilities of revolution would yield proportionately lower increases; a PR of .5, for example, would lead to an increase of .025 in CSP.

The third parameter in this group, b_{12}, governs the rate at which the gap between the *desired* rate of growth and the *actual* rate of growth will be narrowed. We assume that the expansion or contraction process is slower in the capital goods sector than in the consumption sector, and by trial and error we found that .20 yielded a reasonably adaptive behavior pattern.

The last parameter in this group, b_{13}, determines what fraction of TFC is to be allocated to internal security. As in the INS model, the maximum value for this fraction is .3, and this parameter was assigned the same value. Thus, the proportion of force capability devoted to internal security depends directly upon the likelihood of revolution. When it is a virtual certainty, PR = 1.0, the decision-making unit will always raise the internal force capability level to the 30 percent maximum.

The parameters b_{14} through b_{17} control the trading process. The first of these, b_{14}, determines the maximum size of total imports relative to TBC. Inspection of the INS data revealed that nations rarely imported more than one-tenth the value of their TBC, so this value was used as the value for b_{14}.

The next two parameters, b_{15} and b_{16}, were varied across runs of the model, and will be discussed in the next section. The last parameter, b_{17}, was assigned a value of zero for this set of runs. This was done in order to keep the feedback loop between trade and conflict open, so that in the future we will be able to more fully understand the implications of linking these phenomena.

The next three parameters in this portion of the model, b_{18}, b_{19}, and b_{20}, determine the relative importance of the consumption, investment, and defense sectors, respectively, when it becomes clear that the national resource base is not sufficient to meet the desired levels of allocation in all three areas. Under these circumstances, a budget crisis is said to exist and these parameters indicate the way in which the sectors are to be weighted in resolving the dilemma. In this first set of runs, all three parameters were given the same value of 1.0, indicating that the three economic sectors will be cut by equal degrees, if a budget crisis develops.

The set of parameters b_{21} through b_{24} control the conflict generation process. The first of these, b_{21}, determines the degree to which expected conflict will be either systematically amplified or dampened when other factors in the process have no effect. This parameter was assigned the value of 1.0, so that neither a systematic propensity to escalate tensions by over-reaction nor to de-escalate them by under-reaction will be present, but rather the expected level of hostility will be given an equal response.

The second parameter in this series, b_{22}, determines the degree to which differences in FC between the actor and target affect the flow of hostile interaction. Assigning this parameter a value of .25 assures us that it will have the effect of slightly dampening the conflict directed by lesser powers to superior powers, and slightly amplifying the flow in the opposite direction. The third parameter, b_{23}, specifies the amount of hostility that will be ignored when the target nation is an ally. In this set of runs we have assumed that one unit of hostility will be tolerated by an ally, and, therefore, b_{23} was assigned this value. Finally, the parameter b_{24}, which specifies the dampening effects of economic interdependence between the actor and target nation, was assigned the value of zero in this set of runs. As we indicated earlier, it was deemed desirable at this stage to render the feedback loop between trade and conflict inoperative, in order to provide a base line set of runs for future experimentation with this set of relationships.

The last parameter in Table 3–3, b_{25}, specifies the information processing rule to be used in the expectation formation process. This parameter was varied across the simulation runs also, and will be discussed in the final section.

THE EXPERIMENTAL DESIGN

Although we will have a great deal more to say about the experimental design employed in this set of simulation runs in the next chapter, our discussion of the simulation runs would not be complete without a specification of the values assigned to the experimentally manipulated parameters. As we indicated in the previous section, two types of parameters have been varied over the first set of simulation runs. The first type, b_{15} and b_{16}, determine the degree to which non-economic factors are introduced in the trade pricing policy. The second, b_{25}, regulates the manner in which expectations of future behavior are developed by a nation.

The trade-pricing policy was varied across runs in the following way. In twelve of the twenty-four simulation runs, both b_{15} and b_{16} were given the value of zero. In these systems, the terms of trade are purely a function of comparative advantage, and non-economic considerations do not enter into the pricing of goods for export. Hence, a free-trade policy is followed by all nations in these twelve systems. In the second set of twelve runs, certain non-economic considerations are allowed to enter into the export pricing process. In these runs the parameters b_{15} and b_{16} were assigned the values of .20 and 1.0 respectively. The first of these values means that allies will be charged 20 percent less for exported goods and non-allies will be charged 20 percent more. This should encourage greater intra-bloc trade and, in view of other processes at work, greater bloc solidarity on defense coordination. The second value indicates that larger nations will be asked to pay proportionately more for goods by smaller nations, and larger nations will marginally lower their prices for smaller nations. Although this may or may not be true in the referent world, it appears to be characteristic of INS worlds, according to Sherman.[10] Other things being equal, this should encourage trade between larger and smaller nations.

The second type of experimental variation involves the intelligence policy to be used by the nations. In the previous chapter, we discussed five options concerning the rule to be used for developing expectations as to the future behavior of other nations. In this set of runs, we will examine only two of these. In twelve runs, the parameter b_{25} was assigned a value of four, meaning that what we previously called the No Change information processing rule would be used. In effect, this is equivalent to shutting off the expectation formation process entirely, and basing responses on the current situation rather than on some expected future state of affairs. This will be referred to as the Status Quo intelligence policy. In the other twelve runs, this parameter was given the value of zero, indicating that what we previously called the Best

Fit information processing rule would be used. This means that a nation will use the rule that hindsight indicates as the one it *should* have used last period. Hence, in a subset of runs we will permit the nations to adapt to—and learn from—prior experience in their forecasting behavior, and this is referred to as a Future Oriented intelligence policy.

Table 3–4 summarizes the design for our initial simulation runs of the computer model. As we can see, the design specifies that each of the six system configurations described in the earlier part of this chapter was run under the four different combinations of the experimental conditions, producing twenty-four separate international systems.

TABLE 3–4
DESIGN OF SIMULATION RUNS

| | | TRADE POLICY | |
		Free Trade	*Constrained Trade*
INTELLIGENCE POLICY	*Future Oriented*	Systems 1 through 6	Systems 13 through 18
	Status Quo	Systems 7 through 12	Systems 19 through 24

At this point, we have specified the model, the starting conditions, and the parameter values used in this set of simulation runs. All that remains for us to specify, before we examine the results, is the number of time periods in each run. As in the INS runs, twelve periods of simulation time were produced, and, given the initial decisions introduced as inputs, this means eleven periods of computer decision-making. In the next chapter, we will examine the results of this decision-making behavior in order to determine how sensitive the model is to variations in system configurations and parameter values.

THE SIMULATION RUNS

CHAPTER THREE NOTES

1. John R. Raser and Wayman J. Crow, *WINSAFE II: An Inter-Nation Simulation Study of Deterrence postures Embodying Capacity to Delay Response* (La Jolla, Ca.: Western Behavioral Sciences Institute, July, 1964).

Since SIPER does not differentiate between nuclear and conventional weapons, the initial TFC value is a weighted sum of these two weapons categories.

2. *Ibid.*, p. I-1.

3. The Brody-Driver runs, known as INS-8, are described in Richard A. Brody, "Some Systemic Effects of the Spread of Nuclear Weapons Technology: A Study through Simulation of a Multinuclear Future," *Journal of Conflict Resolution, 7,* No. 4 (December, 1963): 663–753.

4. Jagdish Bhagwati, *The Economics of Underdeveloped Countries* (New York: World University Library, 1966).

5. Thomas H. Naylor, et al. *Computer Simulation Techniques* (New York: Wiley, 1966).

6. Jay W. Forrester, *Urban Dynamics,* (Cambridge, Mass.: The M.I.T. Press, 1969), pp. 113–114.

7. Ronald D. Brunner and Garry D. Brewer, *Organized Complexity* (New York: The Free Press, 1971), p. 90.

8. Cleo H. Cherryholmes and Michael J. Shapiro, *Representatives and Roll Calls* (New York: Bobbs-Merrill, 1969), pp. 57–58.

9. Harold Guetzkow, et. al., *Simulation in International Relations* (Englewood Cliffs, N.J.: Prentice-Hall, 1963), Chapter 5, "Structured Programs and their Relation to Free Activity within the Inter-Nation Simulation," pp. 103–149.

10. Allen W. Sherman, "The Social Psychology of Bilateral Negotiations" (unpublished Masters thesis, Department of Sociology, Northwestern University, 1963).

FOUR

Analysis of the Simulation Runs

THE purpose of this chapter is to determine to what degree the behavior of the simulation model is affected by the initial differences between and among the twenty-four simulation runs. In the previous chapter, we indicated that these were of two types: differences in system configuration and differences in parameter settings. Each of these factors will be examined carefully in the following chapter, to determine how sensitive the model is to variations in each.

Focusing on the national level, the analysis will be descriptive and cross-sectional in nature; that is, we will be examining all the simulated nations at the same period in time, and primary emphasis will be given to assessing how much of the variance in national behavior can be accounted for by the initial differences between and among runs rather than to explicating the particular causal linkages that would explain how *initial* differences determine *subsequent* ones.

By necessity, our evaluation must be limited to only a few of the many variables that characterize the performance of a simulated nation under the variety of conditions present in this set of twenty-four runs of the simulation model. Our first task, then, is to indicate what these variables are and why they are important.

THE PERFORMANCE INDICATORS

Selecting a manageable number of key performance indicators is not a simple matter, since the computer model generates values for nearly 100 variables for each nation in each period of time. After some careful consideration, we settled on the following four national characteristics as being central to our assessment.

Level of Productive Resources. The size of a nation's productive resource base is obviously an important national characteristic, since it tells us something about a nation's capability for action in

107

the future. In addition, if we compare its capability to some prior base year's value, we can draw some conclusions about economic growth. We have already seen that, within the simulation model, the level of a nation's TBC is an important major constraint governing a nation's capacity to achieve its political, economic, and military goals. Therefore, we will be interested in seeing how this variable is affected by the initial differences between and among the 24 runs.

Level of Military Capability. The level of military capability a nation maintains in order to defend itself against external and internal threats, is also an important national characteristic. It is both a measure of past decisions, and an important determinant of future decisions on national security affairs. In the simulation model, this is represented by the amount of TFC a nation has accumulated, and we will be very interested in examining the differences between nations on this indicator.

Level of Political Stability. The level of political stability that a nation is able to achieve is also an important performance criteria. By this, we mean the degree to which the national decision-making unit is secure in its position of power. For simulated nations, this is reflected in the POH variable discussed in previous chapters.

Level of International Conflict. The final performance dimension with which we will be concerned in this chapter, deals with the amount of conflictual behavior that nations generate in the course of interacting with other nations. In the simulated worlds, this behavior is represented by the variable, HOST, and since we will not be concerned here with particular dyads, we will use the sum of *all* hostility generated by *each* nation in the period of time under study as our performance indicator, without differentiating as to the target.

This set of four indicators should allow us to examine the basic political, economic, and military aspects of the behavior of simulated nations. Beyond this, there are normative reasons for considering these variables as important. In our judgment, "good" systems will be characterized by high levels of productive capability and political stability, accompanied by low levels of military capability and internation conflict, a "bad" system will exhibit the opposite of these features. It is part of our concern, therefore, to determine under what conditions *more* desirable and *less* desirable outcomes are achieved by the simulation model.

SOURCES OF VARIATION IN THE MODEL'S BEHAVIOR

Before moving to the results of our inquiry concerning the impact of the differences between and among the runs of the model on the simulated nations, a more systematic examination of these differences is necessary. Period seven was selected as our observation point in each of the twenty-four systems, and since each of these systems contains five nations, our data base is composed of 120 observations on each of the four variables discussed above. The factors that would lead to differences between nations on any one of the variables fall into two major groups: historical differences and policy variations.

Historical Differences Between Nations

It may not be obvious why we have chosen to talk in terms of historical differences between such artificial entities as our simulated nations, yet our choice of the term should appear reasonable after some discussion. In a general sense, a nation's history is composed of a series of episodes in which a set of actions is taken (within the context of a set of conditions), with the result that a new set of conditions obtains at the next point in time. From this perspective, our design of the simulation runs offers us thirty nations with different historical backgrounds.

In the first part of the previous chapter, we discussed the different system configurations used in the simulation runs. In essence, a system configuration was defined when we specified: (1) the initial national characteristics of the nations making up the sys-

109

tem; and (2) the set of decisions for each nation concerning initial resource allocation and conflict generation, as well as any subsequent modifications of its alliance affiliations. In the first specification, we determine whether each nation will, for example, be larger or smaller (TBC), more developed or less developed (the generation rates), well armed or poorly armed (TFC), democratic or authoritarian (DL), etc. As we indicated at that time, five different basic nations were selected for this set of runs. The second set of specifications determines the initial priorities on resource allocation and defines the pattern of conflict at the beginning of the system. Since we used six different sets of decisions for each of the original five nations, we can see that, taken together, we have specified thirty different nations with different historical backgrounds. Our a priori expectation is that these initial differences will have an impact on subsequent behavior.

Policy Variations Across Runs

The second major component in our research design involved the systematic variation of parameters that control the Expectation Formation and Trade Pricing processes. We will call these *variations in policy* since a policy is essentially a set of decision rules for dealing with a class of problems in a uniform way. Hence, by changing the parameters in the model we can cause the decision-making units to use different policies. In this set of runs, we have programmed the decision-making units to employ different policies in two areas; the evaluation of intelligence and the pricing of exports.

Alternative Intelligence Evaluation Policies. As we indicated in the previous chapter, one-half of the runs were conducted under the condition that nations would use the No Change information processing rule, while the other half used the Best Fit information processing rule. If we put these differences in a broader context, we see that they amount to differences in the way information about the behavior of other nations is treated. However, we will refer to these as a Status Quo intelligence policy, as opposed to a Future Oriented intelligence policy.

110

The twelve runs in which the No Change rule was used will be considered the utilization of a Status Quo intelligence policy. This designation was chosen in order to capture the basic orientation of the particular information processing rule. Under the No Change rule, intelligence is evaluated in such a way that future behavior is determined to be the same as present behavior; one can easily see how this would lead to a status quo orientation.

The other twelve runs, using the Best Fit rule, are designed as Future Oriented, with respect to the evaluation of intelligence. In essence, this rule leads to anticipatory behavior on the part of nations, based upon projections of the behavior of other nations. Foreign policy decision-makers have been frequently criticized for failing to anticipate developments in the world, so most observers would probably agree that the Future Oriented policy is a more "intelligent" intelligence policy. The Status Quo policy, on the other hand, incorporates a passive orientation to future events, resulting in a re-active pattern of behavior, so often said to be characteristic of foreign affairs bureaucracies.

In short, then, in one set of runs we have nations operating under an intelligence evaluation policy that is forward-looking, trend-seeking, and pragmatic about the specific way in which these evaluations are made. In the other set, the intelligence function is essentially limited to recording the changes that have occurred during the last time period. No extrapolation or inference about changes in the future is made, since the implicit assumption is that things will stay pretty much as they are. Our question is, under which conditions do the nations fare "better" in the simulated world?

Alternative Trade Pricing Policies. As indicated earlier, in one-half of the twenty-four runs, nations set prices on goods for export strictly according to economic considerations, and we will refer to this as a Free Trade policy. It has long been argued that free trade would be beneficial to all nations, while the counter-argument is made, with equal vigor, that only a few nations would benefit from the adoption of this as a world-wide policy

In the remaining twelve systems, we have seen that factors not

111

related to comparative advantage are introduced in the pricing of exports, and we will refer to this as a Constrained Trade policy. The constraints are essentially political in nature, including preferences for allies and special inducements for the *less* developed nations to trade with the *more* developed nations. Once again, we wish to know which of these policies is "best" under what conditions?

Residual Sources of Variation

Given the stochastic processes included in the specification of the environmental processes (described in the first part of chapter two), there is a third source of variation. Since random numbers are used to specify such things as depreciation rates for basic capability and force capability—as well as whether or not a revolution occurs—it is likely that a replication of any of the twenty-four runs would produce a different result, due to stochastic variation. In a situation like this, where stochastic processes are a partial determinant of the behavior of a simulation model, experimenters frequently run many replications of the simulation under the same input conditions in order to randomize these effects.

That strategy was not followed here for three reasons; first, if these stochastic processes are viewed in the context of the complete model, it is clear that they represent a very small portion of the model and, therefore, it is expected that their effects must be modest overall. Second, if these processes are governed by randomly generated numbers, we are assured that their effects will be randomly distributed over our observations. For example, by period seven (the period we will be examining), each system has used up about 100 random numbers, and it is unlikely that this would provide a basis for systematic variance. Third, time and money constraints did not allow us to make the necessary replications. Using the rather modest estimate of five replications per simulation run would mean executing 120 separate simulation runs. This was clearly outside the set of constraints under which this preliminary effort operated. In conclusion, then, we assume that this third source of variation has a small over-all impact on the behavior of the model, and that this is essentially a random, albeit uncontrolled, source of variation.

Analytical Procedures

The results reported in the remainder of this chapter stem from a rather extensive analysis of the simulation data, but only a small portion of it is reported here. For the most part, this stems from discovering that the historical differences are a great deal more important than the policy variations in accounting for variance in the behavior of the model. Thus, the most forthright strategy seems to be an examination of the impact of these historical factors first, and then, having accounted for these effects, the impact of the policy variations should be examined.

THE EFFECTS OF HISTORICAL DIFFERENCES

We will examine each of the four key variables in turn, to assess the over-all impact of historical differences between and among the runs of the simulation model. In this way, we can begin to determine to what degree the model's behavior is dependent upon starting conditions, rather than upon parameter values.

Level of Productive Resources

Figures 4–1 through 4–5 indicate the level of TBC that each nation possessed at the beginning of period seven, in all simulation runs. The 120 observations are first grouped according to nation, and then according to system, so that each column of points contains four points corresponding to the four different policy variants. By inspection, it is obvious that the variation *between* the point columns, and attributable to historical differences, is much greater than the variance *within* the point columns, and mainly attributable to the policy differences.

Using the correlation ratio, we can measure with more precision, the explanatory power of the historical differences. This measure ranges from zero to one and, when multiplied by 100, indicates the amount of variance explained, or accounted for, by the categorical variable. This statistic is commonly used in analysis of variance and is identical in interpretation to the more familiar r^2 statistic.

With respect to TBC, we find that 98.2 percent of the total variance is accounted for by the initial system configuration used. That is, if we adjusted each score by the mean of each nation in each system, we would remove almost all of the variance in these figures. The physical manifestation of this is the very tight cluster of points that correspond to the four policy combinations for each nation-system.

If we examine each nation separately, we find it is not simply a matter of the more developed nations—nations 4 and 5 —experiencing economic growth, while the less developed do not. Nation 2, for example, has increased its resource base in three of the six systems, while nation 4 has declined economically in two systems. Nor is it a simple matter of a particular system being conducive to growth; nation 1 does extremely well on growth in system 1, while nation 2 experiences a severe economic decline in the same system. Thus, we must conclude that the differences in national behavior are due to a complex interaction between national characteristics and system characteristics.

Level of Military Capability

Figures 4–6 through 4–10 indicate the FC levels attained by our simulated nations in period seven, and the pattern is very similar to the one that we found for resource capability. In this case, 97.3 percent of the variance in arms levels is attributable to the initial system configuration. Thus, we are led to conclude that, in comparison, the effect of the policy manipulations is quite small.

However, there is evidence to suggest a regularity in respect to system identity; system 1 tends to have lower levels of armaments for all nations, while system 2 tends to have higher levels for all nations. This would suggest that there is something special about the interaction patterns of these systems, as all the nations in the systems are similarly affected. Bloc members seem to have allocated relatively more to defense in system 6, while bloc leaders appear to have allocated relatively less. Once again, we are led to conclude that the linkages between the initial system configuration and subsequent behavior are important and complex.

114

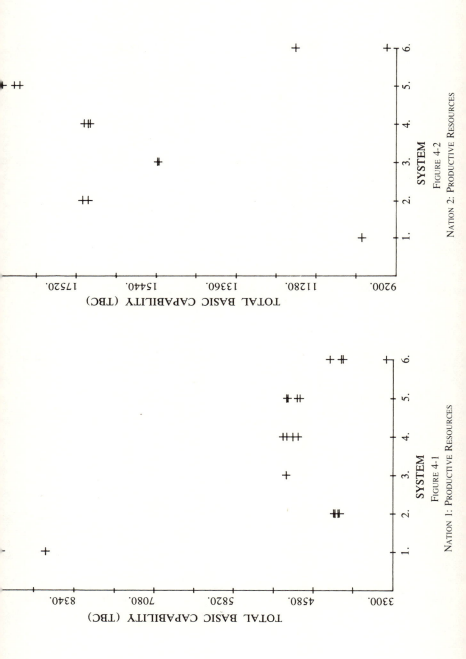

SYSTEM

FIGURE 4-1

NATION 1: PRODUCTIVE RESOURCES

SYSTEM

FIGURE 4-2

NATION 2: PRODUCTIVE RESOURCES

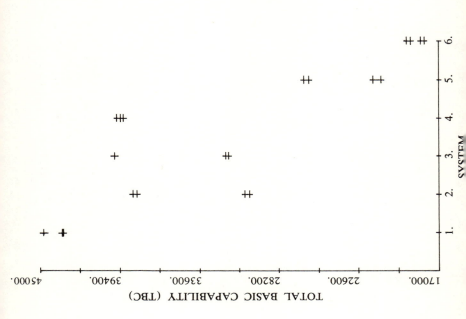

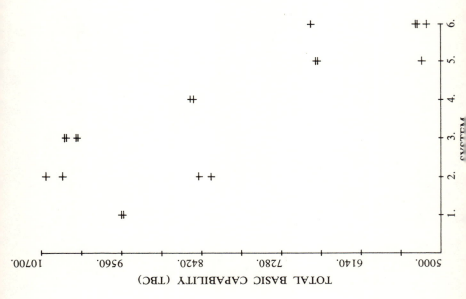

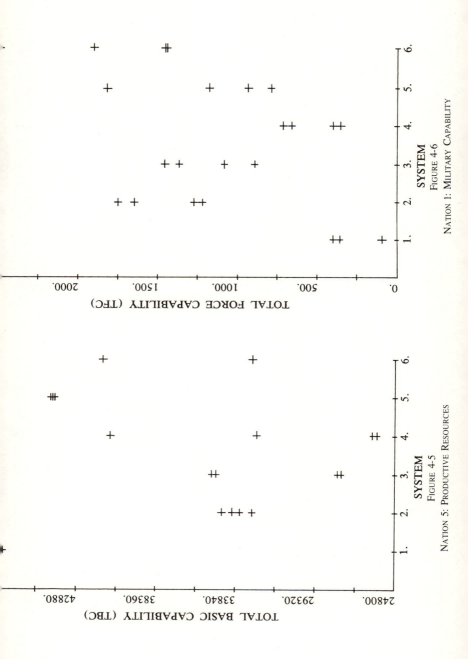

NATION 1: MILITARY CAPABILITY

SYSTEM
FIGURE 4-6

NATION 5: PRODUCTIVE RESOURCES

SYSTEM
FIGURE 4-5

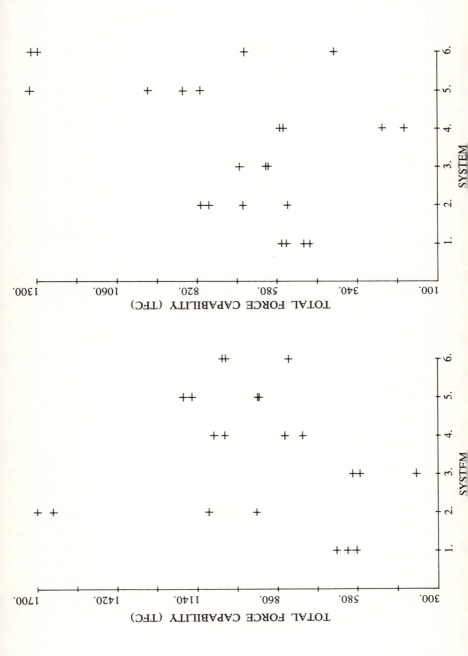

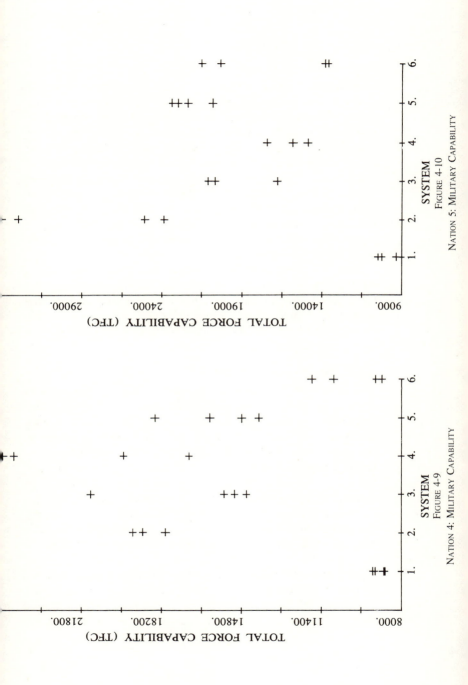

SYSTEM

FIGURE 4-10

NATION 5: MILITARY CAPABILITY

SYSTEM

FIGURE 4-9

NATION 4: MILITARY CAPABILITY

ANALYSIS OF THE SIMULATION RUNS

Level of Political Stability

Although the effects of the historical differences between runs on the level of political stability achieved by period seven are not quite as great as the previous two variables, still 91.3 percent of its variance is accounted for by the system configuration, but the pattern is very mixed. If we examine the category means for each nation, we find that nations 1 and 3 achieved their highest level of political stability in system 4, while nation 2 was more stable in system 1. Nations 4 and 5, on the other hand, achieved their highest level in systems 2 and 4, respectively. An examination of the lowest levels for each nation reveals a similarly disjointed pattern, although there is a slight tendency for all nations to be more stable in system 1.

Figures 4–11 through 4–15 clearly show a wider dispersion of stability levels around the nation-system means, suggesting that the policy variations may have had a greater impact upon this variable than on the previous two. Of course, we will not be able to ascertain whether this is true until the next section, wherein we will concentrate on the policy variations.

Level of International Conflict

Figures 4–16 through 4–20 are graphs of the 120 observations of hostility grouped again by nation-system categories. These categories account for about 83.2 percent of the original variance in this variable, but the pattern is slightly different from our previous observation. Within each column of points, two distinct clusters of points are visible, suggesting that one of the policy variables is having an effect on this, while the other is not. This pattern will be scrutinized closely in the next section.

An examination of the means of each nation-system category suggests that systems 1 and 3 are relatively conflict free for most nations, while systems 2, 4, and 6 tend to generate higher levels of conflict for most nations.

The brief examination of these four variables clearly indicates that the initialization of a simulated system is a very important determinant of the model's subsequent behavior. Such a disclosure is not surprising, given the large number of processes in the

120

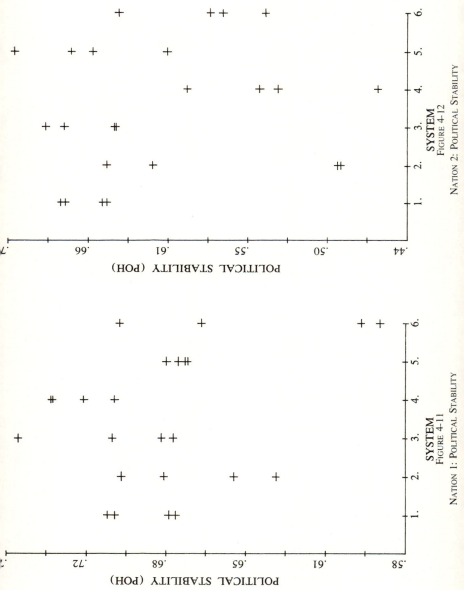

SYSTEM
FIGURE 4-12
NATION 2: POLITICAL STABILITY

SYSTEM
FIGURE 4-11
NATION 1: POLITICAL STABILITY

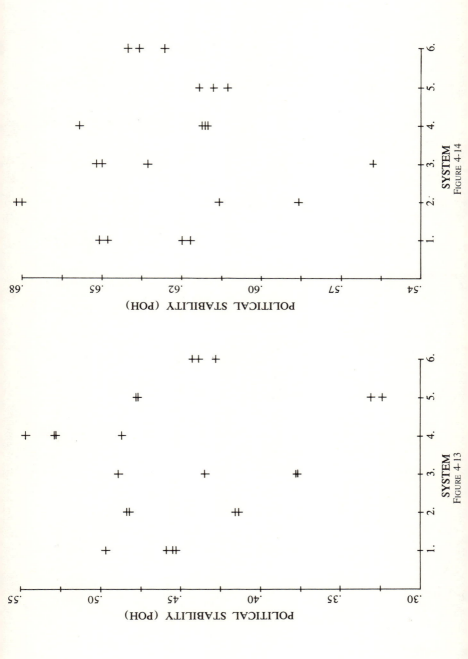

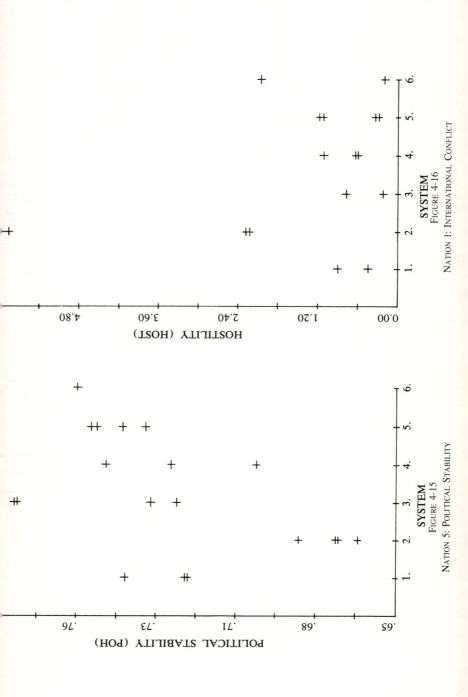

SYSTEM
FIGURE 4-16
NATION 1: INTERNATIONAL CONFLICT

SYSTEM
FIGURE 4-15
NATION 5: POLITICAL STABILITY

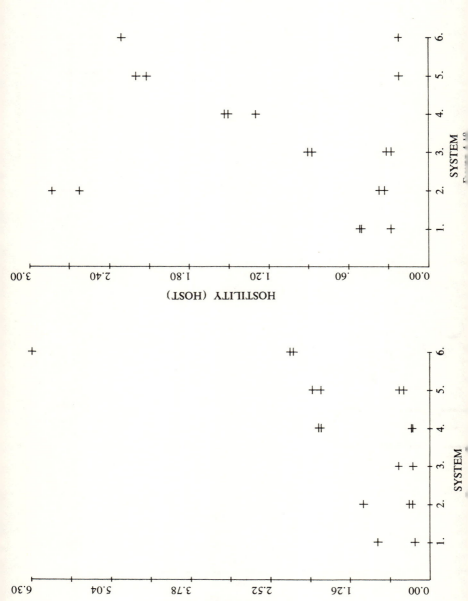

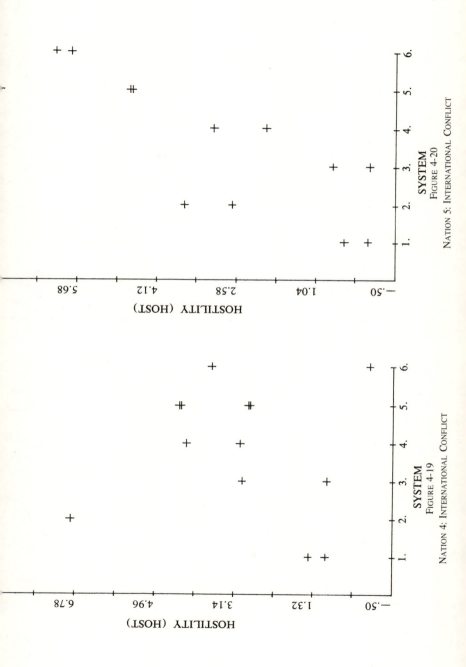

FIGURE 4-19
NATION 4: INTERNATIONAL CONFLICT

FIGURE 4-20
NATION 5: INTERNATIONAL CONFLICT

model that incorporate incremental modifications of earlier decisions. Yet, the magnitude of the effect of these historical differences is surprising. After all, the initial differences between the systems were rather small in comparison to what we could have generated had it been our intention to systematically examine the effects of different initial conditions; later, we may wish to do just that.

When we turn to the matter of explaining precisely how some rather small initial historical differences between and among simulated international systems produce relatively massive subsequent differences, we find ourselves in what has sometimes been referred to as "Bonini's paradox"; that is, the interaction sequence is so complex that a full specification of the linkages connecting the initial state of a system to its subsequent state is not, from a practical standpoint, possible. However, a review of the descriptions contained in the first part of the previous chapter reveals some general patterns in that direction.

Some of the effects observed in this chapter are clearly due to the initial differences among the five nations themselves. On the whole, we would expect large nations to remain large, developed nations to remain developed, closed nations to remain closed, etc. At the same time, however, we should recall that there is a considerable amount of variation in the graphs of the individual nations just examined. Nation 1, for example, has three times the TBC in one system than it has in another.

When we turn to the initial differences in the patterns of resource allocation, the situation becomes more complex. Although not universally true, it appears that the bloc leaders' decisions for the allocation of resources to defense are critical determinants of the future of the system. If, as a result of the first decisions, *one* of the bloc leaders succeeds in securing a large edge over the other in military capability, an intense arms race is prone to develop. This tends, in turn, to lower consumption and investment allocations, leading to political instability, revolution, and economic decline. If *both* leaders maintain parity as to force levels, then, regardless of the *level* of FC, a considerably slower arms accumulation process ensues. In the contemporary world, a major weapons breakthrough is often seen as having a similar destabilizing effect, and if our results are any guide to the nature of that effect, it clearly indicates disaster for all members of the system.

The second major factor that tends to be a powerful determinant of the future of a simulated system is the initial conflict pattern. It appears that high initial conflict between the bloc leaders and the members of opposing blocs acts to exacerbate the armament-tension spiral. Conflict between the bloc leaders themselves does not seem to have such a significant impact, nor does conflict between members of the same or opposing blocs. If this is true in the contemporary world as well, it would suggest that the state of relations between the United States and East Germany, for example, may be more important, in the long run, than the state of relations between the United States and the Soviet Union.

All of these conclusions are tentative and preliminary until the validity of the model has been established. Yet, our discovery of the rather large effect of the initial system configuration on subsequent national behavior has other more direct implications. It is clear that in future runs of the simulation model, greater attention must be given to the specification of the initial characteristics of nations and systems. If, for example, we attempt to reproduce a particular historical or contemporary system, we must take special care to achieve a faithful representation of the initial characteristics of that system. An additional implication of the power of these historical factors is that we will need to account for these factors in the next section, when we examine the effects of the policy variations.

THE EFFECTS OF POLICY VARIATIONS

Although our manipulation of policy-related variables is somewhat restricted in this set of runs, the two areas of concern are nevertheless important and interesting ones. The intelligence evaluation policy governs the way in which information about past behavior of an opponent or ally will be used to generate predictions about its future behavior. As we indicated earlier, the Future Oriented policy involves both an anticipation of future events and a rudimentary kind of learning for the national

127

decision-making unit. The Status Quo policy, on the other hand, ignores the past and assumes the future to be like the present, and, by almost all standards, one makes the a priori judgment that this is a less "intelligent" intelligence policy.

The trade policy manipulations centered on whether non-economic considerations enter into the pricing of goods for export. It is commonly argued that trade policy should be compatible with foreign policy goals, and frequently the needs of national security are invoked as justifications for altering trade flows, by means of the introduction of political factors. In this set of runs, we have identified this policy as Constrained Trade, and it contrasts sharply with the Free Trade policy, whereby trade is based strictly on comparative advantage.

Subsequently, we will need to be mindful of the potential interaction between these two policy areas, anticipating that their effects on the behavior of the model will not be strictly additive. As in the previous section, we will examine, in turn, each of our four key performance variables to ascertain how the behavior of simulated nations is affected by our policy variations. To isolate these effects, we will only be looking at the deviations from the nation-system means; that is, each group of four observations constituting a column of points in the figures of the previous section has been transformed into scores reflecting the deviation from their mean. In this way, we can control for the effects of the nation and system differences discussed earlier.

Level of Productive Resources

Table 4–1 summarizes the effects of the policy variable manipulations on the level of productive resources the simulated national actors had at their disposal during this period. Looking at the amount of variance accounted for by experimental factors, we find that of the 1.8 percent of the variance remaining after we adjust the TBC values by the nation-system means, slightly less than one-fifth of this is attributable to the policy differences between the runs. Most of this can be explained by the intelligence policy, while the trade policy has a relatively minor impact, as does the interaction of the two policies.

TABLE 4–1

ANALYSIS OF VARIANCE IN TOTAL BASIC CAPABILITY

Percent of remaining variance accounted for by:	
Intelligence Policy	16.3
Trade Policy	1.5
Interaction of Policies	0.8
Residual Factors	81.4

Note: Variance remaining after adjusting for nation-system means is 1.8% of original variance.

The magnitude and direction of the effects of the policy manipulations are as follows. Nations employing the Status Quo intelligence policy have resource bases that are about 1500 TBC units larger, on the average, than those using the Future Oriented policy. The use of the Free Trade policy by the simulated nations resulted in a level of productive resources almost 500 units larger, on the average, than those employing the Constrained Trade policy. It appears that both the Future Oriented intelligence policy and the Constrained Trade policy have a negative impact on economic growth, while the Status Quo and Free Trade policies have a positive impact on growth.

When we look at the combined effects of the two policy areas, we find that the sign of the interaction effect is equal to the product of the signs of the two main effects. Thus, we find that, although the Future Oriented and Constrained Trade policies individually, have a negative impact on growth, together they have a positive result, which partially offsets their negative additive effects. The Status Quo and Free Trade policies, both having positive separate effects on growth, also have an additional positive impact, as a result of interaction. The remaining two combinations, Future Oriented and Free Trade and Status Quo and Constrained Trade, which involve combinations of positive and negative separate effects, have a negative joint effect on growth.

Level of Military Capability

Turning to the question of national armament levels, we find in Table 4–2, that of the 2.7 percent of the variance left in force

129

capability levels after adjusting by nation-system means, about 10.6 percent of this can be attributed to policy differences between runs. An overwhelming amount of this explained variance, 9.7 percent, is due to variations in the intelligence evaluation policy, while the trade policy accounts for only 0.4 percent. Their combined effects are responsible for the remaining 0.5 percent of the explained variance.

TABLE 4–2

ANALYSIS OF VARIANCE IN TOTAL FORCE CAPABILITY

Percent of remaining variance accounted for by:	
Intelligence Policy	9.7
Trade Policy	0.4
Interaction of Policies	0.5
Residual Factors	89.4

Note: Variance remaining after adjusting for nation-system means is 2.7% of original variance.

When we examine the direction and magnitude of these effects, we find that a simulated nation using the Future Oriented intelligence policy achieves, on the average, a force capability level approximately 900 units larger than one using the Status Quo policy. Similarly, a nation following a Free Trade policy achieves a force capability level almost 200 units higher than one using a Constrained Trade policy.

The combined effects of the policy variables reveal some interesting patterns. Although the Future Oriented and Free Trade policies both have positive individual effects on the level of national armaments, their interactive effect is negative, perhaps due to a ceiling on the level of armaments which a nation may achieve. On the other hand, both the Status Quo and Constrained Trade policies have a negative effect on armaments, and their combined effect is also negative. The remaining two combinations incorporate policy variants that have positive and negative main effects, but their interaction results in higher levels of armaments than would be expected, if their individual effects were strictly additive.

Level of Politcal Stability

After transforming the data by taking deviations from nation-system means, we find 8.7 percent of the original variance remains. As Table 4–3 reveals, only 1.9 percent of this remaining variance is accounted for by the policy variations, leaving 98.1 percent unaccounted for. Decomposing this 1.9 percent, we find that the intelligence policy accounts for 1.0 percent, the trade policy accounts for 0.1 percent, and their interactive effect accounts for 0.8 percent. The over-all impact of the policy variables on this aspect of the model's behavior appears to be very slight.

TABLE 4–3
ANALYSIS OF VARIANCE IN POLITICAL STABILITY

Percent of remaining variance accounted for by:	
Intelligence Policy	1.0
Trade Policy	0.1
Interaction of Policies	0.8
Residual Factors	98.1

Note: Variance remaining after adjusting for nation-system means is 8.7% of original variance.

The main effects, although small in magnitude, are interesting in their directionality. The Future Oriented policy produces lower levels of political stability than the Status Quo policy, and the Constrained Trade policy similarly produces lower levels of stability than does the Free Trade policy. The interaction effects are similar to those we found in the area of force capability; that is, when the direction of the main effects for both factors is the same—Future Oriented—Constrained Trade and Status Quo —Free Trade—their joint effect is negative. Conversely, when the two policy factors have contradictory influences on the level of political stability, their joint effect is positive.

Level of International Conflict

Of the 16.8 percent of the original variance left in this variable after removing nation-system differences, 61.7 percent of the remaining variance is attributed to the policy differences between runs. Table 4–4 reveals that all of this is due to the different intelligence evaluation policies. The Trade policy had no effect on levels of conflict, nor were any interaction effects present.

TABLE 4–4

ANALYSIS OF VARIANCE IN INTERNATIONAL CONFLICT

Percent of remaining variance accounted for by:	
Intelligence Policy	61.7
Trade Policy	0.0
Interaction of Policies	0.0
Residual Factors	38.3

Note: Variance remaining after adjusting for nation-system means is 16.8% of original variance.

The direction and magnitude of the impact of the alternative intelligence policies is quite straightforward. Nations using a Future Oriented policy generate about one and two-thirds more units of conflict than those following a Status Quo intelligence policy.

Now that we have described the impact of the policy variables on the behavior of the model, we can develop a more comprehensive view of how the policy variables produce these observed effects. As we have noted, the Future Oriented intelligence evaluation policy produces higher levels of armaments and conflict, and lower levels of productive resources and political stability. A complete specification of the causal linkages that explain these results would be as complex as the model itself. However, the heart of this causal network appears to be the connection between the intelligence policy and the levels of armaments and conflict. Seemingly, the Future Oriented evaluation of intelligence tends to lead to higher expected levels of armaments and hostility, thus exacerbating the armaments-tension dilemma that is prone to develop within the simulated nations. Although there is nothing intrinsically escalatory in the information processing rules, which are used when the Future Oriented policy is in force, it seems clear that their operational result is precisely this.

As nations generate more conflict and attempt to maintain higher levels of armaments, fewer resources are left for investment and consumption, resulting in a drop in productive resources and political stability and these conditions, in turn, feedback to further exacerbate the situation. As the resource base declines, a greater proportion of these resources must be allocated to defense so the same absolute level of armaments is maintained. Furthermore, stability may decline to the point of revolution with the result of further losses in productive capabilities.

Although the drawing of policy implications may not be warranted, it appears that the kind of anticipatory behavior incorporated in the Future Oriented intelligence policy is not very beneficial to a nation, in the long run. Strategic planning leads to a succession of worst-case analyses, in which one's dire predictions become self-fulfilling and ultimately self-defeating. Nations that forget the past, ignore the future, and focus only on the dangers of the present seem to be better off.

The Free Trade policy resulted in higher levels of productive resources, military capability and political stability, without noticeably affecting international conflict. These results stem both from the greater trade opportunities present in the system (when prices are not artificially adjusted), and from the increased efficiency of domestic production, when Free Trade permits the shifting of resources from less productive to more productive sectors. The result is that more consumption, investment, and defense value can be obtained with the same resource base, thus raising the levels of resources, stability, and armaments.

Free trade advocates have long argued that unhampered economic exchange between nations would promote peace, prosperity, and stability around the globe. These results indicate that higher levels of prosperity and stability are a consequence of free trade, but if higher levels of armaments are seen as inimical to peace, then truly free trade may be a mixed blessing.

Having described and explained how the model behaves under different historical and policy conditions, we will now address the question of how well the model compares to real world nations and systems.

133

FIVE

Simulated and Referent Nations

IN this chapter, we will present the first of two preliminary efforts to assess the validity of the simulation model. Here we will be concerned with how the two models, SIPER and INS, compare with the contemporary world at a single point in time and at the national level. In the next chapter, we will raise the focus to the level of international systems and broaden the comparison to include static and dynamic analyses of contemporary and historical systems. We will begin with a general discussion of the problems of validating simulation models, and then proceed to outline the specific procedures that were followed, while the remainder of the chapter will be concerned with reporting the results obtained.

The Problem of Validating Simulation Models

Some years ago, Naylor and his colleagues noted that "the problem of verifying simulation models remains today perhaps the most elusive of all the unresolved problems associated with computer simulation techniques,"[1] and this equally holds true today. Before discussing the particular validation strategy we have developed, it would seem useful, therefore, to outline a few of the general reasons why the "validation problem" *is* a problem.

We need to acknowledge at the outset that the problem of validating simulation models is part of the more general question of how theories are to be evaluated empirically. Philosophers of science have not been able to resolve this set of issues, and no attempt to do so will be made here. Social scientists have been able to circumvent this difficulty, to a certain degree, by resorting to largely unarticulated assumptions about the proper way to bridge the gap between the theoretical and empirical. As consensus develops among a group of scholars about the appropriate approach to a particular class of problems, certain standard operating procedures emerge. Certainly, this has been true, for example, of the development of quantitative methods in the social sciences. It has not been true of simulation, however, and therein lies the particular problem of validating simulation models. Without a set of widely accepted standard procedures, each simulator must develop his own validation strategy and do so without being able to appeal to a scholarly consensus as to their appropriateness.

Such a consensus has not been reached because very few scholars have attempted rigorous validation studies. Starbuck and Dutton[2] report, for example, that of the nearly 2,000 publications prior to 1969 that deal with computer simulation, less than half described an operating model, while the majority incorporated either a description of a proposed model or a discussion of more abstract methodological issues. Those publications that did report a working model were further differentiated on the basis of how data were used to demonstrate the realism of the model's outputs. Only about one-fourth of these studies employed quantiative measurement, which they defined as the reporting of "a numerical table of any sort" pertaining to the evaluation of the model's output. Computer simulation is a relatively new technique, and, as expected, in many respects it is undeveloped.

Another aspect of the general problem facing the simulator is the question of purpose. A model may be valid for one purpose, and not another. For example, the electoral simulation designed by Pool, Abelson, and Popkin certainly appears to have had a great deal of validity with respect to predicting the outcomes of presidential elections,[3] but few scholars in the field of electoral studies would credit it with being an explanation of why voters poll as they do. Thus, a model may be valid as a predictive device, while not being valid in an explanatory sense. In addition, there is the objective of developing heuristically useful models and, although only a few may appreciate the value of this somewhat vague objective, it is nevertheless an important one.

A related concern is the question of what type of validity the model possesses. As Hermann has pointed out, there are many different ways in which a model might be valid.[4] It may have face validity, for example, which rests on an intuitive judgment of its soundness, based solely on appearances; or event validity, where the model can produce successfully the same discrete actions or occurrences that are observed in the referent system.

In addition, one who undertakes a validation study must constantly be aware of the two types of mistakes that can be made: (1) accepting the model as valid when it is not; and (2) rejecting the model as *invalid* when in fact it is *valid*. In statistical reasoning, these are referred to as Type I and Type II errors respectively, if the null hypothesis states that the model is invalid. By statistical convention, we try to keep the Type I error probability small—less than .05, for example—but by doing so, we often make the Type II error probability very large. In testing a vaccine where great losses accompany a Type I error, it may be appropriate to concentrate upon minimizing the likelihood of this type of error, but if this is not the case, what kind of balance between the two error probabilities is appropriate?

Finally, there are some problems associated with the concept of validity itself. Although not necessarily intrinsic to the meaning of the term, it has connotations that may suggest that validity is a dichotomous attribute a model either does or does not have. Obviously, a model may be valid in some respects, and not in others, or it may be a close approximation to the referent system, but not an exact replica. In these cases, we want to be able to identify shades of validity, and, in what follows, we will tend to refer to degrees of correspondence rather than validity.

THE VALIDATION DESIGN

As we indicated at the outset of this chapter, the question of concern here is: at a given point in time, do simulated nations exhibit behavior patterns similar to those found in referent world nations? In order to answer this question, we need to specify how these comparisons are to be made, in respect to what particular aspects of national behavior, and with whom. Those questions will be dealt with later in this section.

The Basic Approach

Simulations like SIPER and INS pose special problems when "whole sets of variables in the complex of national and interna-

137

tional life are represented by simplified, generic factors, supposedly the prototypes of more elaborate realities.''[5] As Hermann has observed, the result is that ''comparisons of the simulation's variables and parameters with their assumed counterparts in the observable universe. . . can be particularly troublesome when the definitions must correspond to a simulation variable or parameter that is either an analogue or a prototype intended to combine numerous features of the reference system.''[6] That is, since there is little one-to-one correspondence between the variables incorporated in SIPER and INS and those commonly used to measure the behavior of real world nations, we cannot simply make a direct comparison between the two.

Moreover, if we ask whether any simulated nations behave like the United States, the answer is likely to be no, and we will not have progressed very far. It would seem more useful at this stage of the research to pose the question in a somewhat more general form; do large, developed, democratic simulated nations behave like large, developed, democratic referent nations, such as the United States?

The approach will be to match referent world and simulated nations in terms of their relative standing on several basic attribute variables. Then we will determine the degree to which certain types of national behavior covary with the states' positions in these attribute spaces. Operationally, this means correlating each of the behavior variables with each of the attribute variables, in both the simulated and the referent worlds. If the correlations are similar, then we have a positive answer to the question: do simulated and referent nations that are similar in certain basic attributes exhibit similar behavior profiles?

The above approach was partially inspired by Rosenau's speculations about the impact of basic national characteristics on foreign policy.[7] Specifically, he suggested that size, development, and accountability are important factors in the shaping of a nation's foreign policy. There is additional empirical evidence to suggest that these elements are a source of major variation between nations.[8] For such reasons, we have selected these three variables as our basic national attributes. How are they to be operationalized in the simulated and referent worlds?

138

Size is a measure of magnitude. We commonly mean the bulk or mass of an entity when we refer to its size, but with reference to national systems there is also the connotation of resource potential. Several of the measures that have been isolated in factor analysis of real world data seem to have the common element of resource potential.[9] We will use as our measure of size in the real world data, national population, which has the advantage of being a rather complete and reliable statistical series.[10] In the SIPER and INS data, we will use TBC as our size measure, as it seems to more closely correspond conceptually with population than any other simulation variable we have. Certainly in both the referent and simulated worlds we are measuring the resource potential of nations with these variables.

Measuring development usually involves some assessment of the efficiency of a national economy. When we call a nation *developed,* we are asserting that its economic input-output ratio is relatively lower than other nations, which are considered *undeveloped.* As our aggregate measure of the productivity (output-input) of real national economies, we will use per capita gross national product. With all its shortcomings, this measure is still considered the best single indicator of development.[11] We will use an analogous measure for the simulated nations. If we define the variable gross simulated product as equal to the sum of consumers' goods, investment goods, and security goods produced, and divide this by basic capability, we will have an aggregate measure of the productivity of the simulated nation's economy.[12]

The third attribute variable, accountability, is more difficult to define than the previous two we have chosen. It is unlikely that the differences between the political systems of real nations may be reduced to one dimension without losing a good deal of information about those systems. But it would be folly to try dealing with the full variety of political systems at this stage of our work. Fortunately, we are not without some guidelines in examining national political systems, and the work of Gregg and Banks is particularly noteworthy.[13] The first factor extracted in their factor analysis of the cross-polity survey data was named *access.*[14] It would seem that Gregg and Banks have captured the same

139

phenomenon that Rosenau refers to as accountability, but the nominal perspectives are different. If a citizen has access to the political system, then similarly the political leader is accountable to the citizen. We shall take our measure from another study of the cross-polity survey data in which a factor analysis of the nations within the survey was performed.[15] An inspection of the rotated factor matrix indicates that the nations that load heavily on the first factor are precisely those nations we would describe as having open, accessible, or accountable political systems. We therefore decided to use a nation's loading on this first factor as a measure of the accountability of its political system. The measure of accountability in the simulated worlds is 10 minus the DL of the simulated nation. Obviously the higher the elite's DL, the less accountable it is to the citizenry. Hence, we want to take the difference between the maximum DL, 10, and that of a simulated nation as our measure of the accountability of its political system.

Now that we have indicated the bases upon which we will distinguish between larger and smaller, developed and undeveloped, and open and closed simulated and referent world nations, we turn to determining the type of behavioral phenomena to which these attributes will be related.

From the wide variety of behavior we observe nations exhibiting, we must, by necessity, select particular phenomena for study, and neglect others. Our choices for the exclusion or inclusion of a variable were guided by theoretical, empirical, and practical considerations. The variables chosen should have theoretical significance; that is, they should be essential to virtually any theoretical abstraction drawn from the relevant observable phenomena. Their theoretical import should be confirmed with empirical evidence. Lastly, the variables should be measurable.

Four areas of national behavior are examined: behavior pertaining to political stability, behavior pertaining to economic growth, behavior pertaining to national security, and behavior pertaining to international cooperation and conflict.

The political stability area contains five variables. The first three of these, turmoil, conspiracy, and internal war, have been isolated theoretically and empirically by several authors.[16] We do not think we can improve on Gurr's definitions of these variables.

Turmoil: relatively spontaneous, unstructured mass strife, including demonstrations, political strikes, riots, political clashes, and localized rebellions.

Conspiracy: intensively organized, relatively small-scale terrorism, small-scale civil strife, including political assassinations, small-scale terrorism, small-scale guerrilla wars, coups, mutinies, and plots and purges, the last two on grounds that they are evidence of planned strife.

Internal war: large-scale, organized, focused civil strife, almost always accompanied by extensive violence, including large-scale terrorism and guerrilla wars, civil wars, private wars, and large-scale revolts.[17]

Gurr's indicators of these variables for the referent nations are used in the analysis.

INS and SIPER do not produce any direct measure of turmoil behavior; however we can measure this behavior indirectly. Validation Satisfaction over-all (VSm) is a general measure of the satisfaction of the citizenry with the political system, and if we transform this variable by subtracting it from the level of perfect satisfaction, 10, we receive a measure of the citizenry's dissatisfaction. Although this measure is affective rather than behavioral, we will assume we are measuring potential turmoil. This approximation should be sufficient for our purposes. As to conspiracy and internal war, we find more directly analogous variables in the simulated worlds than with turmoil. We shall call a simulated nation's Probability of Revolution (PR) its conspiracy score, and the Costs of Revolution (CR) it incurs in a particular period, its internal war score for that period.

The fourth variable, stability, does not lend itself so easily to definition or measurement. The prevailing views in the literature seem to fall into two groups: those that see stability as the absence of destabilizing events[18] and those seeing stability, to some degree, as independent of, although not necessarily orthogonal to, instability.[19] The former interpretation is followed here.

The real world measure of stability is based on Gurr's Total Magnitude of Civil Strife index.[20] Since we want to measure stability rather than instability, the index has been transformed by

141

multiplying each nation's value by -1. In the SIPER and INS data, we have (according to evidence gathered by Elder and Pendley) a variable, the probability of continued office holding (POH), that is analogous to stability of the system.[21]

The fifth and last variable in the political stability area is consumption, included here because of the theoretical and empirical relation between economic deprivation and political stability. Consumption is the proportion of national economic resources allocated to consumers' goods. As a real world measure, we will use the gross private consumption expenditures as a percent of gross national product as taken from the *World Handbook of Political and Social Indicators*.[22] In the simulated data sources, we will use the level of consumption goods production expressed as a percent of gross simulated product.

The variables in the second behavior area, economic growth, require less elaboration. The first variable in this area, growth, is an absolute measure of the change in the referent and simulated national product. Consequently, for real nations growth equals the annual increment in gross national product,[23] and for simulated nations it is the period increment in gross simulated product.

The second variable in this group, growth rate, is simply the gross national or gross simulated product at time $t+1$ divided by the gross national or gross simulated product at time t. Hence, when there is no change, the growth rate will equal unity.[24]

The third variable is investment, and here we want to examine the proportion of the national and simulated product located in the investment sector. For the real world, we again turn to the *World Handbook* for the series gross domestic capital formation as a percent of the gross national product.[25] As with consumption, our ratio will be investment goods expressed as a proportion of gross simulated product.

The third area, national security behavior, includes three variables: force capability, defense effort, and defense spending. The first of these, force capability, is an aggregate measure of the coercive power of a nation. In the real world, we have taken the product of defense expenditures and size of their armed forces[26]

142

as our indicator, and in the simulated worlds, we will use total force capability as our measure.

Defense effort, like consumption and investment, is the proportion of the gross national or simulated product that is security goods. The real world data are taken from the *World Handbook of Political and Social Indicators*.[27] This variable may be thought of as a measure of relative defense spending.

Defense spending, the third and last in this group, in the real world is the amount a nation spends in its budget for defense, and in the simulated worlds we will use the amount of security goods produced in a period. The real world data again are taken from the *World Handbook of Political and Social Indicators*.[28]

The last area of interest, which we have called international cooperation and conflict behavior, contains three variables. The first, relative trade, measures the relative importance of the foreign sector to the national economy. As our real world measure, we will take the ratio of total exports and imports to gross national product,[29] and the ratio of total exports and imports to gross simulated product for the simulated nations.

Related to this is the variable trade magnitude, which is an absolute measure of international exchange. Here we simply use the numerator in the above measure as our indicator.[30]

Finally, we shall look at diplomatic conflict. This variable is one of the three basic dimensions of foreign conflict behavior delineated through a factor analysis of a variety of foreign conflict behavior.[31] The variables that loaded most heavily upon this dimension included the sending of threats, accusations, and protests. We shall use Rummel's factor scores as a real world measure of diplomatic conflict.[32] In the SIPER data we have a variable analogous to diplomatic conflict: hostile communications sent. We shall take the total hostile communications sent to all nations as our measure of diplomatic conflict. A content analysis of all international communication in the INS runs was done, and as a result of that analysis, we shall take as our INS diplomatic conflict indicator, the total number of messages sent that were classed as a threat, accusation, or protest.[33]

143

Below is a summary list of the variables we will be examining:

Attribute Variables	Stability Variables
Size	Turmoil
Development	Conspiracy
Accountability	Internal War
	Stability
	Consumption
Growth Variables	Security Variables
Growth	Force Capability
Growth Rate	Defense Effort
Investment	Defense Spending

Cooperation and Conflict Variables

Relative Trade
Trade Magnitude
Diplomatic Conflict

It remains, now, for us to specify how the relationships between the attribute and behavior variables will be compared in the referent and simulated systems.

The Method of Comparison

Two questions need to be answered at this point: who is to be compared to whom, and what correspondence criteria are to be used? Turning to the first question, we should indicate at the outset that we will be working with three sets of observations. One set is derived from a sample of real world nations; a second is drawn from the SIPER runs. The third set of observations stems from the INS runs conducted by Raser and Crow. A brief discussion of each of these follows.

The real world data were drawn from several data sources, and the number of nations for which data were available ranged from 62 to 133, depending upon the variable. Reducing the sample to nations about which we have complete information (a value for each of the behavior and attribute variables) leaves a sample of 41 nations. While this sample is not as large as possible, it should be sufficient for our purposes here. Table 5–1 lists those nations included, and these tend to be a little larger, more developed, and more open, but the bias does not appear to be very large.

TABLE 5–1

REAL WORLD NATIONS INCLUDED IN THE SAMPLE

United States	Peru	Spain
Canada	Chile	Turkey
West Germany	Ceylon	Soviet Union
Belgium	Thailand	Guatemala
Italy	Japan	Dominican Republic
Sweden	Australia	Colombia
Norway	South Africa	Brazil
Portugal	United Kingdom	Argentina
Greece	Ireland	Israel
Yugoslavia	France	Burma
Mexico	Netherlands	Philippines
Cuba	Switzerland	South Korea
Venezuela	Denmark	New Zealand
Ecuador	Finland	

The set of observations for the SIPER model is composed of the same observation points used in the previous chapter. That is, six system configurations composed of five nations each, run under four experimental conditions, and yielding a set of 120 nations. This is not a sample in any clear sense, and we will not treat it as such; instead, we will treat these 120 observations as a population, as it is identified in the statistical sense.

For this analysis, we will pool all 120 observations and not differentiate between subsets on the basis of system configuration or experimental conditions. There are several reasons for this. First, by introducing the attribute variables, we are partially controlling for some of the differences between runs that we observed in the preceding chapter. Second, since we are examining 42 separate relationships (3 attribute x 14 behavior variables), disaggregation by system configuration, for example, would raise this number to 252, in addition to the 42 relationships based on the pooled data. This is clearly unmanageable and, in the end, would probably prove to be more confusing than informative. Third, and

145

most important, since we are dealing with a population of observations, the best over-all measure of the characteristics of that population should be based on the population itself. It is to be expected, of course, that we would probably find different relationships between the relevant variables if we were to break down the 120 observations into subsets for separate analyses. The implication is that some systems or nations or experimental conditons may compare more favorably to the referent system in some respects than others, and, thus, our pooling procedure may lead us to underestimate the ability of the model to replicate real world patterns. However, given our objective of evaluating the over-all behavior of the model, the pooling of the SIPER observations seems appropriate.

The set of observations for the INS nations was drawn from six of the twelve runs conducted by Raser and Crow in the WINSAFE II exercise. These are not the same six runs that served as a partial basis for our parameter estimates, but rather the second set of six runs that made up the twelve original runs. Since each of these runs contained five nations, we have thirty nations in our pooled set. Once again, we wll treat this set as a population, rather than a sample, and for the reasons outlined above, not differentiate between subsets.

To recapitulate, we have three sets of observations; two drawn from models that may or may not be accurate representations of the referent world they are to be compared to, and a sample of contemporary referent world nations. We now turn to a more detailed specification of our procedures for comparison.

The essence of this procedure is to assess and compare, by correlational methods, the degree to which different types of national behavior co-vary with certain national attributes in the three sets of observations. The correlations we will be examining, however, will be partial correlations, rather than simple correlations, in order to eliminate spurious correlations between attribute and behavior variables through spill-over effects. Thus, when we examine the relationship between size and turmoil, we will be controlling for the effects of development and accountability.

146

In the tables that follow, relationships between each attribute and behavior variable will be presented in the following form.

		SIPER	Size Real		INS
Turmoil	r	−9	+5		−63
	|z|		0.85	4.75	
	p		.198	.000	

The first row reports the partial correlations, rounded to the nearest two decimal places and multiplied by 100, found in each of the three data sets, the second and third rows contain information concerning the goodness-of-fit between the SIPER model and the real world, on the left, and the INS model and the real world, on the right. The technical derivation of the measures is given in Appendix Two. Briefly, however, both values reflect the degree of discrepancy between the correlation predicted by the simulation and the correlation observed in the real world sample. The first goodness-of-fit statistic, $|z|$, reflects the size of this discrepancy in terms of standard error units, and, of course, the larger the value, the poorer the prediction. The second statistic, p, is the likelihood that this discrepancy is due to sampling error in the real world coefficient. Hence, the smaller the value of p, the poorer the quality of the model's prediction.

In order to summarize the over-all goodness-of-fit of the two models, the following correspondence categories will be used.

Good: The discrepancy between the predicted (simulated) correlation and the observed (real) correlation, when transformed into units of standard error, has an absolute value of less than 1.0. If the predicted value is correct, the probability of obtaining a discrepancy larger than this is approximately .30.

Fair: The discrepancy between the predicted and observed values measured in standard error units, has an absolute value between 1.0 and 2.0. The probability of obtaining a discrepancy within this range, if the pre-

147

dicted value were correct, is less than .30 but greater than .05.

Poor: The discrepancy between the predicted and observed correlations is greater than ±2.0 units of standard error and has a probability of less than .05 of being obtained if the predicted value were correct.

NATIONAL ATTRIBUTES AND BEHAVIOR

The Area of Political Stability

The correlations and goodness-of-fit values concerning the relationships between our three basic national attributes and the five behavior variables that pertain to political stability are given in Table 5–2.

Looking first at the relationship between size and the behavior variables pertaining to political stability in this table, we find that in both SIPER and real world data, rather weak relationships are found between size and the first four stability variables, while the results are quite different for INS. The evidence that larger nations in INS experience less turmoil and conspiracy (though not less revolution) than smaller nations is quite strong. Revolutions are relatively rare in INS and 30 observations may not yield sufficient non-zero values for a pattern to emerge. The real world results reported here are in substantial agreement with Chadwick's findings.[34]

The general conclusion that size and the stability variables are unrelated in the SIPER and referent worlds is supported by the correlation between size and stability given in Table 5–2.[35] Again, however, larger nations in INS show a moderate tendency to be more stable than smaller nations.

Turning to the relationship between size and consumption, we find little association in the real world, a positive association in the SIPER worlds, and a negative association in the INS worlds. Russet et al., reported in correlation of −.24 between total population (size) and private consumption as a percentage of G.N.P. (consumption),[36] but seemingly the relationship between size and

148

TABLE 5–2
POLITICAL STABILITY RELATIONSHIPS

BEHAVIOR		ATTRIBUTE								
		Size			Development			Accountability		
		SIPER	Real	INS	SIPER	Real	INS	SIPER	Real	INS
Turmoil	r	−9	+5	−63	+8	−11	+28	+9	−5	−17
	|z|		0.85	4.75		1.15	2.39		0.85	0.73
	p		.198	.000		.125	.008		.198	.233
Conspiracy	r	−2	−14	−52	−10	−11	+28	0	−32	−24
	|z|		0.73	2.61		0.06	2.39		2.00	0.53
	p		.233	.005		.476	.008		.023	.298
Internal War	r	+5	−18	−3	+2	−7	+8	+3	−26	−32
	|z|		1.40	0.91		0.54	0.91		1.78	0.39
	p		.081	.181		.295	.181		.038	.348
Stability	r	+12	+8	+33	−9	+13	−4	−80	+28	−46
	|z|		0.18	1.58		1.33	1.03		8.33	4.72
	p		.429	.057		.092	.152		.000	.000
Consumption	r	+26	−13	−39	−73	−38	−18	−18	−2	+19
	|z|		2.41	1.69		3.17	1.31		0.97	1.28
	p		.008	.045		.001	.095		.166	.100

consumption in the referent world disappears when the level of development is held constant. Chadwick also reports a positive correlation (.87) between BC (size) and CS,[37] but since CS is an absolute measure of consumption, it seems likely that this correlation is a result of the effect of size. That is, large nations must spend more on consumption measured in absolute terms than smaller nations spend. Here we are concerned with relative consumption levels.

Due to the fact that consumption, investment, and defense effort are closely related (since they must sum to unity), a discrepancy between the observed and predicted correlations for one of these variables could be a secondary result of an error in the processes that control either of the other two variables. For this reason, a more detailed examination of only these three variables is presented in a later section.

An examination of the relationships between the level of development and the first four measures of political stability reveals that in all three data sources the relationships tend to be quite modest, although the turmoil and conspiracy correlations appear to be somewhat higher in the INS worlds. The correlations in all cases are quite low, however, and these findings are in conformity with Russett's and Taylor's conclusion that ''we know of no study that produced a correlation that exceeded .75 between economic development and any political variable of interest.''[38]

Agreement among the three data sets about the relationship between consumption and development is not apparent. Both the referent and SIPER worlds show consumption to be negatively related to the level of development, while little association is present in the INS worlds.[39] However, the SIPER correlation is substantially different from the real world and INS correlations, while the discrepancy between these latter two is a good deal smaller. Again, discussion of consumption is postponed for reasons indicated above.

With regard to the attribute of accountability, we find apparent agreement in the three data sources that it bears little relationship to the level of turmoil. However, the same cannot be said about the relationships between accountability and conspiracy, and ac-

150

countability and internal war. Real world nations that are more open experience less conspiracy and internal war than those that are more closed.[40] Similar relationships are found in the INS worlds, while no associations whatsoever are present in the SIPER data.

Those results are somewhat surprising since, according to the structure of the model, one would expect to find negative relationships between accountability and these two variables. As indicated in Chapter Two, the probability of revolution (PR, the conspiracy measure) is positively related to the degree of decision latitude (DL), which is the accountability measure inverted. Consequently, we would expect a negative correlation between conspiracy and accountability. Since internal war and conspiracy are structurally linked in a positive way, we would also expect a negative relationship between internal war and accountability. Obviously, other factors are canceling out the effects of this particular relationship, and it is not readily apparent what these are.

Turning to the relationship between accountability and stability, we find that real world nations with more open political systems exhibit a slight tendency to be more stable, while the opposite relationship holds in the simulated worlds.[41] An examination of the programmed hypothesis that relates stability to accountability, which is common to both SIPER and INS, shows clearly why the real world relationship does not emerge in the simulated worlds. The hypothesis states that stability (POH) is positively related to Validator Satisfaction over-all (VSm) and positively related to Decision Latitude (DL), but negatively related to the multiplicative interaction of the two variables.[42] Since we are using a negatively transformed DL as our measure of the accountability of the simulated nations, we would expect stability and accountability to be negatively related.

In view of the empirical evidence gathered from real world data, it would appear that the relationship between accountability and stability postulated by INS theory is improperly framed. However, the weak relationship found in the real world suggests that a reversal of the effect of accountability on stability will not be adequate, but rather that further study of the real world rela-

151

tionships is required before a revision may be proposed. Such a revision might follow the lines of Gurr's work.[43]

The last relationship to be considered in this section involves accountability and consumption. We find little relationship between these variables in the real, INS, and SIPER worlds, although the sign of the SIPER correlation appears odd since there is no a priori reason why the model should produce a negative relationship in any direct way. There are two factors to be kept in mind, however. First, the difference between the real world correlation and the SIPER correlation is rather small, and second, the interdependence of consumption, investment, and defense effort (as indicated earlier) raises the possibility that this somewhat anomalous correlation is due to factors operating in the growth or security areas. For this reason, we will re-examine this relationship in a later section.

We can make some assessment of the overall performance of the models in this area by examining the goodness-of-fit measures in Table 5–2. Placing these values in the appropriate correspondence categories discussed previously, we find the following pattern:

	Correspondence					
	Good		Fair		Poor	
	n	%	*n*	%	*n*	%
SIPER	7	47	5	33	3	20
INS	5	33	5	33	5	33

Over-all, we can see that the two models have not fared badly in this area of national behavior. SIPER was able to predict almost one-half of the real world relationships with reasonable accuracy and an additional one-third with fair accuracy. Two of the three relationships that fall in the poor category are concerned with consumption and its relationships to size and development, while the third deals with the association between accountability and stability.

INS does not do quite as well as SIPER in this area of behavior, having less good correspondences and more poor correspondences than SIPER. Four of the five relationships falling in the poor category deal with the relationships between the attributes of size and development, and the turmoil and conspiracy behaviors. The fifth involves the same accountability-stability relationship that SIPER failed to predict. This suggests that the problem may reside in the environmental processes that both SIPER and INS share.

The Area of Economic Growth

In Table 5–3 we find the correlations and goodness-of-fit measures pertaining to the variables that relate various aspects of economic growth to the basic national attributes. Turning our attention first to the correlations themselves, we discover that larger nations in both the real and simulated worlds have greater absolute growth and higher growth rates. However, the relationship between size and absolute growth is much stronger in the real world than in either of the simulated worlds.[44] On the other hand, the discrepancy between SIPER and the real world, although substantial, is less than the discrepancy between INS and the real world.

Turning to the relationship between size and investment, we find a rather modest negative association in the real and INS worlds, but a strong positive relationship in the SIPER worlds. We will explore this discrepancy in more detail in the section focusing on national allocations toward the end of this chapter.[45]

With regard to the relationship between development and growth, note that a very strong positive relationship appears in the real world data, and no such relationship appears in the SIPER or INS data, although the INS value is positive like the real world value. An examination of the relationship between development and the rate of growth reveals that, in real world nations, there is a moderate negative relationship between development and growth rate, and a slight positive relationship in INS and SIPER nations. The discrepancies between the real world and SIPER coefficients, and the real world and INS coefficients are fairly large. While the real world relationship is not a strong one, it seems odd to discover that more developed countries have lower growth rates than less developed countries. The positive relationship predicted by

153

TABLE 5-3

ECONOMIC GROWTH RELATIONSHIPS

		ATTRIBUTE								
		Size			Development			Accountability		
BEHAVIOR		SIPER	Real	INS	SIPER	Real	INS	SIPER	Real	INS
Growth	r	+33	+87	+13	−9	+62	+21	−15	+5	+33
	$|z|$	5.96	7.22		8.50	3.08		1.22	1.69	
	p	.000	.000		.000	.001		.111	.046	
Growth Rate	r	+24	+39	+15	+5	−30	+15	−8	+9	+21
	$|z|$	1.01	1.81		2.17	2.77		1.02	0.73	
	p	.156	.035		.015	.003		.154	.233	
Investment	r	+44	−5	+21	−17	+21	−6	−3	+7	+25
	$|z|$	3.14	1.58		2.32	1.64		0.61	1.11	
	p	.001	.057		.010	.051		.271	.134	

both SIPER and INS certainly seems more in line with conventional wisdom, so perhaps this discrepancy is due to bias in our sample of real nations.

Shifting to the relationship between development and investment, we find rather weak negative associations in both INS and SIPER, and a slightly stronger positive association in the sample of real nations. It may be the case that simulated nations which are more developed can produce the capital goods necessary to sustain a specified growth rate by allocating less to investment, and they take advantage of this opportunity. Real world nations, on the other hand, appear to increase investment as they become more developed.[46] We will return to this question when we focus on the allocation decisions later.

The last attribute variable we want to look at, accountability, is not strongly related to any of the growth behavior variables in the real or SIPER worlds. The relationship between accountability and growth is a weak positive one in INS, and it would appear that more open INS nations have higher absolute and relative growth, and devote more resources to investment, while the associations are very marginal in the real and SIPER data. These findings are generally in agreement with those of Adelman and Morris: that political variables are of marginal importance in explaining different rates of economic growth.[47]

An examination of the ''boxscore'' of the models in this area of behavior reveals that neither model has done particularly well in

	Correspondence					
	Good		Fair		Poor	
	n	%	n	%	n	%
SIPER	1	11	3	33	5	56
INS	1	11	5	56	3	33

predicting the real world values. Both had only one correspondence that could be considered good, and SIPER had only three that could be considered fair. The remaining five relationships falling into the category of poor correspondence concern the attributes of size and development and the levels of absolute growth

155

and investment, as well as the relationship between development and rate of growth.

INS, on the other hand, does slightly better than SIPER since five of the relationships can be considered as evidencing fair correspondence. The three falling into the poor category deal with the relationship of absolute growth to size and development, and the connection between development and rate of growth. The models do seem to have a common problem in the growth area, suggesting that the explanation may be found in their common structural elements.

The Area of National Security

Turning now to Table 5–4, we find there the correlations and goodness-of-fit measures for the three behavior variables that tap various aspects of national security. Looking first at how these variables are linked to size, we find that all three data sources concur as to a strong positive relationship between the level of force capability and a nation's size.[48] All the correlations are quite high, and the differences between them are small.

Similarly, we find agreement concerning the positive relationship between size and the absolute level of defense allocation, defense spending. However, the goodness-of-fit statistics reveal that the gap between the value predicted by SIPER and the observed value is quite large.

The agreement that characterizes the relationships discussed above is clearly not found in the matter of size and defense effort. Real world nations that are larger spend proportionately more on defense than those that are smaller, while the reverse holds in the SIPER nations. Large INS nations, on the other hand, appear to allocate neither relatively more nor relatively less to defense than smaller INS nations. The major difference, as the goodness-of-fit measures reveal, is between SIPER and the real world, however. In the section on national allocations we will consider this problem at length along with the consumption and investment variables.

Development and force capability are positively related in all three worlds and the differences between the coefficients are relatively small, even though the relationship in INS is somewhat

TABLE 5-4
NATIONAL SECURITY RELATIONSHIPS

ATTRIBUTE

BEHAVIOR		Size				Development				Accountability			
		SIPER	Real	INS		SIPER	Real	INS		SIPER	Real	INS
Force Capability	r	+50	+65	+72		+64	+61	+42		+1	−33	+18
	$\|z\|$		1.36	0.80			0.30	1.56			2.12	3.16
	p		.087	.212			.382	.059			.017	.001
Defense Spending	r	+32	+78	+88		+74	+74	−7		+27	−29	−35
	$\|z\|$		4.29	1.94			.000	6.12			3.46	0.41
	p		.000	.026			.500	.000			.000	.341
Defense Effort	r	−41	+36	+8		+74	+53	+17		+22	−44	−46
	$\|z\|$		4.89	1.78			2.17	2.51			4.18	0.16
	p		.000	.038			.015	.006			.000	.436

weaker. Turning to the relationship between development and defense spending, we find that real and SIPER nations spend more on defense in absolute terms if they are *developed* than if they are *undeveloped*. There is, on the other hand, a very weak negative association in the INS nations, and, as the goodness-of-fit statistics indicate, the INS correlation is substantially different from both the real and SIPER values. Moving on to the last variable in this column of the table, we discover that more developed nations spend relatively more on defense than less developed nations in both the SIPER and real worlds, but there appears to be a much weaker relationship between development and defense effort in the INS world. The goodness-of-fit measures suggest, however, that the relationship found in the SIPER nations is much stronger than the real world relationship. The nature of the real world correlation deserves elaboration.

Russett, in his study of nations, concluded that "no relationship was found between the military expenditure ratio and G.N.P. per capita. . . ."[49] Although Russett gives no coefficient of correlation for the two variables, it is probably not significantly different from the zero order correlation of .33 found in the present sample of 41 nations. All of these nations, by the way, were in Russett's sample of 82. Russett's finding was confirmed by Pryor for the NATO and Warsaw Treaty nations.[50] How is this discrepancy to be explained? The simple correlations between defense effort and size, development and accountability are .43, .33, and −.16 respectively. The partial correlations, on the other hand, are .36, .53, and −.44 respectively for the variable pairs. When we add to this the fact that the level of development is positively related to the degree of accountability (.62), it becomes clear why others have not found the relationships reported here. The more developed a nation is, the more, relatively speaking, it spends on defense; but the more open it is, the less it will spend on defense in relative terms. Hence, there are two contrary forces at work, and it is only through partial correlation that we are able to see their separate effects.

The relationships between accountability and force capability indicate poor predictive power for both SIPER and INS. The real world relationship is a negative one,[51] while both the INS and

SIPER coefficients are weak and positive. The explanation for this divergence may dwell in the relationship between force capability and internal strife. In INS and SIPER, decision-makers may reduce the probability of domestic strife by increasing the proportion of FC allocated to internal security, but an increase in the absolute size of FC does not, per se, decrease internal threats. Hence, simulated nations gain little domestic security from maintaining large force capabilities, regardless of the degree to which they are open or closed. Real world nations, on the other hand, which are more closed, may find it beneficial and necessary to maintain large internal security forces. It has often been suggested, for example, that the national military establishments in Latin American countries are intended to preserve internal, as much as external, security. It is probable that we are capturing the effects of closed real world nations maintaining large force capabilities for internal security purposes. Chadwick has found that "highly responsive political systems tend to use relatively little coercion. . .,"[52] while less responsive political systems may rely on "authoritarian stabilization" and consequently maintain larger armed forces.[53] A revision of the INS conceptualization, along the lines suggested by Gurr, as indicated earlier, is likely to improve correspondence.[54]

The remaining two behavior variables in this area of behavior, defense spending and defense effort, are related in a similar fashion to the attribute of accountability in two of the three sources. In real world and INS nations, the pattern is for nations that are less open to spend relatively and absolutely more on defense than those that are more open. The opposite relationship is found to characterize the SIPER nations.

This relationship in the SIPER data is unexpected, and the source of error is difficult to locate within the computer model at this time. Since consumption, investment, and defense effort are interdependent decisions, we need to view these facets of behavior together, as an error in one necessarily will produce an error in at least one other facet of behavior. Hence, as we indicated earlier, we will consider these three behavior variables in more detail in a later section.

An over-all assessment of the two models' predictive power by

159

means of our correspondence criteria reveals that they are slightly stronger in

	Correspondence					
	Good		Fair		Poor	
	n	%	*n*	%	*n*	%
SIPER	2	22	1	11	6	67
INS	3	33	3	33	3	33

this area than in the growth area. The quality of the INS predictions is mixed, with three relationships in each of the three correspondence categories. The three classified as poor include the relationships between development and the absolute and relative levels of defense expenditure, as well as the association between accountability and the level of force capability.

With six predictions falling in the poor category and only two in the good category, we can see that SIPER's over-all performance is not particularly good in the national security area. Three of the six poor predictions arise from the relationships between defense effort and each of the three attribute variables, and in two of these the predicted values are in the opposite direction from the observed values. The three remaining poor predictions involve under-predicting the observed strong positive association between size and defense spending and erroneously predicting a positive link between development and defense spending, when the observed value is negative, as well as sharing the error that INS made, concerning the relationship between accountability and force capability levels.

Perhaps we will find that the models fare better in the last area of concern, international interactions.

The Area of International Interaction

In the first row of Table 5–5, we find that both SIPER and INS appear to differ from the real world with respect to the relationship of relative trade to size. The negative relationship between size and relative trade present in our sample of contemporary nations has been observed by others, notably Deutsch, Bliss, and Ecks-

TABLE 5-5

INTERNATION INTERACTION RELATIONSHIPS

| | | ATTRIBUTE | | | | | | | | |
| | | Size | | | Development | | | Accountability | | |
BEHAVIOR		SIPER	Real	INS	SIPER	Real	INS	SIPER	Real	INS
Relative Trade	r	−1	−63	−6	−29	+12	−3	−8	+1	+19
	|z|	4.40	4.09		0.91	2.52		0.54	1.09	
	p	.000	.000		.181	.006		.295	.138	
Trade Magnitude	r	+50	+74	+8	−12	+74	+7	0	+6	+30
	|z|	2.42	5.23		5.28	6.36		0.37	1.56	
	p	.008	.000		.000	.000		.356	.059	
Diplomatic Conflict	r	+6	+12	−35	+29	+34	−8	+6	−26	−36
	|z|	0.37	2.92		2.61	0.33		1.96	0.67	
	p	.356	.002		.005	.371		.025	.251	

tein. The observed curvilinear relationship was stated thus: ". . .the foreign trade ratio tends to decline only moderately. . . as country sizes increase from about 1 million to about 10 million. . . This decline is accelerated, however, at population sizes above 10 million".[55] Kuznets similarly says that ". . . the ratio of foreign trade to national income rises as the average size of population declines,"[56] and reasons for this relationship have been suggested elsewhere.[57] Economies of scale enter the foreign trade decisions in such a way as to reduce the advantage of international exchange, relatively speaking, for larger nations. In the SIPER model, the amount of national trade the nation desires to engage in is given as a constant proportion of size rather than as a decreasing proportion. A revision of this formulation to include a curvilinear relationship should remedy this discrepancy between the observed and predicted values.

Both SIPER and real world nations trade more in absolute terms as their size increases, while INS nations do not.[58] There are differences between the strengths of relationship between real world, SIPER, and INS nations, as can be seen from the goodness-of-fit measures; however, on the whole, SIPER's prediction is quite a bit better than the INS prediction.

With respect to the relationship between size and diplomatic conflict, we find the real and SIPER data sources in substantial agreement about the weak positive nature of the relationship.[59] However, in INS we find a weak inverse relationship, and one significantly different from the relationships found in real and SIPER worlds, according to the goodness-of-fit measures. Interestingly, smaller INS nations appear to be the source of more diplomatic conflict than larger INS nations.

Considering the relationship between a nation's level of development and its relative trading activity, we find that in real world and INS data the relationship is essentially absent, while more developed SIPER nations exhibit a tendency to trade relatively less.[60] Interestingly enough, this is precisely the relationship that Sombart proposed.[61] Deutsch and Eckstein have empirically investigated this "law of the declining importance of foreign trade."[62] Their findings relating to real world nations do not support our observed real world value, but rather they agree with the SIPER predictions. By using time series data, rather than cross-sectional data such as ours, they found a clear trend toward a reduction in the relative size of the foreign trade sector, as industrialization advanced. The relationship is not strictly linear, however, since there is a slight increase in trade in the early stages of industrialization. The fact that the SIPER model produces a relationship in cross-sectional data, which appears in longitudinal real world data, might be considered at least a partial correspondence.

We are not so fortunate, however, regarding the relationship between development and the absolute size of the foreign trade sector. More developed real world nations trade more, in absolute terms, than less developed ones, while the level of development of SIPER and INS nations is only weakly related to the absolute size of their foreign trade sector. This finding seems to suggest that some rethinking of the decision processes governing the amount of trade is necessary, as was previously noted. In the reformulation of trade volume decision processes, as discussed above, we shall have to examine carefully the role of development in the processes.

Examining the relationship between development and diplomatic conflict, we find SIPER and the real world in substantial agreement that developed nations engage more in diplomatic conflict than do undeveloped nations.[63] A similar relationship is not found in the INS data, according to Table 5–5. Furthermore, INS appears to be significantly different from both SIPER and the real world in this respect, according to the goodness-of-fit measures, while there is only a slight discrepancy between SIPER and the real world.

As to the relationships between the attribute of accountability and the variables relative trade and trade magnitude, we can report agreement among the three data sources that there is little association in all three data sets.[64] Finally, Table 5–5 reveals that real and INS nations having more closed political systems generate more diplomatic conflict than their more open counterparts, while the amount of conflict that SIPER nations generate is essentially

163

unrelated to the accountability of their political systems. The SIPER prediction is in accordance with Rummel's finding, but not with our sample value.[65]

Shifting our attention to the breakdown on the goodness-of-fit categories, we find that the models have performed somewhat better in

	Correspondence					
	Good		Fair		Poor	
	n	%	n	%	n	%
SIPER	4	44	1	11	4	44
INS	2	22	2	22	5	56

this area than in the previous two. The majority of SIPER predictions are of either good or fair accuracy, with all four of the poor fits concerning the two trade variables and the attributes of size and development.

INS appears to fare a little worse in this area, with five relationships that fall into the area of poor correspondence. Three of these stem from the inability of INS to predict accurately the negative association between relative trade and size, and the positive relationships between the level of trade measured in absolute terms and the size and development attributes. The two remaining erroneous predictions concern diplomatic conflict and its relationship to size and development.

Over-all, then, it would appear that SIPER and INS share some deficiencies in the foreign trade sector of the model and reformulations are in order.

National Attributes and National Allocations

We have already indicated several times in this chapter that some special attention is due three behavior variables: consumption, investment, and defense effort. Indeed, of the nine attribute-behavior relationships that incorporated these three variables, seven were judged to be cases of poor correspondence between SIPER and the real world.

In Table 5–6 we have reproduced the entries relevant to these three variables from Tables 5–2, 5–3, and 5–4. As this table shows, larger SIPER nations spend relatively more on consump-

TABLE 5-6
NATIONAL ALLOCATION RELATIONSHIPS

ATTRIBUTE

BEHAVIOR		Size			Development			Accountability		
		SIPER	Real	INS	SIPER	Real	INS	SIPER	Real	INS
Consumption	r	+26	−13	−39	−73	−38	−18	−18	−2	+19
	|z|	2.41	1.69			3.17	1.31		0.97	1.28	
	p	.008	.045			.001	.095		.166	.100	
Investment	r	+44	−5	+21	−17	+21	−6	−3	+7	+25
	|z|	3.14	1.58			2.32	1.64		0.61	1.11	
	p	.001	.057			.010	.051		.271	.134	
Defense Effort	r	−41	+36	+8	+74	+53	+17	+22	−44	−46
	|z|	4.89	1.78			2.17	2.51		4.18	0.16	
	p	.000	.038			.015	.006		.000	.436	

tion and investment and relatively less on defense than smaller SIPER nations. Larger INS nations spend relatively less on consumption, and relatively more on investment. Real nations, on the other hand, spend relatively more on defense, but again there is no clear evidence as to where the deficit is incurred.

Developed SIPER nations spend relatively less on consumption and investment and relatively more on defense. This is a reversal of the pattern found in our examination of the size attribute. Real nations, which are more developed, seem to follow a similar pattern of decreasing consumption's share of the national wealth and increasing the relative size of the defense sector. Developed INS nations, on the other hand, seem to act only marginally different from undeveloped nations with respect to the allocation of national wealth, although a more moderate version of the consumption defense trade-off found in the SIPER nations is suggested.

Finally, we find that *more* open SIPER nations tend to increase the defense share and decrease the consumption share, as compared to *less* open nations. Real world and INS nations, however, decrease the relative size of the defense sector as their degree of accountability increases.

In seeking the source of these discrepancies, it will be useful to examine the interrelationships among the three behavior variables in each of the three data sources. Figure 5–1 gives the simple correlations between consumption, investment, and defense for the referent and simulated worlds.[66] An examination of these triads clearly shows some basic patterns. In all three data sources the relationship between defense and investment is very weak. It appears that defense and investment are not commonly traded off in any of the worlds, a finding somewhat at variance with Russett's work.[67] He found that over time there was a tendency in the United States for increases in defense to be partially paid for by decreases in investment. However, the real world conclusions here are based on cross-sectional rather than longitudinal data, and Russett himself notes that the U.S. pattern is by no means cross-culturally constant. He finds that Canada, for exam-

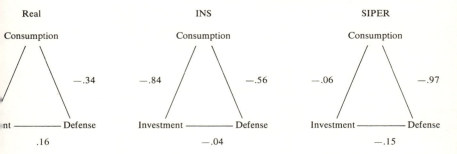

FIGURE 5-1

SIMPLE CORRELATIONS BETWEEN CONSUMPTION, INVESTMENT, AND DEFENSE

ple, exhibits the same behavior that we find above; that is, there is a tendency for increases in defense to be paid for by decreasing consumption.[68]

Real world nations and SIPER nations provide a marked contrast to the relationship of consumption to the other two sectors. As consumption declines, real world nations seem to devote the released resources predominantly to investment, while SIPER nations devote the surplus to defense. It would appear that SIPER nations give national security a higher priority than economic growth and that, to some extent, the opposite is true in the real world. The pattern of INS trade-offs is clearly somewhere in between both SIPER and the real world. As consumption declines in INS nations, investment and defense both increase, with the increases in defense being slightly better correlated to the decreases in consumption than to the increases in investment.

A resetting of SIPER parameters may remedy this noncorrespondence. It will be recalled that a set of parameters discussed in Chapter Two, the budget crisis resolution weights b_{18}, b_{19} and b_{20}, establish the priorities of the expenditure sectors when conflict among goals is encountered. For this set of runs, an equal weight was given each sector. This means that the same proportion will be cut in each sector. By way of example, let us consider a hypothetical case in which a nation wants to allocate its resources in the following manner:

Consumption	4/5 of resources
Investment	1/5 of resources
Defense	1/5 of resources

This would, of course, be a crisis situation. Giving equal weight to the sectors would reduce each sector by one sixth.[69] The new allocations would be:

Consumption	2/3 of resources
Investment	1/6 of resources
Defense	1/6 of resources

Proportionately, consumption has been cut as much as defense or investment, but in absolute terms, it has been cut four times more than the other two sectors.

Since the over-all mean percent levels of allocation are 84, 5, and 11 for the consumption, investment, and defense sectors, respectively, for SIPER nations, it is likely that *in the event of a budget crisis* the type of reduction proposed above would take place. Such reductions would tend to produce the correlations found in the SIPER data.

Increasing the budget crisis resolution weight of the consumption sector, b_{18}, may enable us to replicate the real world pattern without further modification of the computer model. Further study is needed, however, and such study may suggest that a reformulation is necessary. It is interesting to note, however, that SIPER nations (in one sense) act as Bruce Russett suggests real world nations should act. "It is bad to sacrifice future productivity and resources for current defense or war-fighting activities; insofar as possible such activities 'should' be financed out of current consumption".[70]

SUMMARY EVALUATION

The over-all results of our assessment of the SIPER and INS models, in comparison to a sample of contemporary nations, is given in the following table:

Correspondence

	Good		Fair		Poor	
	n	%	n	%	n	%
SIPER	14	33	10	24	18	43
INS	11	26	15	36	16	38

The aggregate profiles of the two models are quite similar. SIPER predicted fourteen relationships with a good degree of accuracy, while the comparable value for INS is eleven, yielding values of 33 and 26 percent respectively. In the middle category, INS predicted 15 relationships with fair accuracy, while only ten of the SIPER predictions fell in this category. SIPER failed to predict eighteen relationships with less than fair accuracy, while the comparable value for INS is sixteen. On the whole then, there appears to be a slight tendency for SIPER predictions to cluster at both ends of the underlying correspondence continuum; that is, SIPER's predictions tend to be quite accurate or quite inaccurate, while the INS predictions are more evenly distributed over the three correspondence categories.

The following table reveals the joint performance of the two models in predicting the forty-two relationships. To a certain extent, this

SIPER
Correspondence

INS	Good	Fair	Poor	Total
Correspondence				
Good	2	6	3	11
Fair	6	3	6	15
Poor	6	1	9	16
Total	14	10	18	42

breakdown suggests that the two models have the same weaknesses, but different strengths. When SIPER produced good predictions with respect to a set of relationships, INS tended to produce only fair or poor predictions; and on those relationships where SIPER was only fairly accurate, INS tended to have good

169

correspondence. On the other hand, relationships predicted inaccurately by SIPER tended to be predicted imprecisely by INS. This supports our previous conclusion that some, perhaps one-half, of our non-correspondences are due to those elements common to the two models; i.e., the environmental processes outlined in the first part of Chapter Two.

Throughout this chapter we have noted ways in which the SIPER model needs to be revised, and they will not be repeated here. This first validation study has pointed out both strengths and weaknesses in the SIPER model, and in the next chapter we will evaluate its performance from another perspective.

CHAPTER FIVE NOTES

1. Thomas H. Naylor et al., *Computer Simulation Techniques* (New York: Wiley, 1966), p. 310.

2. William H. Starbuck and John M. Dutton, ''The History of Simulation Models,'' in John M. Dutton and William H. Starbuck, *Computer Simulation of Human Behavior* (New York: Wiley, 1971), pp. 9–30.

3. Ithiel de Sola Pool, Robert P. Abelson, and Samuel Popkin, *Candidates, Issues, and Strategies* (Cambridge, Mass.: The M.I.T. Press, 1965).

4. Charles Hermann, ''Validation Problems in Games and Simulations with Special Reference to Models of International Politics,'' *Behavioral Science,* 12, (May, 1967): 220–224. See also Charles F. Hermann and Margaret G. Hermann, *Validation Studies of the Inter-Nation Simulation* (China Lake, Ca., U.S. Naval Ordinance Test Station, December, 1963), pp. 26-34.

5. Harold Guetzkow, ''Structured Programs and Their Relation to Free Activity within the Inter-Nation Simulation,'' in Harold Guetzkow et al., *Simulation in International Relations* (Englewood Cliffs, N.J.: Prentice-Hall, 1963), p. 105.

6. Hermann, ''Validation Problems in Games and Simulations,'' p. 222.

7. James N. Rosenau, ''Pre-Theories and Theories of Foreign Policy,'' *Approaches to Comparative and International Politics,* ed. R. Barry Farrell (Evanston, Ill.: Northwestern University Press, 1966), pp. 27–92.

8. Jack Sawyer, ''Dimensions of Nations: Size, Wealth, and Politics,'' *American Journal of Sociology,* 73, No. 2 (September, 1967): 145–172.

9. Rudolph J. Rummel, ''Indicators of Cross-National and International Patterns,'' *American Political Science Review,* 63, No. 1 (March, 1969): 127–147.

10. Population data were taken from Bruce Russett, et al., *World Handbook of Political and Social Indicators* (New Haven: Yale University Press, 1964), pp. 15–21. The choice of this indicator for the size variable is supported by Rummel, ''Indicators of Cross-National and International Patterns,'' p. 134. The indicator is $\log_{10}$ transformed to reduce the skewness of the distribution.

11. For a discussion of the advantages and disadvantages of this indicator see Irma Adelman and Cynthia Taft Morris, *Society, Politics, and Economic Development* (Baltimore: Johns Hopkins University Press, 1967), pp. 84–90.

12. It should be evident that development is a weighted average of the national generation rates.

Development = a_1 * CS generation rate + a_2 * BC generation rate
$\qquad\qquad$ + a_3 * FC generation rate

where the weights a_1, a_2, a_3 are equal to the proportion of the total basic capability of the nation which is allocated to the production of consumer goods (CS), investment goods (BC), and security goods (FC) respectively in a given period.

13. Phillip M. Gregg and Arthur S. Banks, ''Dimensions of Political Systems: Factor Analysis of a Cross-Polity Survey,'' *American Political Science Review,* 59, No. 3 (September, 1965): 602–614.

14. The variables that loaded positively on this factor were: electoral system, constitutional regime, group opposition, status of legislature, horizontal power distribution, representativeness of regime, press freedom, aggregation by legislature, military neutral, conventional ideological orientation, articulation by parties, articulation by associational groups, and modern bureaucracy. *Ibid.*, p. 608.

15. Arthur S. Banks and Phillip M. Gregg, ''Grouping Political Systems: Q-Factor Analysis of a Cross-Polity Survey,'' *American Behavioral Scientist,* 9, No. 3 (November, 1965): 3–6.

16. Rudolph J. Rummel, ''Dimensions of Conflict Behavior Within and Between Nations,'' *General Systems Yearbook,* 8 (1963): 1–50; Raymond Tanter, ''Dimensions of Conflict Behavior Within and Between Nations, 1957-1960,'' *Journal of Conflict Resolution,* 10, No. 1 (March, 1966): 41–64; Ted R. Gurr, ''Causal Model of Civil Strife: A Comparative Analysis Using New Indices,'' *American Political Science Review,* 62, No. 4 (December, 1968): 1104–1124.

17. Gurr, ''A Causal Model of Civil Strife,'' p. 1107.

18. Feierabend and Feierabend computed political stability by counting events of aggressive behavior directed against the political system. See Ivo K. Feierabend and Rosalind L. Feierabend, ''Aggressive Behavior Within Polities, 1948–1962: A Cross-National Study,'' *Journal of Conflict Resolution,* 10, No. 3 (September, 1966): 249–271. The emphasis in this point of view is on the degree to which the continued existence of the system is threatened by violence.

19. Banks and Textor speak more in terms of major constitutional change when they discuss stability, and more emphasis is placed on whether major change has taken place in the political system, rather than the means by which this change was brought about. See Arthur S. Banks and Robert B. Textor, *A Cross-Polity Survey* (Cambridge, Mass.: The M.I.T. Press, 1963).

20. See Gurr, ''A Causal Model of Civil Strife,'' pp. 1107–1109, for a discussion of the construction of this index.

21. Robert E. Pendley and Charles D. Elder, ''An Analysis of Office-Holding in the Inter-Nation Simulation in Terms of Contemporary Political Theory and Data on the Stability of Regimes and Governments'' (Evanston, Ill.: Simulated International Processes project, Northwestern University, November, 1966).

22. Russett, et al., *World Handbook,* pp. 170–171.

23. Absolute economic growth is the product of gross national product in 1957 in U.S. dollars (*ibid.,* pp. 152–154), annual growth of G.N.P. per capita (*ibid.,* pp. 160–161), and annual percentage of increase in population (*ibid.,* pp. 46–48). The indicator is transformed using $\log_{10}(x+1)$ transformation to reduce the skewness of the distribution.

24. Growth rate equals annual growth of G.N.P. per capita (*ibid.,* pp. 160–161) times annual percentage of increase in population (*ibid.,* pp. 46–48).

25. *Ibid.,* pp. 168–169.

26. This data is taken from the *World Handbook of Political and Social Indicators.* FC is the product of total population (*ibid.,* pp. 18–21), military personnel as a percentage of total population (*ibid.,* pp. 74–76), expenditure on defense as a percentage of G.N.P. (*ibid.,* pp. 79–80), and gross national product in U.S

172

dollars (*ibid.*, pp. 152–154). The variable is $\log_{10}(x+1)$ transformed to make the distribution less skewed.

27. *Ibid.*, pp. 79–80.

28. Defense spending equals gross national product in U.S. dollars (*ibid.*, pp. 152–154) times expenditure on defense as a percentage of G.N.P. (*ibid.*, pp. 79–80). Defense spending is $\log_{10}(x+1)$ transformed to make the distribution more normal.

29. *Ibid.*, pp. 164–165.

30. Trade magnitude is the product of foreign trade as a percentage of G.N.P. (*ibid.*, pp. 164–165) and gross national product in U.S. dollars (*ibid.*, pp. 152–154). A $\log_{10}(x+1)$ transformation is applied to the variable to make the distribution less skewed.

31. Rudolph J. Rummel, "Dimensions of Conflict Behavior Within and Between Nations," *General Systems Yearbook,* 8 (1963): 1–50.

32. The factor scores are taken from the appendix of the above article.

33. The analysis was carried out under the direction of Richard W. Chadwick. See Richard W. Chadwick, *Definition of Simulation Threats, Accusations and Protests* (Evanston, Ill.: Northwestern University Department of Political Science, April, 1965). The INS data are from a set of runs conducted by John Raser and Wayman Crow at the Western Behavioral Sciences Institute. See their *Winsafe II: An Inter-Nation Simulation Study of Deterrence Postures Embodying Capacity to Delay Response* (La Jolla, Ca.: Western Behavioral Sciences Institute, July 31, 1964).

34. Richard W. Chadwick, "An Inductive, Empirical Analysis of Intra-and International Behavior, Aimed at a Partial Extension of Inter-Nation Simulation Theory," *Journal of Peace Research,* 6, No. 3 (1969): 193–214. Chadwick reports a correlation of $-.18$ between BC (size) and VSm (turmoil) and a correlation of $-.17$ between BC (size) and pR (conspiracy).

35. Chadwick *(ibid.,* p. 197) reports a correlation of .18 between BC (size) and POH (stability).

36. Russett et al., *World Handbook,* p. 278.

37. Chadwick, "An Inductive, Empirical Analysis," p. 197.

38. Bruce M. Russett and Charles L. Taylor, "Is Political Instability Related to Per Capita Income?" Bendix Corporation Working Paper No. 97 (Ann Arbor: Bendix Corporation, January 23, 1967), p. 6.

39. Russett et al., *World Handbook,* p. 278, report a correlation of $-.44$, which is significant at the .001 level, between private consumption as a percentage of G.N.P. and per capita G.N.P.

40. Chadwick, "An Inductive, Empirical Analysis," p. 197, finds no relationship between DL (accountability) and pR (conspiracy), (r = .08). Since the simple correlation found here between accountability and conspiracy is $-.45$, it appears that Chadwick's indicator of pR, number of attempted revolutions, measures a specific kind of conspiratorial behavior rather than the more general measure developed by Gurr, which is used here.

41. Chadwick *(ibid.,* p. 197), reports the opposite relationship. He found a

positive relationship between DL (inverted accountability) and POH (stability), (r = .30, significant at the .05 level). Chadwick's indicator of POH is the average age of the last two governments. This choice of indicator seems to reflect a conceptualization of stability as the absence of change (see note 19), rather than the one used here, the absence of destabilizing events (see note 18). The lack of intercorrelation between indicators of political stability has been discussed by Russett and Taylor, with the conclusion that "empirically, there is no single dimension of political stability . . . that measures satisfactorily all the phenomena we would like to know about," "Is Political Stability Related," pp. 5–6.

42. The mathematical formulation for this relationship is POH = abVSm − a(DL)(VSm) + cDL − cd, but the verbal statement of the relationship is simply "the higher the decision-latitude, the less immediately is office-holding subject to validator satisfaction;" a statement which does not necessarily require the interaction term in the above equation. Guetzkow, "Structured Programs," pp. 115–116.

43. Gurr, "A Causal Model of Civil Strife," pp. 1104–1124.

44. Kuznets has noted " . . . small countries are under a greater handicap than large in the task of economic growth. Their small size may not permit them to take full advantage of the potential of large-scale production and organization; their defense task vis-a-vis the rest of the world may be proportionately greater; and their reliance on international trade and international division of labour, while greater than for large countries, must still be limited for security reasons, and because many needed goods that are closely interwoven with the country's distinctive culture and indigenous life cannot be imported." Simon Kuznets, "Economic Growth of Small Nations," *The Economic Consequences of the Size of Nations,* ed. E. A. Robinson (New York: St. Martin's Press, 1965), p. 20.

45. It should be noted, however, that according to Ragnar Nurske, "the inducement to invest is limited by the size of the market. In the exchange economy of the real world, it is not difficult to find illustrations of the way in which the small size of a country's market can discourage, or even prohibit, the profitable application of modern capital equipment by any individual entrepreneur in any particular industry." Ragnar Nurske, "The Size of the Market and the Inducement to Invest," *Development and Society,* eds. D. E. Novack and R. Lekachman (New York: St. Martin's Press, 1964), pp. 92–93. This proposition would support the results produced by SIPER.

46. In regard to the relationship between investment and development, Jacob Viner has stated, "it may also be true that as average income through time increases, the percentage of the national income which will be annually saved will increase. But empirical evidence in support of this is lacking, and there are some *a priori* reasons for being skeptical about it." Jacob Viner, "Barriers to Economic Development," D. E. Novack and R. Lekachman, *Development and Society,* p. 83.

47. Irma Adelman and Cynthia Taft Morris, *Society, Politics and Economic Development.* See also Andreas C. Tsantis, "Political Factors in Economic Development," *Comparative Politics,* 2, No. 1 (October, 1969): 63–78.

48. Chadwick, "An Inductive, Empirical Analysis," p. 197, reports a strong positive association between BC (size) and FC (force capability). In addition, Haas and Whiting have commented, "human resources, combined with physical foundations and industrial production, determine the amount of power available to the policy maker in support of means." *Dynamics of International Relations* (New York: McGraw-Hill, 1956), pp. 133–134.

49. Bruce M. Russett, "Measures of Military Effort," *American Behavioral Scientist*, 7, No. 6 (February, 1964): 29.

50. Frederic L. Pryor, *Public Expenditures in Communist and Capitalistic Nations* (Homewood, Ill.: Irwin, 1969), p. 93.

51. Chadwick, "An Inductive, Empirical Analysis," p. 197, reports a real world correlation of $-.03$ between DL (inverse accountability) and FC (force capability).

52. Chadwick, *Ibid.*, p. 207.

53. Gabriel Almond, "Research Note: A Comparative Study of Interest Groups and the Political Process," *American Political Science Review*, 52, No. 1 (March, 1958): 270–282.

54. Gurr, "A Causal Model of Civil Strife."

55. Karl W. Deutsch, Chester I. Bliss, and Alexander Eckstein, "Population, Sovereignty, and the Share of Foreign Trade," *Economic Development and Cultural Change*, 10, No. 4 (July, 1962): 353–366.

56. Kuznets, "Economic Growth of Small Nations," p. 20.

57. Hollis B. Chenery, "Patterns of Industrial Growth," *American Economic Review*, 50, No. 4 (September, 1960): 624–654.

58. Chadwick, "An Inductive, Empirical Analysis," p. 197, reports correlations of .85 between BC (size) and imports and .79 between BC (size) and exports for the real world.

59. Rummel also found significant correlations between population (size) and threats (.32), accusations (.36), and protests (.38), which are significant at the .01 level. In spite of this, Rummel concludes "there is little relationship between a nation's power and its foreign conflict behavior." Rudolph J. Rummel, "The Relationship Between National Attributes and Foreign Conflict Behavior," *Quantitative International Politics*, ed. J. David Singer (New York: The Free Press, 1966), p. 208. The preliminary work of Salmore and Hermann indicates that of the three variables: size, development, and accountability, size best accounts for variation in conflict. Regrettably, the partial correlations are not now available for comparison. Stephen A. Salmore and Charles F. Hermann, "The Effect of Size, Development and Accountability on Foreign Policy." Prepared for delivery at the Seventh North American Peace Research Conference of the Peace Research Society (International), University of Michigan, Ann Arbor, Michigan, November 11–12, 1969.

60. Kuznets has commented, " . . . there is no clear association between the ratio of foreign trade to income (relative trade) and per capita income (development)." Kuznets, "Economic Growth of Small Nations," p. 20.

175

61. Werner Sombart, *Die Deutsche Volkswirtschaft in Neunzehnten Jahrhundert*, 3d ed. (Berlin: Bondi, 1913), pp. 368–376, 528.

62. Karl W. Deutsch and Alexander Eckstein, "National Industrialization and the Declining Share of the International Economic Sector, 1890–1959," *World Politics*, 13, No. 2 (January, 1961): 267–299.

63. Rummel finds little relationship between development and threats, accusations, and protests and concludes that there is "little relationship between a nation's economic development or level of technology and its foreign conflict behavior." "National Attributes and Foreign Conflict Behavior," p. 205.

64. However, Chadwick, "An Inductive, Empirical Analysis," p. 197, finds a negative relationship between DL (inverse accountability) and imports ($r = -.35$) and exports ($r = -.33$). Both of these are significant at the .01 level. Further confirmation of either of these results has not been found.

65. We are in substantial agreement here with Rummel that "the degree of totalitarianism of a government has little relationship to its foreign conflict behavior." "National Attributes and Foreign Conflict Behavior," p. 207.

66. Problems may arise when the variables being correlated have the same denominator, but as Kuh and Meyer state, "the question of spurious correlation quite obviously does not arise when the hypothesis to be tested has initially been formulated in terms of ratios." Edwin Kuh and John R. Meyer, "Correlation and Regression Estimates When the Data are Ratios." *Econometrica*, 23, No. 4 (October, 1955): 400–416.

67. Bruce M. Russett, "Who Pays for Defense?", *American Political Science Review*, 63, No. 2 (June, 1969): 412–426.

68. *Ibid.*, p. 416.

69. The desired level of expenditure is $4/5 + 1/5 + 1/5 = 6/5$, and if each sector is given equal weight, the new value will be 5/6 of its former value, or cut by 1/6.

70. *Ibid.*, p. 416.

SIX

Simulated and Referent International Systems

THE purpose of this chapter is to compare the international systems produced by the SIPER systems to contemporary and historical systems drawn from the real world. In this second validation study, we will be concerned with both static and dynamic properties of these systems, with a focus on certain macro-system properties. Before outlining the specific procedures to be followed, some general discussion of the problems of comparing international systems is in order.

COMPARING INTERNATIONAL SYSTEMS

One basic problem faced in comparing simulated international systems to real world systems centers on the selection of the appropriate referent world. In the previous chapter, we acknowledged that the simulated nations are not designed to represent particular nations, but rather broad classes or genotypes of nations. It follows, therefore, that the simulated international systems considered here are not necessarily models of any past or present international systems. On the other hand, the system configurations we have used are taken from a set of INS runs designed to investigate a contemporary problem, so one might conclude that it was the intention of those who selected these initial values to replicate a contemporary system. This will be treated as an empirical question, however, in this chapter.

Perhaps it is unfortunate that we cannot state unequivocally that we sought, in this series of computer runs, to simulate the nineteenth-century European system or the twentieth-century bipolar world, but the preliminary nature of this research would suggest that selecting such an objective might be premature. International systems take shape through the interaction of the nations comprising the system, and until we have some knowledge as to the dynamic nature of the model, we cannot be sure that our parameter settings and variable initializations will produce the desired system. Moreover, one of the purposes of the present research is to determine the kinds of international systems that result when various formulations prescribing the behavior of nations are drawn together in an interactive context.

In the previous chapter, we were able to partially overcome the validation problem being discussed here by extracting "genotypic" nations by means of controlling statistically major dimensions of inter-nation variability. With a large sample of nations, it was permissible to talk of larger and smaller, more developed and less developed, and more open and less open national systems. That strategy cannot be followed here, since our sample of international systems is not large enough to permit using a procedure analogous to that employed in Chapter Five.

A second problem in making comparisons among international systems arises, and for two reasons. First, there is insufficient data available to allow a micro-level comparison between simulated and real systems; and second, since the simulated systems are fundamentally somewhat abstract, the only feasible strategy is to raise the referent world systems to a similar level of abstraction. Therefore, our analytical focus will be macro in nature.

Another limitation we face in the following analyses, is that it is neither feasible nor efficient to evaluate all twenty-four of the simulated international systems, therefore we must reduce the number of simulated systems to be examined. Given the results reported in Chapter Four concerning the relative impact of the historical and policy variables, the wisest strategy would seem to require us to base our comparisons on the six different system configurations rather than on the four policy variables. Thus, the six SIPER systems examined will be based on an average of the four policy variations. In addition, we will include (for comparative purposes) the six INS systems discussed in the previous chapter.

With these constraints and limitations, let us turn to the question of what properties of the relevant systems are to be compared.

178

SIMULATED AND REFERENT INTERNATIONAL SYSTEMS

System Properties

A system is a collectivity, and, as such, it is useful to think of its properties as falling into one of three categories for collectivities, as defined by Lazarsfeld.[1] Analytical properties are those based on a mathematical operation, which is performed upon a property of each individual member of the system. An example of this type of system property is the average proportion of gross national product the world's nations devote to defense. Structural properties, on the other hand, reflect the ways in which members of the system are related to each other. The distribution of alliance bonds present in an international system might be considered an example of this type of system property. Finally, there are those global system properties that are *not* derived directly from the properties of individual system members, but rather reflect the syntactic nature of the system, and may be thought of as ''gestalt'' properties. In the area of international relations, such system characterizations as multipolar and bipolar seem to fall into this category.

All the system properties we will be examining fall into the analytical category. Some may consider them an inferior type of system property, but, in fact, there is no logical basis for this assertion. It is clear that these three categories reflect different aspects of the nature of a system, and no one category is either *more* or *less* ''systemic'' in nature than the others. From a practical viewpoint, analytical properties have several advantages. They are relatively easy to derive and interpret, and, as a general rule, less information is required to make a reasonably accurate estimate of an analytical system property than in the case of the other two types. On the other hand, since analytical properties essentially characterize a system by its 'average'' member, it may be the case that no system member has these exact characteristics.

Four analytical system properties were selected for examination here. Three of them deal with the way in which the members of a system allocate resources among the three main sectors of economic activity: consumption, investment, and defense, and the

179

fourth reflects the level of economic exchange between system members. These variables were selected because they are important decisional variables in both SIPER and INS, and because enough data are available on past and present systems to make comparisons possible. Let us briefly examine each of these four variables.

Consumption. As we noted earlier, consumption " is the vital process by which the population replenishes or increases its energies and ministers to its wants and needs."[2] Other things being equal, the standard of living of individuals will be higher in a system where a high proportion of productive energies is directed at consumption, than that available in systems with low consumption properties. In all systems, this measure is derived by computing the average percentage of resources devoted to consumption by all system members. In this sense, then, the measure reflects what the average system member devotes to consumption.

Investment. The growth of a system "is possible only if some storage of energies occurs within a system. . . ,"[3] and resources allocated to investment perform just this function. Since growth is an important concern, it follows that the allocation of resources to investment is a system property worth noting. Once again our system level measure is the average percentage of resources devoted to investment for all system members, and reflects the proportion of resources the average system member devotes to achieving economic growth.

Defense. It goes without saying that we are interested in differentiating between systems in which large amounts of resources are channeled toward the production of armaments and in systems where this is *not* the case. Accordingly, the third of our system properties is measured by taking the mean of the member nations' percentage allocations.

Trade. Although not as central to our concerns as the three previous measures, trade has implications in all three of these areas, and it will be interesting to see how the simulated systems stack

180

up against various referent systems. We define this system property, operationally, as the average national ratio of exports and imports to national product expressed as a percentage of national product.

STATIC CORRESPONDENCE OF SYSTEM PROPERTIES

In the following section, we will be comparing six SIPER systems and six INS systems to various referent systems at one given point in time. Thus, our perspective is again cross-sectional. The data for the SIPER and INS systems are drawn from period seven, while the referent system measures are derived from several time spans, depending upon whether or not the referent system is contemporary or historical in nature.

Contemporary Referent Systems

This section of our evaluation is devoted to the consideration of SIPER and INS international systems in comparison to referent systems drawn from the contemporary world. These referent systems are generally of two kinds: the world system, which, in theory, encompasses all of the nations on the globe, but, in practice, is more restricted due to data limitations. We have endeavored, however, to make the sample as large as possible. The other referent systems are essentially subsystems of the world system, and, for the most part, we have specified these subsystems according to Russett's findings.[4] When possible, we will examine four systems: the western community, Eastern Europe, Latin America, and the Afro-Asian subsystem. In certain cases, we will find the need to substitute another subsystem, the Middle East, for one of these. Our choices were guided principally by the availability of reliable data.

The nations that make up these various referent systems are listed in Table 6–1 with the value for each system property based on a sample of nations as large as could be assembled from existing data sources. For the most part, the referent data for this part of the analysis are drawn from the *World Handbook or Political and Social Indicators*.[5]

181

TABLE 6–1
CONTEMPORARY REFERENT SYSTEMS

Latin America (LA)

Paraguay	Peru	Dominican Republic
Haiti	Chile	Nicaragua
Argentina	Venezuela	Ecuador
Brazil	Bolivia	Cuba
Honduras	Guatemala	El Salvador
Columbia	Uruguay	Mexico
Costa Rica	Panama	Trinidad & Tobago

Western Community (WC)

Netherlands	Belgium	Denmark
Ireland	Norway	Switzerland
Finland	Austria	Sweden
Portugal	Cyprus	Canada
West Germany	United Kingdom	Greece
Italy	France	Spain
Turkey	United States	Iceland

Afro-Asian (AA)

Taiwan	Laos	South Vietnam
Cambodia	South Korea	Burma
Indonesia	Pakistan	Libya
Morocco	China	Thailand
Cameroon	Malaya	Ethiopia
India	Afghanistan	Somalia
Tunisia	Philippines	Sudan
Ceylon	Rhodesia-	South Africa
Kenya	Nyasaland	Ghana
Nepal	Liberia	Tanganyika
	Nigeria	

Eastern Europe (EE)

East Germany	Bulgaria	Poland
Soviet Union	Hungary	

Middle East (ME)

Jordan	Iraq	Israel
Iran	Syria	Egypt
Lebanon		

World (All of the above Nations Plus)

Yugoslavia	Australia	New Zealand

Consumption Allocation. Table 6–2 indicates the average percentage of resources devoted to consumption in the simulated and referent systems. On the average, INS systems devote 91.2 percent of their economic activity to consumption, and all of the INS systems are within a narrow range of 89.3 percent to 92.7 percent. There is a good deal more variety in the percentage values in the SIPER systems; the minimum level is 80.7 percent and the maximum is 90.2 percent. On the average, SIPER systems devote 84.6 percent of their economic production to consumption. The referent data presented in Table 6–2 indicates the consumption level in the world system and each of four subsystems separately.

TABLE 6–2

AVERAGE CONSUMPTION ALLOCATION IN
SIMULATED AND CONTEMPORARY SYSTEMS

SIPER		Referent*		INS	
All Systems	84.6%	World	70.3%	All Systems	91.2%
System 1	90.2	WC	67.4	System 1	89.3
System 2	82.1	EE	63.6	System 2	92.0
System 3	86.1	LA	74.7	System 3	92.7
System 4	85.7	AA	72.5	System 4	91.2
System 5	80.7			System 5	91.2
System 6	82.5			System 6	91.0

*See Table 6–1 for composition of world system and its subsystems.

It is clear that the correspondence of INS and SIPER to the referent systems is not as good as it might be. SIPER and INS systems differ only slightly with regard to consumption levels, and both types of systems devote substantially more resources to this area than do the referent systems. The closest correspondence seems to be SIPER system 5 and the Latin American subsystem. The respective consumption levels are 80.7 percent and 74.7 percent, but even here, there is a significant gap between the simulated and referent systems. The simulated systems generally appear to be more like the less developed referent systems than the more developed referent systems, since the referent systems most comparable to both INS and SIPER simulated systems are the Latin American and Afro-Asian subsystems.

183

Investment Allocation. Table 6–3 presents the relevant data for the comparison of investment levels in the international systems. Again we are looking at the six INS systems, six SIPER systems, and the world system with four of its subsystems.

TABLE 6–3

AVERAGE INVESTMENT ALLOCATION IN
SIMULATED AND CONTEMPORARY SYSTEMS

SIPER		Referent*		INS	
All Systems	4.5%	World	18.8%	All Systems	7.1%
System 1	5.7	WC	20.5	System 1	6.4
System 2	4.6	EE	26.0	System 2	5.2
System 3	3.8	LA	17.5	System 3	4.9
System 4	4.0	AA	14.8	System 4	9.1
System 5	4.5			System 5	10.2
System 6	4.5			System 6	7.2

*See Table 6–1 for composition of world system and its subsystems.

The INS and SIPER systems are different in their investment levels. The average investment level is about 7.1 percent for the INS systems and about 4.5 percent for the SIPER systems. In the contemporary world, by contrast, investment constitutes almost 19 percent of all economic activity, and the referent subsystems are all substantially higher in this regard than any of the simulated systems. The correspondence is clearly not good here for either SIPER or INS, but we do find further evidence for the suggestion that the simulated systems are most like the Latin American and Afro-Asian subsystems.

Defense Allocation. Table 6–4 presents the information with regard to the relative levels of defense allocation for the six INS systems, six SIPER systems, and the referent world system, as well as four of its subsystems.

On the average, INS systems channel about 3.4 percent of their economic resources to the area of defense, and this compares favorably with the referent world figure of about 3.7 percent. In

TABLE 6–4

AVERAGE DEFENSE ALLOCATION IN
SIMULATED AND CONTEMPORARY SYSTEMS

SIPER		Referent*		INS	
All Systems	10.9%	World	3.7%	All Systems	3.4%
System 1	4.2	WC	3.8	System 1	6.9
System 2	13.6	ME	8.6	System 2	3.9
System 3	10.2	LA	1.9	System 3	2.8
System 4	9.2	AA	3.5	System 4	2.9
System 5	15.0			System 5	1.7
System 6	13.4			System 6	2.4

*See Table 6–1 for composition of world system and its subsystems.

general, the correspondence of the INS systems in this sphere of activity is good.

The same cannot be said, however, with regard to the SIPER systems, whose average level of system defense activity is more than twice as high as that observed in the INS or referent systems. The average percentage of resources devoted to defense for the SIPER systems is about 10.9, which compares favorably only to the Middle East subsystems. It seems evident that SIPER systems are highly militarized in general, but there are notable exceptions. System 1, with a percentage value of 4.2, is not substantially different from the referent world system. Nevertheless, it is clear that, on the whole, the correspondence of the SIPER systems to contemporary referent systems, with respect to levels of defense allocation, is not as good as one might wish.

Trade Proportion. Table 6–5 gives the relevant information concerning levels of trade in the INS, SIPER, and referent systems. It appears that the INS systems are characterized by a very low level of economic interaction among the components of the system. The average trade proportion is 4.5 percent, ranging from 1.4 percent to 11.4 percent. This does not compare at all favorably with any of the patterns found in the referent data.

The SIPER systems have, on the average, a slightly higher trade level than the INS systems. The average trade proportion for

185

TABLE 6–5

AVERAGE TRADE PROPORTION IN SIMULATED
AND CONTEMPORARY SYSTEMS

SIPER		Referent*		INS	
All Systems	7.1%	World	38.8%	All Systems	4.6%
System 1	6.9	WC	38.5	System 1	3.2
System 2	7.6	ME	46.1	System 2	1.4
System 3	7.1	LA	37.3	System 3	1.4
System 4	6.5	AA	37.8	System 4	11.4
System 5	7.3			System 5	6.6
System 6	7.7			System 6	3.4

*See Table 6–1 for composition of world system and its subsystems.

the SIPER systems is 7.1 percent and there is very little variation between the specific systems. However, these values are somewhat misleading, since we have averaged out the effects of the alternative trade policies. One of the free trade systems, for example, achieved a trade level of 13 percent. Nevertheless, we are led to conclude that both kinds of simulated systems are considerably less active in the trade sector than the referent systems. As can be seen in Table 6–5, the trade levels found in the referent systems are significantly higher than any of those found in the simulated systems.

At this point, the following would appear to be true: both SIPER and INS systems exhibit higher levels of consumption and lower levels of investment and trade than contemporary referent systems. However, in the area of defense, SIPER systems, on the whole, allocate more resources to armaments than contemporary referent systems, while INS systems are not noticeably different from the referent systems in this area.

This set of observations suggests that the simulated systems are different from the contemporary world in some fundamental respects. Let us turn our attention to the consideration of some past international systems.

Historical Referent Systems

The strategy used here will be to select a subsystem of the

international system and trace its development over time with respect to the four basic variables. The sample includes nations from Europe and North America: the United Kingdom, Germany, Italy, Norway, Sweden, the United States, Canada, Denmark and France, and it may be considered representative of the subsystem that we consider historically the West.

Consumption Allocation. The information concerning levels of consumption in the simulated and referent subsystem is given in Table 6–6. In this table, we list the average consumption percentages for the INS and SIPER systems and the comparable values for the referent subsystem at different periods of time over the last century. There is a strong downward trend in the level of consumption in the referent system over the century. This stems from the widely noted negative relationship between the level of consumption and the level of economic development. Thus, it would appear that the SIPER system consumption level compares favorably with that of the referent subsystem in the middle of the

TABLE 6–6

AVERAGE CONSUMPTION ALLOCATION IN
SIMULATED AND HISTORICAL SYSTEMS

SIPER		Referent*		INS	
All Systems	84.6%	1860–79	83.4%	All Systems	91.2%
System 1	90.2	1880–99	80.5	System 1	89.3
System 2	82.1	1900–19	76.7	System 2	92.0
System 3	86.1	1920–39	77.4	System 3	92.7
System 4	85.7	1940–59	64.1	System 4	91.2
System 5	80.7	1960–69	60.0	System 5	91.2
System 6	82.5			System 6	91.0

*The referent data are taken from Simon Kuznets, *Modern Economic Growth* (New Haven: Yale University Press, 1966), pp. 236–239.

nineteenth century. At that time, the referent subsystem was devoting approximately 83 percent of its economic resources to consumption. The over-all SIPER consumption level, 84.6 percent, is close to the referent level, and this may add credibility to the hypothesis that the SIPER systems are pre-modern in nature.

187

The INS systems represent a level of consumption that exceeds the earliest period of referent data by about 10 percent, and this may suggest that they represent systems older and less developed than the SIPER systems or the referent subsystem. However, it appears in general that the simulated systems, judged on the basis of their consumption levels, are early or mid-nineteenth century western in nature.

Investment Allocation. Further evidence for the hypothesis that the simulated systems represent essentially pre-modern systems can be found in Table 6–7. Here we have the relevant information concerning the investment levels in the INS, SIPER and referent systems. There appears to be a trend in the referent subsystem for

TABLE 6–7

AVERAGE INVESTMENT ALLOCATION IN
SIMULATED AND HISTORICAL SYSTEMS

SIPER		Referent*		INS	
All Systems	4.5%			All Systems	7.1%
System 1	5.7	1860–79	13.0%	System 1	6.4
System 2	4.6	1880–99	13.7	System 2	5.2
System 3	3.8	1900–19	16.0	System 3	4.9
System 4	4.0	1920–39	15.3	System 4	9.1
System 5	4.5	1940–59	21.9	System 5	10.2
System 6	4.5	1960–69	22.4	System 6	7.2

*The referent data are taken from Simon Kuznets, *Modern Economic Growth*, pp. 236–239.

the investment percentage to increase as one approaches the present and this is also associated with economic growth. The investment level in the referent subsystem between 1860 and 1879 is approximately 13 percent. Our data do not permit us to estimate the level of investment in the referent subsystem prior to 1860, but it seems likely that the level would approach the SIPER and INS levels.[6] Again, the pre-modern system hypothesis is supported.

Defense Allocation. Table 6–8 presents the comparative levels of defense allocation for the systems under consideration. As one

188

TABLE 6–8

AVERAGE DEFENSE ALLOCATION IN
SIMULATED AND HISTORICAL SYSTEMS

SIPER		Referent*		INS	
All Systems	10.9%			All Systems	3.4%
System 1	4.2	1860–79	1.6%	System 1	6.9
System 2	13.6	1880–99	1.2	System 2	3.9
System 3	10.2	1900–19	2.2	System 3	2.8
System 4	9.2	1920–39	3.4	System 4	2.9
System 5	15.0	1940–59	9.9	System 5	1.7
System 6	13.4	1960–69	6.5	System 6	2.4

*The years 1870, 1890, 1910, 1929, 1948, and 1969 were selected as representative of the twenty year periods. The 1870 through 1929 data are from Quincy Wright, *A Study of War* (Chicago: University of Chicago Press, 2d ed., 1965), pp. 666–672, and the 1948 and 1969 data are from Stockholm International Peace Research Institute, *Yearbook of World Armaments and Disarmament, 1968/69* (New York: Humanities Press, 1970), pp. 194–214.

might expect, there is not such a clear trend in the referent data as with the other variables. The INS systems compare favorably in their level of defense activity with the 1920 to 1939 inter-war period in the referent subsystem. SIPER systems, however, compare more favorably with the World War II and Cold War period of 1940 to 1959. Neither the INS nor the SIPER systems exhibit the kind of defense levels that our data suggest characterized the nineteenth-century referent subsystem. Rather than Pax Britannia we appear to have systems preparing for, or engaging in, major conflict. If we may be permitted to speculate, it could be that the simulated systems are not unlike Napoleonic Europe. From what we know, it might be inferred that system defense allocation levels were considerably higher in the Napoleonic period than in the rest of the nineteenth century.

Trade Proportion. The final characteristic to be examined historically is the level of trade in the systems. Table 6–9 presents the data concerning the level of this kind of activity for the simulated and referent systems, and, with our previous indicators, we find a substantial change taking place over time in the referent subsystem. In the earliest period for which we have data, the trade proportion is about one third of current levels, and while still

TABLE 6–9

AVERAGE TRADE PROPORTION IN
SIMULATED AND HISTORICAL SYSTEMS

SIPER		Referent*		INS	
All Systems	7.1%			All Systems	4.6%
System 1	6.9	1860–79	14.0%	System 1	3.2
System 2	7.6	1880–99	33.3	System 2	1.4
System 3	7.1	1900–19	44.8	System 3	1.4
System 4	6.5	1920–39	40.4	System 4	11.4
System 5	7.3	1940–59	28.8	System 5	6.6
System 6	7.7	1960–69	39.7	System 6	3.4

*The nineteenth-century data were drawn from Kuznets, *Modern Economic Growth,* pp. 310–316. The years 1913, 1928, 1957, and 1966 were chosen to represent the twenty year periods after 1900, and these data are from Karl W. Deutsch and Alexander Eckstein, ''National Industrialization and the Declining Share of the International Economic Sector, 1890–1959,'' *World Politics,* 13, No. 2 (January, 1961): p. 275 and United Nations Statistical Office, *Statistical Yearbook, 1967* (New York: United Nations Publications, 1967).

higher than the levels found in the simulated systems, the comparisons are much more favorable. Low levels of trade are characteristic of pre-industrial international systems,[7] and this finding is consistent with our previous ones concerning the pre-modern nature of the simulated systems.

On the basis of the evidence gathered concerning four basic system properties, it appears that the simulated systems, both INS and SIPER, resemble in certain fundamental respects early nineteenth-century Europe and North America. Because our data extend back only one hundred years, this conclusion rests on the projection of trends backward through time. Nevertheless, the evidence suggests that a re-examination of the model is in order. Since the problem is common to both SIPER and INS, this may suggest that it is due to the elements they share.

190

We have, to this point, emphasized the continuity of international systems by limiting our analysis to an examination of single slices of time. In the next section we will turn to the consideration of the rate and direction of change in these system properties.

DYNAMIC CORRESPONDENCE OF SYSTEM PROPERTIES

Dynamic correspondence may be said to exist between two systems to the degree that they are changing in similar ways. For our purposes, there are two aspects of this transformation process that are particularly salient: (1) the direction of systematic change (e.g., are the systems becoming more or less militarized?); and (2) the rate of systemic change (e.g., how rapidly are the systems becoming more or less militarized?). In order to make a preliminary judgment, we will again use the four system properties introduced in the previous sections. In this case, however, we will be examining the average rates of change, expressed as a percentage increase or decrease, in each of the measures over a specified interval of time.

In addition, we will confine our attention to the SIPER and referent systems. Due to the irregularity of behavior, INS systems do not lend themselves to the kind of analysis being undertaken here. Rates and direction of change are very erratic and, consequently, no clear conclusions may be drawn from the INS data with regard to the transformation of systems.[8] If the central focus of this research were the validity of the INS systems, we would pursue this point further, but since that is not the case, we will simply omit the consideration of the INS systems from this part of the analysis. Suffice it to say that this behavior pattern casts doubt upon the INS's dynamic validity.

Once again we will be examining the six basic SIPER systems in comparison to a set of states drawn from western community subsystems. Once again, we were limited by the availability of reliable data to the nations listed below. In the short-term comparisons, the measurements of system properties are based on all of the following nations.

191

Austria	Greece	Portugal
Belgium	Iceland	Spain
Canada	Ireland	Sweden*
Denmark*	Italy*	Switzerland
Finland	Luxembourg	Turkey
France*	Netherlands	United Kingdom*
West Germany*	Norway*	United States*

The values used in the long-term comparisons were derived from the more limited subset of nations whose names are followed by an asterisk.

Short-Term Comparisons: Contemporary Systems

In this section, an effort will be made to assess the dynamic correspondence of the simulated systems to the subsystems of nations listed above.[9] We will assume that one period of simulated time is approximately equal to one year of real time. Since the referent world data are drawn from the years 1957 to 1966, the system values reflect the average annual rate of change over a ten year period.

Table 6–10 gives the rates of change (expressed in percents) in all four of the system properties for the six SIPER systems and the referent system. Looking first at the trends in consumption, we find that the simulated systems vary considerably in their rates of change, but all are in agreement with the referent system that consumption is receiving a declining share of economic resources. The over-all decline in the simulated systems is somewhat more rapid than in the referent system, however. System 1 very nearly matches the referent trend, while System 5's rate of decrease is considerably larger than that found in the referent world. Over-all, then, consumption seems to be declining somewhatfaster in the simulated worlds than in the referent world.

Shifting our attention to trends in the allocation of resources to investment, we again find a good deal of variability in the rates of change in the simulated systems and unanimity with regard to the direction of change. The simulated systems vary from a low of 1.5 percent decrease per period to a high of 9.1 percent decrease per

192

TABLE 6–10

TRENDS IN ALLOCATION IN SIMULATED

AND CONTEMPORARY SYSTEMS

SYSTEM	INVESTMENT CONSUMPTION		DEFENSE	TRADE
Referent	−0.1%	+1.0%	−1.9%	+1.9%
Simulated				
All Systems	−1.7	−5.9	+17.5	+0.9
System 1	−0.4	−1.5	+12.7	−2.8
System 2	−1.6	−7.1	+16.9	−1.6
System 3	−1.4	−5.1	+14.2	+3.0
System 4	−1.2	−4.0	+13.9	+7.6
System 5	−3.7	−8.4	+25.5	−2.2
System 6	−2.1	−9.1	+21.8	+1.4

period, with an overall average decline of 5.9 percent. This compares rather unfavorably with the 1.0 percent per year increase in the investment proportion of the referent system. Once again, System 1 compares most favorably with the referent system, while System 5, although not the most deviant of the systems, is nevertheless very different from this referent world.

Turning to the trends in defense allocation, we find all the simulated systems devoting an increasing share of their resources to defense, and these rates of increase in some systems are of alarming proportions. System 1 is lowest, with a rate of increase of 12.7 percent per period, while System 5 is highest, with a rate of 25.5 percent per period. In contrast to this, we find that the proportion of resources being allocated to defense by the WC was declining at a rate of 1.9 percent per year. The conclusion seems to be that the simulated systems are caught in intense arms races, while the referent world is not involved at this time.

Both the simulated and referent worlds reveal an over-all increase in the ratio of trade to total product, although the trend is slight in both cases. As we can see, however, breaking down the over-all simulated value by system reveals that in three of the systems, trade expressed as a proportion of product is on the increase while it is decreasing in the remaining three systems.

193

The most prominent finding in this set of comparisons is a very high rate of increase in the proportion of resources devoted to defense; and this is characteristic of virtually all the simulated systems. As we suggested earlier, the indication is, then, that our simulated systems are generally experiencing intense arms races. This would explain why consumption is decreasing faster than it is in the contemporary systems, and why investment is also decreasing, while it is rising in the contemporary world. The need for additional armaments draws resources away from both of these sectors, with investment apparently bearing most of the burden.

While it is clear that the nations that make up our simulated systems are accumulating arms at a rapid rate, relative to the late 1950's and early 1960's, these rates are not atypical of what other nations have exhibited at other times. The United States, for example, in the years 1938–1943, raised its proportion of resources going to defense by an average annual rate of 171.8 percent. Thus, although the simulated nations are arming at a relatively fast pace, it is far from the limit of mobilization speed a nation can attain.

The previous conclusions were based on the assumption that one period of simulated time is approximately the equivalent of one year of real time. In the next section we will assume a different time scale. This was brought about because most of the rates of change in the simulated systems are faster than in the referent systems, and, in turn, may cast doubt upon the assumption that one simulation period equals one year of real time. A second reason for changing the time scale is that, although the model fails to reproduce some important aspects of contemporary short term trends, it could, nonetheless accurately replicate more long-term trends.

Long-Term Comparisons: Historical Systems

Resetting the time scale so that one simulation period equals one decade of real time enables us to assess the model's ability to replicate long-term trends in the allocation of resources. However, the relative scarcity of reliable data for our four variables for the 100 year period 1860 to 1960 means that we will need to restrict our analysis of the referent world to a small number of nations and a half dozen time points.

The referent rates of change are derived from data that includes the following nations: Denmark, France, Italy, Norway, Sweden, United Kingdom, and the United States, with observations about every twenty years. Thus, the simulated systems will be compared to a referent system composed of nations at the top of the development spectrum throughout the century. Given our previous conclusion that the simulated nations resemble (in some respects) less developed, rather than more developed, nations, the comparison may not be wholly appropriate. However, since we are dealing with rates of change in behavior, rather than levels of behavior, it may nevertheless prove informative.

Table 6–11 presents the over-all rates of change in the four variables of both the referent and simulated worlds. The referent values are expressed as percent change per decade, while the simulated values are percent change per period of simulation time. A comparison of the referent values in this table to those in Table 6–10 reveals, with one exception, substantial agreement between the short-term and long-term trends. The exception is, that during

TABLE 6–11

TRENDS IN RESOURCE ALLOCATION IN SIMULATED
AND HISTORICAL SYSTEMS

SYSTEM	INVESTMENT		DEFENSE	TRADE
	CONSUMPTION			
Referent*	−2.6%	+6.0%	+22.9%	+4.2%
Simulated				
All Systems	−1.7	−5.9	+17.5	+0.9
System 1	−0.4	−1.5	+12.7	−2.8
System 2	−1.6	−7.1	+16.9	−1.6
System 3	−1.4	−5.1	+14.2	+3.0
System 4	−1.2	−4.0	+13.9	+7.6
System 5	−3.7	−8.4	+25.5	−2.2
System 6	−2.1	−9.1	+21.8	+1.4

*The rates of change for the referent world were estimated from the data contained in Tables 6–6 through 6–9, and adjusted to reflect the average percent change per decade.

195

the late 1950's and early 1960's, defense was declining slightly, while the century trend is in the opposite direction.

Comparing the rates of change in the simulated and referent worlds, we find the fit on consumption, defense, and trade to be reasonably good, although the referent rates are now consistently faster than the simulated rates. Since the *annual* rates of change in the referent world were found to be too *low* and the *decade* rates of change are too *high,* this may suggest that a time scale of one-half decade of real time to one period of simulated time might yield comparable rates of change in these three areas.

No such remedy will suffice in the area of investment, however. The trend in investment is clearly upward in the century spanned by the referent data, while it is clearly downward in the simulated data. Apparently, in the referent world, decreases in consumption have been sufficient to allow increases in both investment and defense, but in the simulated systems, the over-all decrease in consumption does not free enough resources for increases in defense, therefore investment also declines.

As we look back over the structure of the model in light of these results, it would appear that the assumed constancy of the generation rates is a troublesome assumption. Given that these values represent collectively the level of economic development, perhaps it is not unreasonable to assert that in the real world these may be relatively constant over a ten year period, but it is clearly false when we examine industrialized nations over a century. In these nations, the decline in the proportion of resources devoted to consumption has been more than offset by increases in productivity. This, in turn, has allowed them to avoid the political consequences of a declining standard of living (such as revolution and political instability) while at the same time releasing resources for use in capital formation and armaments acquisition.

CONCLUSION

The over-all results reported in this chapter seem to support the following conclusion: on the *average,* the simulated systems are characterized by a low level of economic development and growth, coupled with a high level of conflict and arms competition. The nations that make up these systems are reducing the standard of living of their populations and using up capital equipment faster than it can be replaced, in order to finance increased arms expenditures. Many nations in the past have followed a similar strategy in times of stress, particularly when they faced a very real threat of war, and the same seems to be true of our simulated nations.

CHAPTER SIX NOTES

1. Paul F. Lazarsfeld, "Evidence and Inference in Social Research," in May Broadbeck, ed., *Readings in the Philosophy of the Social Sciences,* (New York: Mcmillan, 1968), pp. 608–634.

2. Robert L. Heilbroner, *Understanding Macro-Economics* (Englewood Cliffs, N.J.: Prentice-Hall, 1966), p. 13.

3. F. Kenneth Berrien, *General and Social Systems* (New Brunswick, N.J.: Rutgers University Press, 1968), p. 80.

4. Bruce M. Russett, *International Regions and the International System* (Chicago: Rand-McNally, 1967).

5. Table 43, "Private Consumption as a Percentage of G.N.P.," Table 47, "Gross Domestic Capital Formation as a Percentage of G.N.P., Table 23, "Expenditure on Defense as a Percentage of G.N.P.," and Table 46 "Foreign Trade (Exports and Imports) as a Percentage of G.N.P." in Bruce M. Russett, et al., *World Handbook of Political and Social Indicators* (New Haven: Yale University Press, 1964), were the source of data for the consumption, investment and defense and trade variables.

6. See Simon Kuznets, "Quantitative Aspects of the Economic Growth of Nations: VI. Long-Term Trends in Capital Formation Proportions," *Economic Development and Cultural Change,* 9, No. 4 (July 1961, Part II): 1–124 for an extended discussion of investment in pre-modern and modern societies.

7. Simon Kuznets, "Quantitative Aspects of the Economic Growth of Nations: X. Level and Structure of Foreign Trade: Long-Term Trends," *Economic Development and Cultural Change,* 13, No. 1 (July, 1965, Part II): 1–106.

8. Regressing various INS Behavior variables on time yielded very large standard errors for the regression coefficients. The standard deviation of the rates of change were also very large, indicating the absence of any simple linear trends.

9. The referent rates of change were estimated from annual observations (1957 to 1966) of consumption, investment, trade and gross national product. The data were taken from the 1958 to 1967 editions of United Nations Statistical Office, *Statistical Yearbook* (New York: United Nations Publications). The table, "Expenditure vs. Gross National Product" was the source in each volume. The defense expenditure data for the same years came from Stockholm International Peace Research Institute, *Yearbook of World Armaments and Disarmament, 1968–69* (New York: Humanities press, 1970), pp. 194–214.

SEVEN

Conclusion

IN this concluding chapter, I want to do four things: summarize the contents of the book, offer an over-all evaluation of the model, indicate directions for its future development, and suggest why I think this work is a significant contribution to the field of world politics.

SUMMARY OF CONTENTS

Following the introductory chapter, we outlined a set of plausible decision-making rules which we postulated are used by national decision-making units. The resulting decisions deal with such matters as the setting of national goals, the allocation of resources, the exchange of goods with other nations, the requesting and granting of foreign aid, and the generation of internation conflict. In addition, we specified a set of environmental processes that determine the consequences of decisions and redefine the decision-making environment for the next round of decision-making. Among these consequences are increases or decreases in economic and military power, as well as changes in political stability. Together these two kinds of processes form a closed theoretical system, in which the national actors attempt to cope with an environment that is constantly changing, chiefly as a consequence of their prior actions.

In Chapter Three, we specified the parameter values and variable initializations used for this first set of twenty-four runs. At that time, we suggested that the variation in parameters, representing policy differences, and the variation in initial system configurations, representing different historical paths, would enable us to make a preliminary assessment of the sensitivity and validity of the model.

The next chapter addressed itself to the sensitivity of the model

199

and we found that, with respect to some basic performance indicators, the initial system configurations or history of the simulated world is a much more important determinant of the model's behavior than the parameter variations. These findings are in accord with Herbert Simon's observation that complex behavior stems from a complex environment, not a complex entity. In this particular case, we observed a corollary of this general theorem: variation in behavior is due more to variation in the *environment* than to variation in the *entity*. The general implications for the study of world politics are that (1) apparent differences in national behavior are not necessarily evidence of different national objectives or decisional calculi, and (2) we are not likely to discover empirically the similarity of nations, with respect to these latter factors, until we have controlled or partialled out differences in their environments.

In Chapter Five, we examined the results of the first two validation studies. Restricting ourselves to a single time slice and focusing on a broad range of behavior, we were able to see how the nations, generated by the SIPER and INS simulation models, compare to a sample of contemporary referent nations. We discovered that both models have strengths and weaknesss, and that there is a tendency for them to have the *same weaknesses,* but *different strengths*.

Shifting our focus to the level of international systems and employing both static and dynamic analytical modes, we were able to shed some light on the synchronic and diachronic correspondence of the simulation model to contemporary and historical referent world systems. We discovered that in some basic respects the simulated systems are more like systems composed of states in the early stages of industrialization than to fully developed states. We noted also that there is a strong tendency for the simulated systems to become overburdened with arms, with serious economic and political consequences.

OVER-ALL EVALUATION OF THE MODEL

Among the strengths of computer simulation models, there is

one characteristic of the model *qua* model not explicitly mentioned before . . . simply that it works. For those not familiar with complex, feedback-directed models that are fully self-contained and self-productive, it may seem an unremarkable accomplishment. While it is true that a working model is not necessarily a worthy model, it is also true that working models of this type are not so easy to construct.

Consider the pitfalls: if a model is of the sort that provides its own input for the next round of processing, without the aid of exogenous inputs to put it back on the track, very small errors can result in very large errors as time goes by. If any denominator takes on the value of zero, the program stops executing. If a variable, assumed to be positive at all times, manages to acquire a negative value somewhere along the way, whole groups of processes contained in the model may begin to work in the reverse of the intended direction. Where there are many feedback loops, one must guard against the possibility of escalatory or de-escalatory spirals that quickly lead the model to collapse. These are just a few of the many things that the designer of a simulation model must be aware of and guard against.

Shifting the evaluation from the model *qua* model to model *qua* theory, the validation studies suggest that we have been successful in replicating some patterns of behavior found in the referent world. The studies also revealed some weaknesses, which we will discuss in more detail shortly. On balance, the macro-theory contained in the model has been given a rather demanding series of tests. We have asked it to predict the direction and magnitude of a wide range of relationships not explicitly included in the basic structure of the model. We have also asked it to predict specific levels and rates of change of a few critical variables. Under the circumstances, the model has done well, and can serve as a point of departure for future work, some of which will be discussed in the next section.

Almost inevitably, however, attention shifts away from those phenomena that a theory *can* account for, to those it *cannot* account for. In the long run, this would seem to be beneficial to theory construction, since it may lead to revisions and refinements of a theory, which ultimately expand the theory's ability to account for diverse pheomena. The practice of giving special attention to errors is an integral part of both the *inductive* and *deductive* research strategies. In the *inductive* approach, residual values are often examined to determine whether the form of a relationship needs to be changed or a new variable added to the equation. An analogous procedure is followed in the *deductive* approach, wherein hypothesized values and relationships deduced from a set of assumptions fail to materialize in the empirical world. An effort is then made to infer from the systematic nature of these discrepancies the incorrectness or insufficiency of the assumptions.

For this reason, the remainder of this section will be devoted to an examination of the model's major weaknesses. This may lead the reader to assume a more negative attitude toward the model than it deserves.

In the previous pages, we have discovered a few key problems in the behavior of the model, and it is apparent that these must be dealt with before undertaking major extensions of the model. These problems, in order of increasing complexity and severity, are: low levels of international trade, low levels of growth, and high levels of armaments.

Trade Autarky

The generally low level of trade in the simulated systems prevents the simulated nations from deriving full benefit from the obvious advantages of exchanging relatively cheap goods for relatively expensive goods. In the referent world, this generally results from the erection of high tariff barriers by all nations (as in the 1930's after the United States enacted the very restrictive Hawley-Smoot tariff act). This kind of economic nationalism is not altogether incompatible with high levels of conflict and armaments.

In the simulation model, we can lower these tariff barriers substantially by simply raising the parameter that governs the setting of import limits. Increasing the volume of trade may, in turn, alleviate some of the resource scarcity problems. We know also that the pricing of exports affects the volume of trade, for trade was substantially higher in those systems where a free trade policy was in force. The depressive effect of the introduction of non-economic factors into the pricing of exports is probably made more acute by the small size of the international systems. That is, systems of ten or twenty nations offer much greater opportunities for trade, even if a constrained trade policy is in force. Of course, only future experimentation with the model will reveal whether this problem is as tractable as thought.

Economic Stagnation

Although the growth patterns of the simulated nations vary widely, the over-all tendency is for little or no growth to occur, and in some cases a substantial decline in resources is evident. Some who are ecologically minded may find this no-growth state of affairs a normatively pleasing one, but from the standpoint of replicating the contemporary world, it represents a failure on the model's part. The conclusion this work suggests is, that as long as an arms race (and the tensions that produce it) are present, no-growth may lead to a substantial decline in the standard of living resulting in much political instability. The real danger may lie in the premise that national security can become such a pre-eminent concern of national decision-makers that they display more willingness to sacrifice future growth and the standard of living than does the population of the nation. As long as some growth occurs, that conflict remains latent, but when growth stops or slows substantially, the conflicting desires of the decision-makers and the population may emerge with consequences resembling those predicted by the simulation model.

It is possible, therefore, that the problem confronting the simulated nations is precisely the problem that many feel the globe is facing today and if so, its predictions are disturbing. In order to maintain national security, increasing amounts of resources are devoted to defense, leading ultimately to disinvestment and a lowering of the standard of living. Disinvestment leads to a loss of productive capital, while the lowering of the standard of living leads to political instability and revolution. Both of these factors combine to lower the absolute level of productive resources, which means that an increase in the proportion of resources devoted to defense is necessary to merely maintain current armaments levels. The vicious circle is complete, and the results are disastrous.

There are several ways this situation may be ameliorated, one being to restructure the way in which growth takes place in the model, so that changes in economic productivity can occur, and historically this is the solution adopted by modern nations. One way for this to be represented in the model entails a slight reconceptualization of some of the variables and a few alterations in some basic relationships.

The first thing we must provide for is a means by which the generation rates can change. The most logical and empirically sound assumption is that allocation to investment in excess of depreciation leads to higher generation rates. Fortunately, there has been a substantial amount of research on this relationship upon which we can draw. In this reconceptualization, TBC can become the pool of human resources, and it will rise as the standard of living (consumption) rises. This, in turn, enables us to integrate some of the relationships between birth rates and death rates, and the standard of living. By themselves, these relatively minor changes may or may not eliminate the problem of economic stagnation, but they will certainly allow us to make more direct comparisons between simulated and referent nations and enable us to draw upon a fairly substantial body of empirically supported knowledge.

The other two solutions to the problem involve a reformulation of those processes related to national security, or an alternation of the initial system configuration in order to determine if an initially low level of arms and conflict will prevent the development of an arms race and encourage economic growth.

Military Escalation

We have found a consistent tendency for the simulation model to produce arms races, although we also found that certain system configurations are more likely to lead to high armaments levels than others. In addition, we were able to determine that when nations base their behavior on how they expect other nations to behave, the tendency to escalate arms is given additional impetus. While these factors all contributed to the rate of the arms race, the over-all trend of increasing arms remained unaffected.

At this juncture, three possibilities seem worth considering. First, it may be that we have successfully captured the essence of the decisional calculus decision-makers use in making their assessments of national security needs, and our results merely reflect the true state of the contemporary world. What may be missing are some additional constraints that tend to slow the accumulation of arms in non-war periods, or some mechanisms (such as war itself) that tend to bring arms races to an end, at least temporarily, after the war is over. In either case, we would direct our attention to processes other than those concerned directly with national security.

A second possibility is that some fine tuning is required. That is, the decision processes are essentially correct, but some of the parameter values are in error. For example, the parameters specifying the priority that each of three categories of resource allocation has (in the event that resources are not sufficient and cuts must be made) may be instrumental. Perhaps a simple adjustment of these parameters, giving investment a somewhat higher priority than defense, will slow the pace of the arms race.

A third possibility is that the processes in this part of the model are wrong in a fundamental respect. For example, some contend that the acquisition of armaments by the United States has little to do with what other nations are doing, and is largely attributable either to the needs of the miliary-industrial complex generally, or to the defense bureaucracy specifically. If these arguments turn out to be true, then a substantial alteration in the national security processes will be in order.

These avenues of exploration are, of course, not mutually exclusive, and we have already begun to explore some of them. This brings us to the question of the future development of the model.

FUTURE DEVELOPMENTS

In addition to the alterations and reformulations outlined above, several major extensions of the model are in order. First, it is necessary to lift the tight bipolarity assumption, so that the model is capable of representing systems of nations more like those with which we are familiar. One way of doing this is simply to assume that a non-allied nation operates like our bloc member nations, but without urging from a bloc leader, as to a suggested level of armaments. Under these conditions, the non-allied nation would survey its environment for potential threat and attempt to adjust its armaments accordingly. This is by no means the only plausible process for non-allied nations to use in their attempt to maintain national security, but it does have an element of face validity.

Since it is clear that geographical considerations have had (and continue to have) an impact upon the way in which nations interact, our attempts to replicate real world patterns will be handicapped until we explicitly introduce spatial considerations. Some initial steps have already been taken in this direction, and the results look promising. Recently, Michael Mihalka and I have developed a computer simulation model that includes as a central element a "map" of the world, along with processes that stipulate how and when borders are to be changed and territorial annexation is to occur.[1] In this newer model, still under development, decision-making units "see" their positions in relation to potential allies and enemies, and act accordingly. Although the "region" we are currently working with is entirely abstract, it is now a rather small step to move towards representation of *real* geographical regions and *real* nations. Ultimately, it is envisioned that the model reported in this book, and the one under development, will be combined.

This new model complements in several other respects the one we have been discussing in the previous pages. Whereas the SIPER model gives a heavy emphasis to the internal dynamics of nations, the new model, tentatively called MACHI,[2] is concerned solely with the external relations of political entities. Among other features, this model includes processes that determine under what conditions nations will ally with other nations. Although these alliance processes are still quite rudimentary, there are resources that have not been fully exploited, the first being Leavitt's computer simulation model of alliance formation, based on a comprehensive survey of the alliance literature.[3] The second is the continuing empirical investigation of alliances in the last century and a half that is being carried on by the Correlates of War Project. Since I am closely associated with the project, I foresee that current and future studies of alliances should provide an important empirical base for the processes governing the formation and dissolution of alliances.

Another major area that may be incorporated into the model in the future, is a more differentiated conflict sector. The MACHI model includes war as an instrument of national policy, and research on levels of conflict short of war is now being carried out by the Correlates of War Project. It is hoped that, in the immediate future, findings emerging from that research will be integrated into the model.

The last major extension of the model scheduled for the not-too-distant future involves the modeling of specific nations for a specified period of time. Two periods seem to be particularly promising at this point: the major power systems of 1870 to 1914 and 1950 to 1974. What is required (and only now becoming available) is a substantial data base, and fortunately a large proportion of the necessary data will soon be available through the Correlates of War Project.

All of these developments will not be realized in a few years, and perhaps not in a decade, for the problems are complex and the procedures new, but a beginning has been made.

OVER-ALL CONTRIBUTION

It is not enough to simply say what I hope the model will *become,* and drop the matter at that. It is also necessary to indicate what the utility of the model *is,* as it presently stands. As I see it, there are several potential uses of the model, aside from its potential for further theoretical development.

The SIPER model can be used, in the same way the INS model was used, as a quasi-laboratory setting wherein one aspect of a complex process can be singled out for analysis. The model can provide a dynamic experimental context for determining the im-

207

pact of alternate decision-making processes, including both short-run and long-run consequences. For example, the present conflict generation process is oriented entirely toward factors such as hostility, military force, and alliances, which are directly concerned with national security. There is a long-standing argument, however, that nations experiencing internal instability and conflict will attempt to alleviate this situation by raising international tensions. Behind this loose set of postulates is a set of decision-rules that specify broadly when, and under what conditions, a nation will be more or less belligerent. If these rules are well-specified and programmed, they can easily be substituted for those presently in the model, and the implications of such an alteration can be determined.

The national security processes are also susceptible to reformulation along this kind of external-versus-internal determinant differentiation. The present processes assume that nations are intensely aware of the ''security dilemma'' in which an anarchical international system places them, and they attempt to guarantee their continued survival by the traditional means of arms and alliances. Those who think that internal considerations are the main determinants of national security policy (either, for example, through the influence of powerful special interest groups or self-serving bureaucracies) would postulate a very different set of decision-rules than those presently contained in the model. Substitution could lead to a more comprehensive evaluation of the short-run and long-run consequences of each.

By altering the factors describing the initial state of a simulated international system, such as the distribution of power and the alliance configuration, it is possible to gain insights into the over-all impact of environmental factors upon the behavior of nations. Our results, to date, suggest that these effects are very powerful indeed, but a much more systematic evaluation would be useful.

The model can serve as a means of integrating new knowledge into a coherent and consistent framework, making it possible to give a preliminary assessment of the larger and long-term implications of a new discovery. It also points out areas in our knowledge base that are not well explored, but are nevertheless important. Further, as it now stands, the model can serve as a point of departure for new models, for as I found it easier to develop the SIPER model with the INS model in hand, so others may find this model a convenient starting point for their own modeling efforts.

The over-all contribution of this work to the field of world politics is, then, primarily theoretical and methodological, rather than empirical. A few "islands of theory," to use Guetzkow's phrase, have been brought together in one dynamic context. This work demonstrates how complex theories of international relations are constructed and evaluated, and, by incremental revisions and extensions, these theories and models provide the basis for movement toward a satisfactory general theory of world politics.

In addition to offering a specific process formulation or methodological innovation that scholars may find useful or interesting, this book represents an initial attempt to synthesize the traditional and scientific approaches to world politics. A few years ago, Haas issued a plea for bridge building in the field of international relations.[4] Perhaps, in this work, I have been able to erect the first pier for such a much-needed span.

CONCLUSION

CHAPTER SEVEN NOTES

1. A complete description of this model, along with some experimental results, is being prepared for presentation at the 1976 meetings of the International Political Science Association. The paper is titled, "Machiavelli in Machina: A Computer Simulation of Multi-State System Dynamics."

2. The model was informally given the name "Chicken Coop" due to the six-sided figures used to portray a specific indivisible piece of territory. The resulting map pattern, with which war gamers will be familiar, has the appearance of chicken wire, and an observant passerby, upon seeing the map, inquired whimsically whether it was a computer designed chicken coop. As the model developed, it became clear that our colleagues might misperceive the seriousness of our pursuit, so a more suitable name was adopted, MACHI refers to one of the guiding spirits in the design of the model, Niccolo Machiavelli, although it might be concluded that the designers are subtly and immodestly suggesting that they have progressed from subsonic to supersonic performance.

3. Michael R. Leavitt, "A Computer Simulation of International Alliance Behavior," (Ph.D. dissertation, Department of Political Science, Northwestern University, 1971).

4. Michael Haas, "A Plan for Bridge Building in International Relations," in K. Knorr and J. N. Rosenau, eds., *Contending Approaches to International Politics* (Princeton, N.J.: Princeton University Press, 1969), pp. 158–176.

System Configuration Values

THE following six tables contain the input values that were used to generate the six basic international systems. These values were taken from the first decision-making period in six of the WIN-SAFE II runs of the INS model. Each table corresponds to one system and is broken down into three parts. The first part indicates the initial allocation of resources to consumption, investment, and defense and the percent of TFC devoted to internal security. The second part displays the initial pattern of conflict behavior, and the third part lists the characteristics of each of the simulated nations at the beginning of the next period when the computerized decision processes take over. The seventh table in this appendix reports the alliance changes which were exogenously introduced.

TABLE A–1
SYSTEM 1

DECISIONS

Nation

Resource Allocations (%)	1	2	3	4	5
Consumption	94.9	95.9	93.0	88.2	89.2
Investment	5.0	2.9	5.9	10.3	8.
Defense	0.1	1.2	1.1	1.5	2.
Internal Security (%)	20.0	20.0	15.0	4.4	10.

CONFLICT

Sending Nation

Receiving Nation	1	2	3	4	5
1	0	0	0	0	0
2	0	0	0	0	0
3	0	0	0	0	0
4	0	1	0	0	1
5	0	0	0	0	0

CONSEQUENCES

Nation

	1	2	3	4	5
Total Basic Capability	7725	13128	9350	33270	35168
Total Force Capability	105	790	810	2865	4057
Validator Satisfaction	5.5	3.0	3.5	4.0	6.0
Prob. of Office-Holding	0.8	0.6	0.5	0.7	0.9
Decision Latitude	6.0	5.0	3.0	5.0	7.0
Prob. of Revolution	0.0	0.4	0.4	0.6	0.0

TABLE A–2
SYSTEM 2

DECISIONS

Nation

Resource Allocations (%)

	1	2	3	4	5
Consumption	93.3	95.0	90.5	85.3	88.3
Investment	4.0	3.3	7.7	8.2	8.7
Defense	2.7	1.7	1.8	6.5	3.0
Internal Security (%)	15.0	0.0	30.0	20.0	20.0

CONFLICT

Sending Nation

Receiving Nation

	1	2	3	4	5
1	0	1	0	1	1
2	0	0	0	2	0
3	0	1	0	0	0
4	7	3	0	0	0
5	3	1	2	0	0

CONSEQUENCES

Nation

	1	2	3	4	5
Total Basic Capability	7050	17332	9320	32360	35700
Total Force Capability	390	1103	873	6340	3240
Validator Satisfaction	4.0	5.5	2.0	5.0	5.0
Prob. of Office-Holding	0.8	0.7	0.4	0.8	0.9
Decision Latitude	6.0	4.0	3.0	5.0	7.0
Prob. of Revolution	0.6	0.0	0.6	0.0	0.0

TABLE A–3
SYSTEM 3

DECISIONS			*Nation*		
Resource Allocations (%)	1	2	3	4	5
Consumption	96.7	95.6	92.2	85.3	89.2
Investment	0.0	3.5	5.6	7.9	6.
Defense	3.3	0.9	2.2	6.8	4.
Internal Security (%)	15.0	20.0	0.0	10.0	10.0

CONFLICT			*Sending Nation*		
Receiving Nation	1	2	3	4	5
1	0	0	0	0	0
2	0	0	1	0	0
3	0	1	0	0	1
4	2	2	1	0	1
5	0	0	0	0	0

			Nation		
CONSEQUENCES	1	2	3	4	5
Total Basic Capability	7350	16530	9120	32620	37060
Total Force Capability	465	850	900	6130	5340
Validator Satisfaction	5.5	5.0	3.0	4.5	5.5
Prob. of Office-Holding	0.8	0.7	0.5	0.7	0.9
Decision Latitude	6.0	5.0	3.0	5.0	7.0
Prob. of Revolution	0.0	0.0	0.7	0.0	0.0

TABLE A–4
SYSTEM 4

DECISIONS			*Nation*		
Resource Allocations (%)	1	2	3	4	5
Consumption	90.0	95.6	94.4	88.2	91.9
Investment	10.0	4.4	5.6	5.9	6.2
Defense	0.0	0.0	0.0	5.9	1.9
Internal Security (%)	10.0	30.0	10.0	10.0	10.0

CONFLICT			*Sending Nation*		
Receiving Nation	1	2	3	4	5
1	0	1	0	1	0
2	0	0	1	0	0
3	0	0	0	2	1
4	0	1	0	0	3
5	0	0	0	2	0

			Nation		
CONSEQUENCES	1	2	3	4	5
Total Basic Capability	6800	17560	9320	33620	34620
Total Force Capability	90	900	720	6190	3660
Validator Satisfaction	3.0	5.0	3.5	5.0	6.0
Prob. of Office-Holding	0.7	0.7	0.5	0.8	0.9
Decision Latitude	6.0	4.0	3.0	5.0	7.0
Prob. of Revolution	0.7	0.0	0.7	0.0	0.0

TABLE A–5
SYSTEM 5

DECISIONS			Nation		
Resource Allocations (%)	1	2	3	4	5
Consumption	93.3	91.2	95.0	90.0	85.4
Investment	6.7	7.1	5.0	5.9	6.9
Defense	0.0	1.7	0.0	4.1	7.7
Internal Security (%)	2.0	10.0	10.0	10.0	10.0

CONFLICT			Sending Nation		
Receiving Nation	1	2	3	4	5
1	0	0	0	0	0
2	0	0	0	0	1
3	0	0	0	1	0
4	1	2	0	0	1
5	1	2	4	0	0

			Nation		
CONSEQUENCES	1	2	3	4	5
Total Basic Capability	7850	17800	9100	33620	39320
Total Force Capability	90	1110	720	5115	7784
Validator Satisfaction	6.5	2.0	6.0	4.0	6.5
Prob. of Office-Holding	0.9	0.5	0.7	0.7	0.9
Decision Latitude	6.0	4.0	3.0	5.0	7.0
Prob. of Revolution	0.0	0.6	0.0	0.6	0.0

TABLE A–6
SYSTEM 6

DECISIONS	Nation				
Resource Allocations (%)	1	2	3	4	5
Consumption	92.0	91.2	91.1	88.2	90.3
Investment	2.7	5.3	8.9	7.4	6.0
Defense	5.3	3.5	0.0	4.4	3.7
Internal Security (%)	10.0	0.0	0.0	5.0	0.0

CONFLICT	Sending Nation				
Receiving Nation	1	2	3	4	5
1	0	0	0	0	0
2	4	0	0	0	0
3	0	0	0	1	0
4	2	2	3	0	0
5	0	0	4	2	0

	Nation				
CONSEQUENCES	1	2	3	4	5
Total Basic Capability	7150	12984	7970	25576	36660
Total Force Capability	690	1270	680	5235	5013
Validator Satisfaction	4.5	2.0	2.0	2.5	7.0
Prob. of Office-Holding	0.8	0.6	0.4	0.6	0.9
Decision Latitude	6.0	5.0	4.0	5.0	7.0
Prob. of Revolution	0.0	0.7	0.7	0.7	0.0

TABLE A–7
ALLIANCE CHANGES

System 1:	In period 7 nation 3 leaves the 1–3–5 bloc to join the 2–4 bloc.
System 2:	In period 4 nation 3 leaves the 1–3–5 bloc to join the 2–4 bloc. In period 7 nation 1 leaves the 1–5 bloc to join the 2–3–4 bloc.
System 3:	In period 4 nation 2 leaves the 2–4 bloc to join the 1–3–5 bloc. In period 6 nation 3 leaves the 1–2–3–5 bloc to join nation 4.
System 4:	In period 3 nation 3 leaves the 1–3–5 bloc to join the 2–4 bloc. In period 6 nation 1 leaves the 1–5 bloc to join the 2–3–4 bloc. In period 6 nation 2 leaves the 1–2–3–4 bloc to join nation 5.
System 5:	No alliance changes.
System 6:	In period 5 nations 1 and 3 leave the 1–3–5 bloc to join the 2–4 bloc.

APPENDIX TWO

Derivation of the Goodness-of-Fit Measures

THE goodness-of-fit statistics reported in chapter five measure the discrepancy between the observed and predicted partial correlations in two different, but complimentary, ways. In this appendix we will show the logic underlying their usage and their derivation from more conventional statistical procedures. In addition, attention will be directed to the interpretation and implications of these procedures.

The logic of the goodness-of-fit procedures is as follows. If we treat the partial correlations which emerge from the SIPER and INS results as predictions of what we should find in the referent world, then the goodness-of-fit question becomes ''if the SIPER (or INS) model is correct as to the association between the relevant variables, how likely it is that we would have obtained a sample correlation as discrepant as, or more discrepant than, the one actually obtained?'' If the predicted (model) and observed (sample) correlations are very different, and it is highly unlikely that such a difference can be attributed to sampling error, then we would conclude that the model lacks credibility. This kind of validation logic is commonly used by those who postulate certain probability models, deduce what the observed frequencies should be, and perform a chi-square goodness-of-fit test. The p-value that is reported is the probability that the differences between the probability model's predictions and the observed distribution is attributable to sampling error in generating the observed distribution. In general, a p-value (or probability-value) is defined as the probability that a *sample value* would be as extreme as the value actually *observed,* given that the *predicted value* is correct. It is commonly viewed as a measure of credibility of the hypotheses being tested,[1] and it is our basic goodness-of-fit measure.

In order to show how these p-values are obtained in the present case, a review of some statistical background material may be helpful. A correlation coefficient, r, when subjected to the following transformation

$$\tfrac{1}{2}\log_e \frac{1 + r}{1 - r}$$

is normally distributed with a mean of

$$\tfrac{1}{2} \log_e \frac{1 + p}{1 - p}$$

and a standard deviation of

$$\sqrt{\frac{1}{N - k - 1}}$$

where p is the true correlation, N is the size of the sample upon which the correlation is based, and k is the number of dependent and independent variables. The complete equation for obtaining the standard normal variable, Z, is

$$Z = \frac{\tfrac{1}{2}\log_e \dfrac{1 + r}{1 - r} - \tfrac{1}{2}\log_e \dfrac{1 + p}{1 - p}}{\sqrt{\dfrac{1}{N - k - 1}}}$$

This Z value indicates how large the discrepancy is between the predicted and observed values in terms of units of standard error. These are the first values that are reported beneath the correlations contained in the tables in chapter five.

From a table of the normal distribution we can determine how likely it is that the discrepancy between an observed r and a posited p would be as large as, or larger than, the one obtained if p were the correct parameter value. This probability is exactly equivalent to the p-value previously discussed. That is, it is the probability that the sample correlation, r, would be as extreme as the value actually obtained if the value predicted by the model, p, were correct.

In the present application, we have two predicted values for p, one derived from the SIPER data and one from the INS data. These values are treated as predicted values for the partial correlations and each set of values is tested against the observed correlations to determine how likely it is that a value as extreme as the observed value would be obtained if the predicted value were correct.

An example from Table 5–2 may further clarify our precedures.

		SIPER	Size Real		INS
Turmoil	r	−.09	+.05		−.63
	|Z|		0.85	4.75	
	p	.198		.000	

These values indicate the partial correlations and the associated goodness-of-fit measures for the size-turmoil relationship. Substituting the values of the correlations for the values of ρ ($-.09$) and r ($+.05$) in the above equation, with N equal to forty-one and k equal to four, we find that the discrepancy between the value predicted by SIPER and the observed value is -0.85 standard error units. Since we are not interested here in the direction of the discrepancy but rather its magnitude, only the absolute values of Z are reported in the tables. Consulting a table of the normal distribution, we find that approximately 20 percent of the expected correlations would be more deviant than the predicted value (in the same direction) than the actual observed value. However, since this value is based on a one-tailed test, we would need to double this probability if the direction of the discrepancy is ignored; that is, nearly 40 percent of the sample correlations would be farther away from the predicted correlation in terms of absolute distance than the observed correlation.

If we substitute the INS prediction for the SIPER value we find that the difference between the INS value and the real sample value corresponds to 4.75 units of standard error, which has an associated p-value considerably less than .001.

We are now in a position to interpret these results. It is clear that, with respect to this relationship, the empirical evidence supports (or more accurately, fails to refute) the SIPER model more than it does the INS model. The very small p-value for the INS-real comparison indicates a very low level of credibility for the INS model, while the larger SIPER p-value indicates that it is more plausible.

The p-values have a meaning in their own right. If we denote the *null* hypothesis as "the model is *invalid*" and the *alternate* hypothesis as "the model is *valid*", then these p-values are related to the probability of committing a Type II error if the alternate hypothesis is erroneously rejected in favor of the null hypothesis. If, for example, we were to use the decision rule that any discrepancy between predicted and observed values greater than one standard error unit constituted grounds for rejecting the model as valid, then, on the average, we could expect to incorrectly reject a valid model about one-third of the time (approximately one-sixth on each end of the distribution). Thus, if the p-values are doubled they indicate the likelihood of rejecting a valid model, a Type II error.

In general, the higher the probability of making a Type II error, the lower the probability of making a Type I error, so if we set the acceptable level of Type II error low, in order to minimize rejecting valid models, we can expect to classify a significant number of models as valid when they are not (Type I error). Conversely, setting the acceptable level of Type II error high will reduce the likelihood of accepting invalid models, but it also increases the likelihood of rejecting valid models. Thus we introduce in chapter five the three-fold categorization of correspondence in order to summarize the overall results. These reflect degrees of compromise between Type I and Type II errors. The reader, of course, has the option of selecting his own level of acceptable Type II error and interpreting the findings of chapter five accordingly.

APPENDIX 2 NOTES

1. See Thomas H. Wonnacott and Ronald J. Wonnacott, *Introductory Statistics,* (New York: John Wiley, 1969), pp. 179–181 for a discussion of the p-value concept.

APPENDIX THREE

The Computer Program

THE computer program was written in FORTRAN IV, and was originally designed to operate on the Control Data Corporation 6400–6500–6600 computing systems. A slightly revised version of the program is available from the International Relations Archive, Inter-University Consortium for Political Research which is located at the Institute for Social Research at the University of Michigan. This version of the program is compatable with IBM computing systems. The program is composed of eight subroutines and a main executive routine. Figure A–1 indicates the sequence in which the subroutines are executed in one period of simulated time. Two solid lines represent iterative passage of control from one routine to another while a single solid line indicates that a routine is called only once in each cycle.

A period of simulated time begins at about one o'clock on the execution clock in Figure A–1. The first routine called, DMER1, is concerned with revising aspiration levels and setting export prices. TRADER, the next routine called by the executive routine, negotiates and concludes trades between the simulated nations. DMER2 revises the national product decisions in accordance with trade commitments, resolves budget crises should they arise, and assesses the need for foreign aid. The granting of aid and the expression of hostility are handled by DMER3. CALCER calculates the consequences of decisions made and prepares the system for the next period. OUTPUT, as the name implies, transfers summary information about the period to the appropriate output device.

The program has several input-output options. The user may specify at what intervals data is to be read in and the model set back on some prescribed track. For example, it is possible to specify that after each period of decision-making, data are read from the input tape, and this information is substituted for the model-generated data before the next period begins. In this way

223

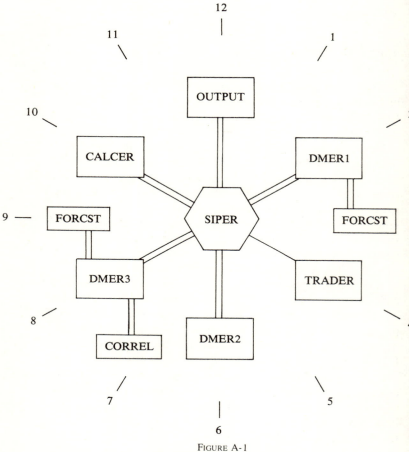

FIGURE A-1
PROGRAM EXECUTION SEQUENCE

single-period differences between referent and simulated behavior may be studied.

On the output side, there is provision for specifying detailed print-out of all decision-making or specific portions of the decision-making cycle. In addition, summary information may be printed and/or written on tape at the end of each period.

The estimates of space, time, and cost are as follows. The program requires approximately 50,000 octal memory locations, and one period of decision-making for a five-nation world requires approximately one-half of a second of central processer time. Our cost estimate for a Control Data Corporation 6500 computing system is less than one cent per nation per period. This estimate does not include compilation costs or peripheral processing costs, which may vary.

Glossary

AID International assistance in the form of grants which may include consumption, investment, or defense goods.

AIDREQ The request made by an alliance member to its alliance leader for assistance.

ALGRO The aspiration level for economic growth; the rate of growth which the nation considers desirable at a point in time.

ALLY The relationship between nations where each is committed to assist the other in the event of an attack on one of them.

ALPOH The aspiration level for political stability; the desired probability that the decision-makers will retain their decision-making positions.

ALSEC The aspiration level for national security; the proportion of its resources a nation desires to allocate to defense needs to counter expected threat.

APOW The expected threat-countering capability of a leader's alliance.

BC Basic capability; value which has the characteristic of being able to produce more value.

BCGR Basic capability generation rate; the basic capability value produced by the commitment of one unit of resources (TBC) to the investment sector.

BCP The proportion of national resources (TBC) devoted to the investment sector for the production of BC value.

CR The loss of TBC units associated with the occurrence of a revolution within a nation.

CS Consumption satisfaction; value which has the characteristic of being able to satisfy population wants and needs.

GLOSSARY

CSGR	Consumption satisfaction generation rates; the consumption satisfaction value produced by the commitment of one unit of resources (TBC) to the consumption sector.
CSmax	The amount of CS value that would be produced if all national resources were devoted to the consumption sector.
CSMF	The fraction of a nation's resources that must be devoted to CS production in order to achieve CSmin.
CSmin	The minimum level of CS value production necessary to maintain the nation.
CSP	The proportion of national resources (TBC) devoted to the consumption sector for the production of CS value.
DBC	The depreciation rate for national productive resources.
DDL	Exogenous, random changes in a nation's DL.
DFC	The depreciation rate for total force capability.
DL	Decision latitude; the degree to which decision-makers are dependent upon validator support for their continuation as decision-makers.
DTIE	The degree to which an alliance member has followed its alliance leader's suggestions concerning defense expenditures.
EDEP	Economic dependence; the degree to which an alliance member is economically dependent on its alliance leader.
ETIE	The degree to which two nations are economically coupled through trade linkages.
EXPRC	The set of national export prices indicating the terms of trade for each commodity pair with each potential trade partner.
FC	Force capability; the value which has the characteristic of being able to destroy other value.
FCCUE	The suggestion as to level of defense expenditure which an alliance leader makes to an alliance member.

FCGR	Force capability generation rate; the force capability value produced by the commitment of one unit of resource (TBC) to the defense sector.
FCic	The amount of total force capability (TFC) devoted to internal security.
FCP	The proportion of national resources (TBC) devoted to the defense sector for the production of FC value.
FicP	The proportion of total force capability (TFC) devoted to internal security.
GR	The set of national generation rates including CSGR, BCGR, and FCGR.
GRO	The rate of growth in productive resources (TBC) from one period to the next.
HOST	The aggregate flow of threats, accusations, and protests between nations.
IDEP	Ideological dependence; the amount of moral suasion that an alliance leader can exert over an alliance member by the manipulation of symbolic rewards.
IMLIM	The national import limit for a specific good.
INS	The Inter-Nation Simulation
IPOW	An alliance member's estimate of its threat-countering capability in the next time period.
NEED	The alliance leader's estimate of each ally's need for foreign aid in relation to all aid requests received in a given period.
OPOW	The level of threat expected from the opposing bloc in the next time period.
POH	Probability of office-holding; the overall measure of the stability of the national political system.
PR	Probability of revolution; the degree to which the validators are organized in opposition to the decision-makers.
SURPLUS	The amount of resources left for allocation after primary goal needs have been met.
TAID	The total value of aid that is to be sent to another nation.

229

GLOSSARY

TBC   Total basic capability; national resources available for the production of value.

TFC   Total force capability; the amount of national force capability available for use in any given period of time.

TOTIM   The total amount of imports that will be allowed to enter the nation in any given period.

TRADE   The exchange of commodities by two nations.

VScs   Validator satisfaction with regard to consumption satisfaction; the degree to which validators give support to decision-makers in response to CS value flow.

VSm   Validator satisfaction over-all; the aggregate support of decision-makers by validators.

VSns   Validator satisfaction with regard to national security; the degree to which validators are content with the international position of their nation.

BIBLIOGRAPHY

Adelman, Irma and Cynthia Taft Morris. *Society, Politics, and Economic Development*. Baltimore: Johns Hopkins University Press, 1967.

Alger, Chadwick. "Use of the Inter-Nation Simulation in Undergraduate Teaching." in Harold Guetzkow *et. al. Simulation in International Relations*. Englewood Cliffs, N.J.: Prentice-Hall, 1963, 150–189.

Alker, Hayward. "Decision-Makers' Environments in the Inter-Nation Simulation." In William D. Coplin, ed. *Simulation in the Study of Politics*. Chicago: Markham Publishing Company, 1968, 31–58.

Alker, Hayward and Cheryl Christensen. "From Causal Modelling to Artificial Intelligence." In Jean A. Laponce and Paul Smoker, eds. *Experimentations and Simulation in Political Science*. Toronto: University of Toronto Press, 1972, 177–224.

Almond, Gabriel. "Research Note: A Comparative Study of Interest Groups and the Political Process." *American Political Science Review*. 52, No. 1 (March, 1958), 270–282.

Aron, Raymond. *Peace and War*. New York: Praeger, 1967.

Banks, Arthur S. and Robert B. Textor. *A Cross-Polity Survey*. Cambridge, Mass.: The M.I.T. Press, 1963.

Banks, Arthur S. and Phillip M. Gregg. "Grouping Political Systems: Q-Factor Analysis of a Cross-Polity Survey." *American Behavioral Scientist*. 9, No. 3 (November, 1965), 3–6.

Bartos, Otomar J. "Prediction of Trades in Inter-Nation Simulation." Evanston, Ill.: Dept. of Sociology, Northwestern University, 1963.

Berrien, F. Kenneth. *General and Social Systems*. New Brunswick, N.J.: Rutgers University Press, 1968.

BIBLIOGRAPHY

Bhagwati, Jagdish. *The Economics of Underdeveloped Countries*. New York: World University Library, 1966.

Bremer, Stuart A. and Michael Mihalka. "Machiavelli in Machina: A Computer Simulation of Multi-State System Dynamics." Paper to be presented at the 1976 meetings of the International Political Association, Edinburgh, Scotland.

Brody, Richard A. "Some Systemic Effects of the Spread of Nuclear Weapons Technology: A Study Through Simulation of a Multi-Nuclear Future." *Journal of Conflict Resolution*. 7, No. 4 (December, 1963), 665–753.

Brody, Richard A., Alexandra H. Benham, and Jeffrey S. Milstein. "Hostile International Communications, Arms Production, and Perception of Threat: A Simulation Study." Stanford, Ca.: Institute of Political Studies, Stanford University, July, 1966.

———,———,and———"Hostile International Communication, Arms Production, and Perceptions of Threat: A Simulation Study." *Peace Research Society (International) Papers,* 7 (1967), 15–40.

Browning, Rufus P. "Hypotheses about Political Recruitment: A Partially Data-Based Computer Simulation." William D. Coplin, ed. *Simulation in the Study of Politics*. Chicago: Markham Publishing Company, 1968, 303–326.

———. "Simulation: Attempts and Possibilities." In Jeanne N. Knutson, ed., *Handbook of Political Psychology*. San Francisco: Jossey-Bass Inc., 1974, 383–412.

Brunner, Ronald D. "Some Comments on Simulating Theories of Political Development." In William D. Coplin, ed. *Simulation in the Study of Politics*. Chicago: Markham Publishing Company, 1969, 329–342.

Brunner, Ronald D. and Garry D. Brewer. *Organized Complexity*. New York: The Free Press, 1971.

Burgess, Philip and James Robinson. "Alliances and the Theory of Collective Action: A Simulation of Coalition Processes." In James N. Rosenau, ed. *International Politics and Foreign Policy*. New York: The Free Press, 1969, 640–653.

Caspary, William. "The Causes of War in INS-8." Evanston, Ill.: Northwestern University, ditto, 1962.

232

————. "Simulation Studies in Inter-Nation Conflict: Part II, Application." Presented at the meeting of the Midwest Sociological Association, April 19, 1963.

Chadwick, Richard W. "Definition of Simulation Threats, Accusations, and Protests." Evanston, Ill.: Northwestern University Dept. of Political Science, April, 1965.

————. "An Empirical Test of Five Assumptions in an Inter-Nation Simulation about National Political Systems." *General Systems Yearbook.* 12 (1967), 177–192.

————. "An Inductive, Empirical Analysis of Intra- and International Behavior, Aimed at a Partial Extension of Inter-Nation Simulation Theory." *Journal of Peace Research.* 6, No. 3 (1969), 193–214.

————. "Theory Development through Simulation: A Comparison and Analysis of Associations Among Variables in an International System and an Inter-Nation Simulation." *International Studies Quarterly.* 16, No. 1 (March, 1972), 83–127.

Chenery, Hollis B. "Patterns of Industrial Growth." *American Economic Review.* 50, No. 4 (September, 1960), 624–654.

Cherryholmes, Cleo. "Developments in Simulation of International Relations in High School Teaching." *Phi Delta Kappa.* (January, 1965), 227–231.

————. "Some Current Research on Effectiveness of Educational Simulations: Implications for Alternative Strategies." *American Behavioral Scientist.* 10, No. 2 (October, 1966), 4–7.

Cherryholmes, Cleo and Michael J. Shapiro. *Representatives and Roll Calls.* New York: Bobbs-Merrill, 1969.

Cohen, Kalman J. and Richard M. Cyert. "Simulation of Organizational Behavior." In James G. March, ed. *Handbook of Organizations.* Chicago: Rand McNally, 1965, 305–334.

Coleman, James S. "Mathematical Models and Computer Simulation." In Robert E.L. Faris, ed. *Handbook of Modern Sociology.* Chicago: Rand McNally, 1964, 1027–1062.

Crecine, John P. *Governmental Problem-Solving.* Chicago: Rand McNally, 1969.

Crow, Wayman. "A Study of Strategic Doctrines Using the

Inter-Nation Simulation.'' *Journal of Conflict Resolution.* 7, No. 3 (September, 1963), 580–589.

Crow, Wayman and John Raser. *A Cross-Cultural Simulation Study.* La Jolla, Ca.: Western Behaviorial Science Institute, 1965.

Cyert, Richard M. and James G. March. *A Behaviorial Theory of the Firm.* New York: Prentice-Hall, 1963.

Deutsch, Karl W. *The Analysis of International Relations.* Englewood Cliffs, N.J.: Prentice-Hall, 1968.

Deutsch, Karl W. and Alexander Eckstein. ''National Industrialization and the Declining Share of the International Economic Sector, 1890-1959.'' *World Politics.* 13, No. 2 (January, 1961), 267–299.

Deutsch, Karl W., Chester I. Bliss, and Alexander Eckstein. ''Population, Sovereignty, and the Share of Foreign Trade.'' *Economic Development and Cultural Change.* 10, No. 4 (July, 1962), 353–366.

Driver, Michael J. ''A Cognitive Structure Analysis of Aggression, Stress, and Personality in an Inter-Nation Simulation.'' Lafayette, Ind.: Purdue University, August, 1965.

Druckman, Daniel. ''Ethnocentrism in the Inter-Nation Simulation.'' *Journal of Conflict Resolution.* 12, No. 1 (March, 1968), 45–68.

Durkheim, Emile. *Professional Ethics and Civil Morals.* London: Routledge and Paul, 1957.

Dutton, John M. and William H. Starbuck, eds. *Computer Simulation of Human Behavior.* New York: Wiley, 1971.

Easton, David. *A Framework for Political Analysis.* Englewood Cliffs, N.J.: Prentice-Hall, 1965.

Etzioni, Amitai. *Political Unification.* New York: Holt, Rinehart and Winston, 1965.

Feierabend, Ivo K. and Rosalind L. Feierabend. ''Aggressive Behavior Within Polities, 1948-1962: A Cross-National Study.'' *Journal of Conflict Resolution.* 10, No. 3 (September, 1966), 249–271.

Forcese, Dennis. ''Power and Military Alliance Cohesion.'' Unpublished Ph.D. dissertation, Washington University, 1968.

Forrester, Jay W. *Urban Dynamics*. Cambridge, Mass.: The M.I.T. Press, 1969.

Gift, Richard E. "Trading in a Threat System: The U.S.-Soviet Case." *Journal of Conflict Resolution*. 13, No. 4 (December, 1969), 418–437.

Gregg, Lee W. and Herbert A. Simon. "Process Models and Stochastic Theories of Simple Concept Formation." In John M. Dutton and William H. Starbuck, eds. *Computer Simulation of Human Behavior*. New York: Wiley, 1971, 127–146.

Gregg, Phillip M. and Arthur S. Banks. "Dimensions of Political Systems: Factor Analysis of a Cross-Polity Survey." *American Political Science Review*. 59 (September, 1965), 602–614.

Guetzkow, Harold. "Simulation in International Relations." *Proceedings of the IBM Scientific Computing Symposium on Simulation Models and Gaming*. (1964), 249–278.

_____. "Some Uses of Mathematics in Simulation of International Relations." In John M. Claunch, ed. *Mathematical Applications in Political Science*. Dallas: Southern Methodist University Press, 1965, 21–40.

_____. "Some Correspondences between Simulations and 'Realities' in International Relations." In Morton A. Kaplan, ed. *New Approaches to International Relations*. New York: St. Martin's Press, 1968, 202–269.

Guetzkow, Harold. et al. *Simulation in International Relations*. Englewood Cliffs, N.J.: Prentice-Hall, 1963.

Gurr, Ted R. "Causal Model of Civil Strife: A Comparative Analysis Using New Indices." *American Political Science Review*. 62, No. 4 (December, 1968), 1104–1124.

_____. *Why Men Rebel*. Princeton, N.J.: Princeton University Press, 1970.

Haas, Ernst B. and Allen S. Whiting. *Dynamics of International Relations*. New York: McGraw-Hill, 1956.

Haas, Michael. "A Plan for Bridge Building in International Relations." In Klauss Knorr and James N. Rosenau, eds. *Contending Approaches to International Politics*. Princeton, N.J.: Princeton University Press, 1969, 158–176.

235

Heilbroner, Robert L. *Understanding Macro-Economics*. Englewood Cliffs, N.J.: Prentice-Hall, 1966.

Hermann, Charles F. "Validation Problems in Games and Simulations with Special Reference to Models of International Politics." *Behavioral Science*. 12 (May, 1967), 216–231.

_____.*Crises in Foreign Policy: A Simulation Analysis*. Indianapolis: Bobbs-Merrill, 1969.

_____."Threat, Time, and Surprise: A Simulation of International Crisis." In Charles F. Hermann, ed. *International Crisis: Insights from Behaviorial Research*. New York: The Free Press, 1972, 187–211.

Hermann, Charles F. and Margaret G. Hermann. *Validation Studies of the Inter-Nation Simulation*. China Lake, Ca.: U.S. Naval Ordinance Test Station, December, 1963.

_____."An Attempt to Simulate the Outbreak of World War I." *American Political Science Review*. 61, No. 2 (June, 1967), 400–416.

Hermann, Charles F., Margaret G. Hermann, and Robert Cantor. "Counter-attack on Warning or Delay." Presented at the Midwest Political Science Association Meetings. Chicago, Ill., April 27-29, 1972.

Hermann, Margaret G. "Testing a Model of Psychological Stress." *Journal of Personality*. 34, No. 3 (September, 1966) 381–96.

Homans, George C, *Social Behavior: Its Elementary Forms*. New York: Harcourt, Brace, and World, 1961.

Hoole, Frank. "Societal Conditions and Political Aggression." Bloomington, Ind.: Indiana University, mimeo, 1972.

Jensen, Lloyd. "Foreign Policy Elites and the Prediction of International Events." *Peace Research Society (International) Papers*. 5 (1966), 199–209.

_____."Predicting International Events." *Peace Research Reviews*. 4, No. 6 (August, 1972), 1–65.

Kaplan, Morton A. *System and Process in International Politics*. New York: Wiley, 1957.

Krend, Jeffrey. "A Reconstruction of Oliver Benson's 'Simple Diplomatic Game'." Evanston, Ill.: Simulated International Processes Project, Northwestern University, 1970.

236

_____."Computer Simulations of International Relations as Heuristics for Social Status, Action and Change." Evanston, Ill.: Simulated International Processes Project, Northwestern University, 1972.

_____."War and Peace in the International System: Deriving an All-Computer Heuristic." Proceedings, Summer Simulation Conference, San Diego, Ca., 1972.

Kuh, Edwin and John R. Meyer. "Correlation and Regression Estimates when the Data are Ratios." *Econometrica*. 23, No. 4 (October, 1955), 400–416.

Kuznets, Simon. "Quantitative Aspects of the Economic Growth of Nations: VI. Long-Term Trends in Capital Formation Proportions." *Economic Development and Cultural Change*. 9, No. 4 (July, 1961, Part II), 1–124.

_____."Quantitative Aspects of the Economic Growth of Nations: X. Level and Structure of Foreign Trade: Long-Term Trends." *Economic Development and Cultural Change*. 13, No. 1 (July, 1965, Part II), 1–106.

_____.Economic Growth of Small Nations." In E.A.G. Robinson, ed. *The Economic Consequences of the Size of Nations*. New York: St. Martin's Press, 1965, 14–34.

Lagerstrom, Richard P. and Robert C. North. "An Anticipated-Gap Mathematical Model of International Dynamics." Stanford, Ca.: Institute of Political Studies, Stanford University, April, 1969.

Lasswell, Harold D. "Introduction: The Study of Political Elites." In Harold D. Lasswell and Daniel Lerner, eds. *World Revolutionary Elites*. Cambridge, Mass.: The M.I.T. Press, 1965, 4–6.

Laulicht, Jerome. "A Vietnam Peace Game: A Computer Assisted Simulation of Complex Relations in International Relations." *Computers and Automation*. 16, No. 3 (March, 1967), 14–18.

Lazarsfeld, Paul F. "Evidence and Inference in Social Research." In May Brodbeck, ed. *Readings in the Philosophy of the Social Sciences*. New York: Macmillan, 1968, 608–634.

Leavitt, Michael. "A Computer Simulation of International Alliance Behavior.'' Unpublished Ph.D. dissertation, Dept. of Political Science, Northwestern University, 1971.

McGowan, Patrick. ''Some External Validities of the Inter-Nation Simulation.'' Evanston, Ill.: Northwestern University, 1972.

MacRae, John and Paul Smoker. ''A Vietnam Simulation: A Report on the Canadian/English Project.'' *Journal of Peace Research*. 4, No. 1 (1967), 1–25.

Meier, Dorothy. ''Progress Report: Event Simulation Project.'' Evanston, Ill.: Simulated International Processes Project. Northwestern University, 1965.

Meier, Dorothy and Arthur Stickgold. ''Progress Report: Analysis Procedures,'' St. Louis, Mo.: Event Simulation Project, Washington University, 1965.

Miller, George A., Eugene Galanter, and Karl H. Pribram. *Plans and the Structure of Behavior*. New York: Holt, Rinehart and Winston, 1960.

Modelski, George. ''Simulations, 'Realities' and International Relations Theory.'' *Simulation and Games*. 1, No. 2 (June, 1970), 111–134.

Nardin, Terry and Neal Cutler. ''Reliability and Validity of Some Patterns of International Interaction in an Inter-Nation Simulation.'' *Journal of Peace Research*. 6, No. 1 (1969), 1–12.

Naylor, Thomas H. *Computer Simulation Experiments with Models of Economic Systems*. New York: Wiley, 1971.

Naylor, Thomas H. et al. *Computer Simulation Techniques*. New York: John Wiley, 1966.

Noel, Robert. ''Evolution of the Inter-Nation Simulation.'' Harold Guetzkow et al. *Simulation in International Relations*. Englewood Cliffs, N.J.: Prentice-Hall, 1963, 69–102.

North, Robert C. ''Decision-making in Crisis: An Introduction.'' *Journal of Conflict Resolution*. 6, No. 3 (September, 1962), 197–200.

Nurske, Ragnar. ''The Size of the Market and the Inducement to Invest.'' In D.E. Novack and R. Lekachman, eds.

238

Development and Society. New York: St. Martin's Press, 1964, 91–96.

Organski, A.F.K. *World Politics.* New York: Knopf, 1958.

Osgood, Charles. *An Alternative to War or Surrender.* Urbana: University of Illinois Press, 1962.

Pelowski, Allan L. "An Event-Based Simulation of the Taiwan Straits Crisis." In Jean A. Laponce and Paul Smoker, eds. *Experimentation and Simulation in Political Science.* Toronto: University of Toronto Press, 1972, 259–279.

Pen, Jan. *A Primer of International Trade.* New York: Vintage Books, 1966.

Pendley, Robert E. and Charles D. Elder. "An Analysis of Office-Holding in the Inter-Nation Simulation in Terms of Contemporary Political Theory and Data on the Stability of Regimes and Governments." Evanston, Ill.: Simulated International Processes Project, Northwestern University, November, 1966.

Pirro, Ellen. "Frustration-Aggression: A Casual Model Analysis." Evanston, Ill.: Northwestern University, 1972.

Pool, Ithiel de Sola and Allen Kessler. "The Kaiser, the Tsar, and the Computer: Information Processing in a Crisis." *The American Behavioral Scientist.* 8, No. 9 (May, 1965), 31–38.

Pool, Ithiel de Sola, Robert P. Abelson, and Samuel Popkin. *Candidates, Issues, and Strategies.* Cambridge, Mass.: The M.I.T. Press, 1965.

Pruitt, Dean. "Two Factors in International Agreement." Evanston, Ill.: Northwestern University, ditto, 1961.

———."An Analysis of Responsiveness between Nations." *Journal of Conflict Resolution.* 6, No. 1 (March, 1962), 5–18.

Pryor, Frederic L. *Public Expenditures in Communist and Capitalistic Nations.* Homewood, Ill.: Irwin, 1969.

Raser, John. "Personal Characteristics of Political Decision-Makers: A Literature Review." *Peace Research Society (International) Papers.* 5 (1966), 161–181.

Raser, John and Wayman Crow. *Capacity to Delay Response:*

239

Explication of a Deterrence Concept, and Plan for Research Using the Inter-Nation Simulation. La Jolla, Ca.: Western Behavioral Science Institute, 1963.

————.*WINSAFE II: An Inter-Nation Simulation Study of Deterrence Postures Embodying Capacity to Delay Response.* La Jolla, Ca.: Western Behavioral Science Institute, July, 1964.

————."A Simulation Study of Deterrence Theories." In Dean Pruitt and Richard C. Snyder, eds. *Theory and Research on the Causes of War.* Englewood Cliffs, N.J.: Prentice-Hall, 1969, 136–149.

Raser, John, Donald Campbell, and Richard Chadwick. "Gaming and Simulations for Developing Theory Relevant to International Relations." *General Systems Yearbook.* 15 (1970), 183–204.

Rashevsky, Nicholas. *Mathematical Theory of Human Relations: An Approach to a Mathematical Biology of Social Phenomena.* Bloomington, Ind.: Principia Press, 1947.

Reinken, Donald L. "Computer Explorations of the 'Balance of Power'." In Morton A. Kaplan, ed. *New Approaches to International Relations.* New York: St. Martin's Press, 1968, 459–482.

Remy, Richard C. "Trade and Defense in the IPS and Selected Referent Systems." Evanston, Ill.: Northwestern University, 1967.

Robinson, James, Leroy Anderson, Margaret Hermann, and Richard C. Snyder. "Teaching with Inter-Nation Simulation and Case Studies." *American Political Science Review.* 60, No. 1 (March, 1966), 53–65.

Robinson, James, Charles Hermann, and Margaret Hermann. "Search Under Crisis in Political Gaming and Simulation." In Dean Pruitt and Richard C. Snyder, eds. *Theory and Research on the Causes of War.* Englewood Cliffs, N.J.: Prentice-Hall, 1969, 80–94.

Robinson, James and Alan Wyner. "Information Storage and Search in Inter-Nation Simulation." Columbus, Ohio: Ohio State University, mimeo, 1965.

Rosenau, James N. "Pre-Theories and Theories of Foreign Policy." In R. Barry Farrell, ed. *Approaches to Comparative and International Politics*. Evanston, Ill.: Northwestern University Press, 1966, 27–92.

Rummel, Rudolph J. "Dimensions of Conflict Behavior Within and Between Nations." *General Systems Yearbook*. 8 (1963), 1–50.

————."A Social Field Theory of Foreign Conflict Behavior." *Peace Research Society (International) Papers*. 4 (1965), 131–150.

————."The Relationship between National Attributes and Foreign Conflict Behavior." In J. David Singer, ed. *Quantitative International Politics*. New York: The Free Press, 1966, 187–214.

————."Indicators of Cross-National and International Patterns." *American Political Science Review*. 63, No. 1 (March, 1969), 127–147.

Russett, Bruce M. "Measures of Military Effort." *American Behavioral Scientist*. 7, No. 6 (February, 1964), 26–29.

————.*International Regions and the International System*. Chicago: Rand McNally, 1967.

————."Who Pays for Defense?" *American Political Science Review*. 63, No. 2 (June, 1969), 412–426.

————."A Macroscopic View of International Politics." In James N. Rosenau, Vincent Davis, and Maurice A. East, eds. *The Analysis of International Politics*. New York: The Free Press, 1972, 109–124.

Russett, Bruce M. and Charles L. Taylor. "Is Political Instability Related to Per Capita Income?" Bendix Corporation Working Paper No. 97. Ann Arbor: Bendix Corporation, January 23, 1967.

Russett, Bruce M. et al. *World Handbook of Political and Social Indicators*. New Haven: Yale University Press, 1964.

Salmore, Stephen A. and Charles F. Hermann. "The Effect of Size, Development, and Accountability on Foreign Policy." Paper delivered at the Seventh North American Peace Research Conference of the Peace Research Society (International). University of Michigan, Ann Arbor, Michigan, November 11–12, 1969.

Sawyer, Jack. "Dimensions of Nations: Size, Wealth, and Politics." *American Journal of Sociology.* 73, No. 2 (September, 1967), 145–172.

Schelling, Thomas C. *The Strategy of Conflict.* Cambridge, Mass.: Harvard University Press, 1963.

Shapiro, Michael J. "Cognitive Rigidity and Perceptual Orientations in an Inter-Nation Simulation." Evanston, Ill.: Northwestern University, 1966.

Shapiro, Michael J. and G. Matthew Bonham. "Cognitive Process and Foreign Policy Decision-Making." *International Studies Quarterly.* 17, No. 2 (June, 1973), 147–174.

Sherman, Allen W. "The Social Psychology of Bilateral Negotiations." Unpublished Masters thesis, Dept. of Sociology, Northwestern University, 1963.

Simmel, Georg. *The Sociology of Georg Simmel,* trans. and ed. by Kurt H. Wolf. Glencoe, Ill.: The Free Press, 1950.

Simon, Herbert A. *The Sciences of the Artificial.* Cambridge, Mass.: The M.I.T. Press, 1969.

Singer, J. David. "Threat-perception and the Armament-Tension Dilemma." *Journal of Conflict Resolution.* 2, No. 1 (March, 1958), 90–105.

——. "The Level-of-Analysis Problem in International Relations." In Klauss Knorr and Sidney Verba, eds. *The International System: Theoretical Essays.* Princeton, N.J.: Princeton University Press, 1961, 77–92.

Singer, J. David and Melvin Small. "Alliance Aggregation and the Onset of War, 1815–1945." In J. David Singer, ed. *Quantitative International Politics.* New York: The Free Press, 1968, 247–286.

Skinner, Donald D. and Robert D. Wells. *Michigan Inter-Nation Simulation.* Ann Arbor: The Department of Political Science and the Center for Research on Learning and Teaching, University of Michigan, 1965.

Smoker, Paul. "Trade, Defense, and the Richardson Theory of

Arms Races: A Seven Nation Study." *Journal of Peace Research*. 2, No. 2 (1964), 65–76.

_____."A Preliminary Empirical Study of an Inter-Nation Integrative Subsystem." *International Associations*. 17, No. 11 (1965), 638–646.

_____."A Study of an Arms Race." Masters thesis, University of Lancaster, England, 1966.

_____."Nation-State Escalation and International Integration." *Journal of Peace Research*. 4, No. 1 (1967), 60–75.

_____."An International Process Simulation: Theory and Description." Evanston, Ill.: Simulated International Processes Project, Northwestern University, 1968.

_____."International Processes Simulation: An Evaluation." Presented at the Events Data Conference, East Lansing, Michigan, Michigan State University, 1970.

Sombart, Werner. *Die Deutsche Volkswirtschaft in Neunzehnten Jahrhundert* 3d ed. Berlin: Bondi, 1913.

Soroos, Marvin. "Patterns of Cross-National Activities in the International Processes Simulation and a Real World Reference System." North Carolina State University, 1971.

_____."Crisis Behaviors in the International Processes Simulation and the Berlin Reference System." Raleigh, N.C.: North Carolina State University, 1971.

_____."International Involvement and Foreign Behaviors in the International Processes Simulation and a Real World Reference System." Unpublished Ph.D. dissertation, Dept. of Political Science, Northwestern University, 1972.

_____."An Interpretation of Patterns of Discrepancies Between the International Process Simulation and an International Reference System." In Joseph Bendak, ed. *The Simulation of Intersocietal Relations*. Forthcoming.

Starbuck, William H. and John M. Dutton. "The History of Simulation Models." In John M. Dutton and William H. Starbuck. *Computer Simulation of Human Behavior*. New York: Wiley, 1971, 9–30.

Stockholm International Peace Research Institute. *Yearbook of*

World Armaments and Disarmament, 1968-69. New York: Humanities Press, 1970.

Tanter, Raymond. "Dimensions of Conflict Behavior within and between Nations, 1957-1960." *Journal of Conflict Resolution.* 10, No. 1 (March, 1966), 41–64.

Targ, Harry and Terry Nardin. "The Inter-Nation Simulation as a Predictor of Contemporary Events." Evanston, Ill.: Northwestern University, 1966.

TEMPER: Technological, Economic, Military, and Political Evaluation Routine. Bedford, Mass.: Raytheon Company, Vols. 1–7, 1965–1966.

Tsantis, Andreas C. "Political Factors in Economic Development." *Comparative Politics.* 2, No. 1 (October, 1969), 63–78.

United Nations Statistical Office. *Statistical Yearbook.* New York: United Nations Publications.

Viner, Jacob. "Barriers to Economic Development." In D.E. Novack and R. Lekachman, eds. *Development and Society.* New York: St. Martin's Press, 1964, 81–90.

Weede, Erich. "Conflict Behavior of Nation-States." Paper delivered at the Midwest meeting of the Peace Research Society (International) on April 17, 1969.

Wonnacott, Thomas H. and Ronald J. Wonnacott. *Introductory Statistics.* New York: Wiley, 1969.

Wright, George. "Inter-Group Communication and Attraction in Inter-Nation Simulation." Unpublished Ph.D. dissertation, Washington University, St. Louis, Mo., 1963.

Wright, Quincy. *The Study of International Relations.* New York: Appleton-Century-Crofts, 1955.

Zinnes, Dina A. "A Comparison of Hostile Behavior of Decision-Makers in Simulate and Historical Data." *World Politics.* 18, No. 3 (April, 1966), 474–502.

Zinnes, Dina A. and Francis W. Hoole, eds. *Quantitative International Politics: An Appraisal.* New York: Praeger, forthcoming.

Index

245

Library of Congress Cataloging in Publication Data

Bremer, Stuart A
    Simulated worlds.

    Bibliography: p.
    Includes index.
    1. International relations—Research.   I. Title.
JX1291.B73   327.01'84   76-49547
ISBN 0-691-05661-7